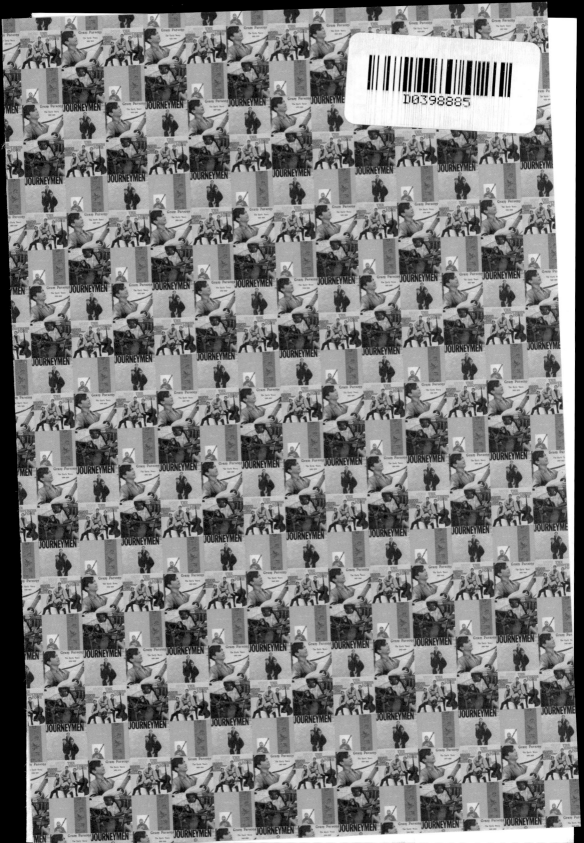

WHICH SIDE ARE YOU ON?

An Inside History of the Folk Music Revival in America

DICK WEISSMAN

continuum

NEW YORK • LONDON

2005

The Continuum International Publishing Group Inc
15 East 26 Street, New York, NY 10010

The Continuum International Publishing Group Ltd
The Tower Building, 11 York Road, London SE1 7NX

Printed in the United States of America

Library of Congress Cataloging-in-Publication Data
    Weissman, Dick.
        Which side are you on? : an inside story of the folk music revival in America /
    Dick Weissman.
        p.   cm.
    Includes bibliographical references (p.   ) and index.
    ISBN 0-8264-1698-5 (hardcover : alk. paper)
    1. Folk music—United States—History and criticism.   I. Title.
    ML3551.W43   2005
    781.62′13′00904—dc22

                                                              2005018994

Continuum Publishing is committed to preserving ancient forests and natural
resources. We have elected to print this title on 30% postconsumer waste recycled
paper. As a result, this book has saved:

18 trees
860 lbs of solid waste
7,799 gallons of water
3,137 kw hours of electricity
1,689 lbs of air pollution

Continuum is a member of Green Press Initiative, a nonprofit program dedicated to
supporting publishers in their efforts to reduce their use of fiber obtained from
endangered forests. For more information, go to www.greenpressinitiative.org.

Contents

Photographs and Illustrations may be found between pages 144 and 145

Preface

In 1931, Florence Reece, the wife of a Kentucky coal miner, wrote one of the classic topical songs preserved in the folk revival. The song contrasted the lot of the working class and the bosses, and asked the listener to choose sides. The song was used again during the civil rights movement, with words appropriate to that situation.

I chose to use the song as the title for this book because, on another level, it seems to symbolize the seemingly endless schisms, factions, and controversies in the folk music world. It all began with the arguments between the pioneering folklorists as to "who had gotten there first." Next within the radical folk song movement was the controversy about whether folk music could be an appropriate platform for raising working-class consciousness, or whether the workers should be upgraded by more traditional musical gestures. There was also the controversy about whether folk music itself should take any political positions at all. Some folklorists thought that trying to make folk songs contemporary by addressing political issues was a violation of folklore itself.

Further arguments developed over whether "Negro spirituals" represented an original creation, or were simply derived from earlier white spirituals. Folklorist George Pullen Jackson devoted his entire career to this issue.

The use of folk songs for political purposes resurfaced after World War II with the formation of People's Songs. Folk music soon became embroiled in the politics of the McCarthy era, when some of its major performers were accused of unpatriotic activities on behalf of the Communist Party. Some, notably Pete Seeger, were threatened with prison sentences.

As the Red Scare died down, the controversies moved to the question of authenticity and commerciality in the performance of folk songs. Pop-folk groups like the Weavers, and later the Kingston Trio, were accused of selling out the music. When Alan Lomax returned to the United States in

1958 he accused the urban folksingers of not truly understanding folk music styles.

During the sixties, magazines and performers fought over the issue of whether white performers could sing black blues. Different magazines developed supporters for opposing views. Even bluegrass was not immune from internecine warfare. The traditional performers hated the long-haired hippies who performed "newgrass," their own fusions of country, rock 'n' roll, and jazz. They were accused of "ruining the music," and some festivals disallowed bluegrass performers.

Some of these controversies persist today. There are still folklorists who think music must be separated from politics, there are still traditional bluegrass musicians that don't like innovation in their music, and there are still blues critics and fans who don't think that it's appropriate for white boys to sing the blues.

One is tempted to heed Rodney King's plaintive cry of "Can't we just get along?" Yet there is something almost charming about a musical style that commands so much devotion among its performers, critics, and fans that they are ready to joust with opponents of their views.

Whichever "side you are on," I hope this book stimulates you to take a look at the folk music revival as an ongoing process, which continues today. Like it or not, without some level of evolution, in a world of Play Stations, cell phones, computers, internet blogs, and drug commercials, there would not be any folk music at all.

Introduction

The very words *folk music revival* have an odd ring to them. What was being revived? Was it some long-lost artifact recovered by musical archeologists or folklorists? Was the music itself actually no longer in existence, but something to be recaptured or recapitulated by Egyptologists? And who were the doctors in charge of the revival? For that matter, which revival are we talking about? And, by the way, who or what are/were the folk?

In the first chapter of this book I cover the folklorists, the people who collected American folk music. The folklorists themselves engendered their own set of controversies, as the reader will soon see. In any case, this process began in earnest around the turn of the twentieth century. It was preceded by some interest in the music of the African Americans that surfaced during and shortly after the American Civil War.

The folklorists of the early twentieth century were essentially preservationists whose goal was to set down folk songs, or at least the text of the songs, before modern civilization entirely eroded or destroyed them. So the first "revival" was an attempt to bring these songs to the attention of the scholarly public. As we will shortly see, the folklorists were not always happy with the products of the "folk," and they took it upon themselves to revise and combine texts, and to eliminate from the fold songs that were regarded as bawdy or salacious. It wasn't simply a question of preserving what they heard or discovered, there was also an editing or culling process going on. In addition to mostly ignoring bawdy songs, the early American collectors had little or no interest in songs from most immigrant groups (except for the English, Irish, and Scotch). Songs expressing political ideas were also suspect.

Another group of folk enthusiasts were simply interested in bringing American folk songs to the attention of the American middle class, and preparing musical arrangements that enabled the songs to be sung by people who were not familiar with them. This notion was based on the assumption that such people were capable of reading written music, especially music written for the piano.

Another faction of folk proselytizers were record companies, which were simply interested in recording any material that could possible be salable. During the 1920s and early 1930s the large record companies did a considerable amount of fieldwork, setting up recording studios all over the southern United States, and actually placing ads in newspapers asking local talent to audition. In this way many significant blues and early country music artists emerged from obscurity or extremely localized notoriety to become relatively famous, although generally not receiving commensurate financial rewards.

The federal government entered the scene when Carl Engel established an Archive of Folk Song at the Library of Congress in 1928. Engel hired R. W. Gordon to staff the archive, who was later succeeded by John Lomax, and later by Alan Lomax. When Franklin Roosevelt was elected president of the United States in 1932, partly because of his own appreciation of folk music, a number of government agencies joined the hunt for traditional music.

By the 1930s the politically radical segment of American society had discovered that there was a body of folk music that advocated social change, a musical style that we generally refer to as "protest music." Earlier, the Industrial Workers of the World (known as the Wobblies), an anarchist-syndicalist union that was active in the early part of the twentieth century, had parodied hymn tunes with lyrics advocating social change and making fun of the bosses. As we will see in the second chapter of this book, the protest music of the 1930s involved music of southern textile workers and coal miners. These were workers who were part of the Southern Appalachian community, and they used their musical heritage to craft new songs that protested against poor working and living conditions. After some initial hesitation that these songs were too déclassé, or represented inferior musical creations, a group of New York classical musical composers seized on this music as a vehicle for promoting radical causes and social change. Charles Seeger was one of these composers, and during the 1930s he went to work for various agencies of the federal government who collected folk songs all over the United States.

By the late 1930s a community of professional folksingers had developed in New York City who saw folk music both as a way to make a living, and as a vehicle to promote radical causes. Leadbelly, Woody Guthrie, and Josh White all had some badge of authenticity that attested to their folk credentials. Pete Seeger came from a family of classical musicians. Richard

Dyer-Bennet was also classically trained, and Burl Ives was positioned to appeal to a more middle-class image of a folksinger.

This was pretty much where the revival stayed, until the end of World War II, and the climate of the cold war caused folksingers' associations with radical causes to be considered "Un-American." The folksingers, especially Pete Seeger, responded by supporting Henry Wallace's Progressive Party, a left-wing political party that advocated a friendlier relationship with Russia, and an end to the cold war. In a peculiar twist of fate, a year after the 1948 election, which produced only a million votes for the Progessive Party, Pete Seeger formed a folk combo called the Weavers, enlisting folk diva Ronnie Gilbert, Seeger's old radical associate Lee Hays, and guitarist-singer Fred Hellerman. The Weavers became the first folk-pop group, carrying traditional folk songs and some new folk-oriented tunes to the very top of the American Hit Parade.

Inevitably, the Weavers' radical associations were revealed, and they were summoned before the U.S. Congress, blacklisted from performances and radio play, and lost their Decca Records recording contract. Suddenly folk music became persona non grata, and anyone who was seeking popular music success wanted to stay as far away from folk music as possible.

The music was restored to national attention and popularity through two unlikely sources. First there was calypso-folksinger Harry Belafonte, a young and attractive black singer who had a mediocre career as a jazz vocalist. Belafonte sparked a calypso music boom, and he included a generous helping of folk songs in his repertoire and recordings. A series of pop-folk groups emerged during the mid-1950s, including the Tarriers and the west-coast–based groups the Easy Riders and the Gateway Singers, but it was the Kingston Trio who really set off the folk-pop boom when their recording of the old folk song "Tom Dooley" became a number-one pop hit in 1958. An industry infrastructure rapidly developed to promote and merchandise the music. This involved booking agents, personal managers, music publishers, record companies, and concert promoters. As with any other popular music style, clearly there was money to be made.

I will discuss the folk-pop era in detail later, but from 1960 to 1964 a dozen popular groups recorded and toured widely throughout the United States. This was the crest of what is generally regarded as the folk revival, and it involved much more than groups wearing button-down shirts selling millions of records. The folk-pop groups opened the door, and a large number of revivalists walked through that door performing blues, bluegrass, mountain music, foreign language folk songs, cowboy songs—in short, just about any conceivable variety of American folk music.

The culture of the folk revival involved many aspects that complemented or resulted from the music itself. There was a folk dance community that stemmed from such groups as the American Square Dance Group, a New York folk dance troupe that dated from the late 1930s. When the folk revival was in full bloom, acoustic music stores developed to serve the needs of the professional and amateur musicians, and there was also a related coffeehouse culture. The first acoustic music stores were the Folklore Center in New York's Greenwich Village and McCabe's in Santa Monica, California. These stores, which flourished in the late 1950s, were soon followed by similar stores everywhere from Denver to Boston. Specific instruments were highly prized and sought after and so were certain repair people who specialized in fixing old guitars, banjos, and mandolins. Many of the music stores also gave lessons, and this in turn created a group of musicians far beyond its original base. Musicians were also employed as teachers at these stores, enabling them to perfect their talents and exchange information about various musical styles. Some of the acoustic music stores also had performance spaces and held regular concerts of folk music.

The coffeehouses sometimes employed performers; many of the folk revivalists got their start at coffeehouses or clubs that served alcohol and featured folk music as their musical attraction.

But even beyond the music, the coffeehouses and the music stores created a sense of community for folk music enthusiasts who gathered to exchange ideas. Certain sections of cities, like Greenwich Village in New York or North Beach in San Francisco, became gathering places for the revivalists. The Newport Folk Festival began in 1959. It originally fused both folk and pop-folk elements, but later became more focused on traditional music and essentially inspired the many other folk festivals that have since proliferated.

Before considering the aftermath of the 1960s folk revival, and the spawning of a number of other musically affiliated styles, let's consider the connection between the actual music and the various groups discussed so far.

It seems to me that one can look at each of the factions described above as people who had their own ulterior motives in promoting the music. We could even say that they all had a vested interest in the plundering of the music to promote preconceived aims. The original folk song collectors were primarily interested in promoting a romanticized version of the folk, one that involved the "nobility" of the illiterate and semiliterate. This was best done by focusing on American versions of traditional ballads from the British Isles.

Then as now, the record companies were mostly interested in product—obtaining it, marketing it, and pocketing the proceeds. The people who compiled music in singable form, like John Jacob Niles or Carl Sandburg, wanted to promote their careers as performers. Radicals such as Alan Lomax and Charles Seeger wanted to use the music as a vehicle for social change. They sang what music fit this image, and they wrote new music loosely or directly based on traditional music to promote these ends. The folk-pop artists, like all pop artists, wanted to make hit records in order to generate lucrative performing opportunities. Virtually all of the different promoters of folk music, pop or not, soon became aware of the economic value of the songs as copyrights, and many of them, from collectors like the Lomaxes to performers such as John Jacob Niles or the Kingston Trio, copyrighted songs that they did not in fact write in order to generate income.

In fairness, we should point out that the pursuit of these goals was not necessarily an entirely cynical operation. Certainly many of the factions mentioned did indeed have some love for the music and some concern about their own efforts at popularizing it. Possibly one key to the situation is the problem of how few of the folk were involved in folk music. Virtually none of the folklorists, the politically oriented performers, or the folk-pop singers learned songs in their own families or "folk" communities. They were outsiders who for musical, political, economic, or psychological reasons were fascinated by the songs.

This brings us to the aftermath of the folk music revival of the 1960s. The fallout of the pop-folk performances, as well as the concertizing of such people as Pete Seeger and the reissue of 1920s and 1930s folk and blues recordings on such record labels as Riverside and especially Folkways Records, was the development of a group of urban revivalists who generally scorned the pop-folk performances, and placed a high value on the notion of *authenticity*. For many of these musicians and performers, authenticity consisted of learning the repertoire of such a performer as Mississippi John Hurt and performing it as closely as possible to Hurt's original recordings. When it turned out that such musicians as Hurt, Skip James, Son House, Bukka White, Dock Boggs, and Pete Steele were still alive, societies formed to bring these performers to urban locales, and summer folk festivals were established to present these performers. The festivals themselves became venues for the discovery of new folksingers, and a corps of urban folksingers—such as Joan Baez, Judy Collins, and Odetta—developed who were regarded, if a bit grudgingly, as relatively authentic folksingers, as opposed to pop-folk artists. Other performers, notably the New Lost City Ramblers, developed around the concept of reproducing the performances of the original mountain string bands. Performers such as Dave Van Ronk and a young Bob Dylan developed more or less original styles that were indebted to the work of earlier performers, but moved more and more in their own directions.

It became obvious that there were only so many traditional songs that singers could perform and inevitably performers began to write their own material. This gave rise to the singer–songwriter tradition, still a viable musical medium forty years later. Bob Dylan, Tom Paxton, John Stewart (in and out of the Kingston Trio), Joni Mitchell, and many other artists who had come out of the folk revival became singer–songwriters. There were also less commercially oriented writers, like Malvina Reynolds and Ella Jenkins. When Dylan moved over into amplified music, and the Beatles' popularity exploded, many of the folksingers amped up, and bands like the Jefferson Airplane, the Buffalo Springfield, and the Byrds combined folk-oriented lyrics and some folk music influences with the rock 'n' roll idiom.

To telescope thirty years of musical history into a few brief paragraphs, the various pop music styles like disco, new wave, and heavy metal coexisted with the singer–songwriters. By the end of the 1960s, the folk-rock period was over. Although a few of the artists, such as Crosby, Stills, Nash, and Young, remained well-known, folk began to infiltrate American popular music in other ways. Gram Parsons was a pop-folk singer who transformed himself into a country-rock artist. He briefly joined the Byrds, had a country-rock band called the Flying Burrito Brothers, and afterward worked with, and heavily influenced, country singer Emmy Lou Harris, who had started out as a folksinger herself. This foreshadowed artists like Mary Chapin Carpenter and Nanci Griffith whose careers were ostensibly, at least initially, as country artists, but whose song subjects and musical styles certainly were rooted in folk music. Periodically, such singers as Suzanne Vega and Tracy Chapman would emerge in the pop music charts with songs that reflected, at the very least, a strong folk sensibility.

Bluegrass and blues music have developed strong identities of their own, and musical experimentation is transforming these forms into ways that seem more relevant to younger audiences. The *O Brother, Where Art Thou?* soundtrack album has sold over seven million copies, and produced a boom of its own in mountain music and bluegrass styles. The blues hold forth at massive music festivals all over the world, and B. B. King, for one, has even entered the mainstream media in a way that was unthinkable forty years ago when he was a virtual unknown among white audiences.

Ani DiFranco is sort of a punk-folk artist, and she in turn inspired a number of other artists who crossed a variety of musical lines. Although folk music as a strong political force had essentially died with the end of the Vietnam War and the civil rights movement, there were and continue to be a number of singers like Anne Feeney and Charlie King whose songs focus on political commentary. As we move farther into the twenty-first century there is yet another folk music revival occurring among young, somewhat punk-oriented artists who are playing acoustic string band music and imitating the musical styles of the artists of the 1920s and 1930s, adding their own rock touches to the mix.

This leads back to where we started. I will examine the relationships, which were often complex, that developed between the various music genres that owed a bit or a good deal of their origins to the folk music revival. Along the way I will explain how so many of the factions described tried to manipulate the music to represent their own points of view or economic self-interest, and I will look at some of the well-known and not so well-known figures in American folk music.

Before we go into all of that, I should probably take a page to outline my own involvement in the revival, so that the reader will get some perspective on the judgments that I will make here. I was born in Philadelphia, and my involvement in folk music began in 1948, when I was thirteen years old and attended the Progressive Party convention in Philadelphia. I saw Pete Seeger perform there and started to buy recordings of folk music. I had played piano as a very young boy and I bought my first banjo in 1951. I immediately broke a couple of strings trying to tune it to the piano notes that Seeger mentioned in his banjo method. I went to Goddard College in Vermont the next year, and was taught how to play by a friend of mine named Lil Blos. Without going into too much detail, a stalled career in sociology at Columbia University graduate school led to my teaching guitar and banjo and my first recording dates. In 1961 I joined with John Phillips and Scott McKenzie in a pop-folk group called the Journeymen. We toured widely and recorded three albums for Capitol Records. After the Journeymen disbanded in 1964, I went on to become a contract songwriter for several music publishers, played on dozens of record dates and for radio and television commercials, and produced records for several major record labels. In 1972 I moved to Colorado, where I went to music school, began performing as a musician in a variety of contexts, and began to write books and musical instruction folios. Since then I have written two movie scores, have made several solo CDs, taught about the music business for twelve years, and continue to be active in writing and performing music.

This is not an autobiographical work. But the way that my background fits into the book is that I started out as someone who was deeply involved in traditional music. I began to write songs and instrumental pieces, jumped into the pop-folk movement as a musician and singer, became a songwriter and record producer, and moved to Colorado when I began to have misgivings about the music that I was playing in order to make a living. Unlike anyone who has written about the revival to date, I was involved in the pop-folk scene and the studio scene, and I've been a persistent fan of a good deal of traditional folk music. I've even been known to write the occasional protest song, and like some of the people I describe, I have at times let commercial considerations overcome my feelings about the music. But, as the saying goes, enough about me.

chapter 1

Guardians of the Folk: The Folklorists and Folk Song Collectors

It might seem that defining a folk song should not have been a difficult proposition. In fact, it turned out to be a controversial pursuit. The German romanticists fantasized that folk songs were not written by a single person, but were created communally. The British folk song scholars saw a folk song as a creation of a single individual, which became transformed as it went from one person, or location, to another over a period of time. Both factions agreed that in order for something to be defined as "folk" it needed to pass into what was referred to as "oral transmission." In other words, the songs were passed along from one person to another without a written text and without the music being written down in formal music notation. Both factions also hypothesized that for a song to be called a folk song, it needed to exist for a long period of time. This time span was not specified, but it was regarded as a sort of litmus test that a song must pass in order to enter the realm of the folk.

Over time the British view became accepted by folk song scholars. However, additional controversies developed about such issues as whether written music could possibly be classed as folk songs. Since all singers of folk songs, even rural ones, were clearly not illiterate, did learning a song or using part of a version on a printed sheet immediately disqualify the song from the folk song canon?

On a more contemporary level, can a pop song be classed as a folk song? Some songs dating from the nineteenth century minstrel era, like "Boatmen Dance," did indeed pass into oral tradition and were changed around by the folk. Because many of these songs were composed by professional entertainers in their capacity as working musicians, did this disqualify these songs as folk songs?

Some of the people who have written about folk music, like Oscar Brand, himself a professional folksinger, describe a sort of authenticity of spirit that moves a song into the folk song category. Although this is a reasonable way to look at the performances of such a contemporary singer as, for example, Joan Baez, it has the inherent problems of requiring judgment calls to be made by the scholar/critic/listener. When people such as the Kingston Trio or Joan Baez began to pursue folksinging as a professional career, the whole thing became more complicated. Folklorists, music critics, and musicians each had their own standards of what constituted authenticity, and what represented values that revolved around entertainment, commerciality, and exploitation by the media. This is a subject that we will return to in our discussions of the folk music revival of the 1960s.

FRANCIS JAMES CHILDE AND THE EARLY AMERICAN COLLECTORS

The early American ballad scholars followed the English model and expanded upon it. Harvard scholar Francis James Childe was only interested in American versions of English ballads. Childe focused on songs that preceded the invention of the printing press, which according to Filene had come to Britain in 1475. This conveniently avoided the subject of broadside ballads, which couldn't possibly have been printed before the existence of printing presses. Because of this restriction, Childe, whose first collection was published in 1882, necessarily limited himself to English and Scottish sources, which he researched with the help of overseas contacts and the American ambassador to England. Childe's research lasted for forty years and he printed 305 different titles and many variants, none of which included melodies. It was Childe's student, George Lyman Kittredge, who was the professor and mentor of John Lomax, one of the primary collectors of "living" folk music in the United States.

Editing

Like most of the following generation of folk song collectors who followed him, Childe did a certain amount of judicious editing of his texts. He omitted texts that he thought to be immoral or tasteless and occasionally edited some of what he collected. Over the years, editing accomplished several different goals. It enabled the collector to cleanse texts so that anything bawdy or salacious could be expunged. In later years it also enabled the collector to copyright the version collected, as opposed to the form that the original song may have taken. When the pop-folk boom began in the late 1940s this became an important issue, because copyrighting songs resulted in royalties for whichever songwriter and music publisher were credited with composing and copyrighting the song.

The First Collectors

The first collectors of American folk songs, people who went out in the field to find the songs, were "Cowboy Jack" Tharp and John Lomax, who collected cowboy songs at the end of the nineteenth century and the beginning of the twentieth century, and Howard Odum. Odum was a sociologist who was interested in the songs of African Americans because he thought that they might provide a window to help him to understand that culture and the people who created them.

Once again the reader might imagine that collecting folk songs is a relatively simple and direct matter. The reader making such assumptions is wrong. A lengthy and rather ugly controversy developed between Lomax and Tharp, amounting to the question of who got there first and who was copying the other. Tharp claimed that he began collecting cowboy songs in 1889 and rode across New Mexico and Texas looking for songs. In any case, in 1908 he had a New Mexico printer make up two thousand copies of what folklorist D. K. Wilgus has described as a "red paper-bound pamphlet of fifty pages," containing twenty-three songs.

Tharp sold the collection for fifty cents and his collection was the first group of cowboy songs in print to include music. Five of the songs were his own compositions, and Lomax, apparently unaware of this, reprinted one of the songs in his own collection of cowboy songs published in 1910. To aggravate the matter, Lomax printed the other four songs in the 1916 edition of his book. In later editions of the Lomax book, he omitted some but not all of Tharp's songs. Wilgus quotes a letter in which Lomax claims that Tharp actually "cribbed" songs from Lomax's book, and he tries to cast doubt on Tharps's authorship claims. As Wilgus puts it, "the weight of the evidence lies with Tharp."

The *Journal of American Folklore* was established in 1888 and by 1893 it was printing folk songs. But possibly the most significant publication of the early collectors was Howard W. Odum's article in the *American Journal of Religious Psychology and Education,* published in 1906. He printed one hundred African American religious songs in this article, and followed with 115 secular songs in a 1911 article in the *Journal of American Folklore.*

Prior to Odum's work, African American songs were virtually invisible outside of the collections in the 1867 slave songs book and the songbooks published by the Fisk Jubilee Singers and a similar group from Hampton Institute. The *Journal* had printed a few black songs, but nothing extensive. Odum was one of a group of southern sociologists working out of the University of North Carolina who formed a sort of 1920s and 1930s think tank to study the culture of the rural southern United States.

Another interesting aspect of Odum's work was that he became extremely taken by one of his informants, a man by the name of Left Wing Gordon. Odum proceeded to write a series of three novels about Johnson, published from 1928 to 1931. The novels are written in dialect and mix verses from songs with the storyline. This put Odum about forty or fifty ideological years ahead of any white novelists, let alone social scientists.

John Lomax

John Lomax was an indefatigable promoter of American folk music of all kinds. In his early collecting days he romanticized the American cowboy in much the same way that Herder had imagined the idyllic lifestyle of his own rural informants. From 1916 until 1931, Lomax gave up collecting folk songs because he simply could not make a living at it. Eventually he replaced Robert W. Gordon as the head of the folk archive at the Library of Congress, a position that paid him all of a dollar a month. Lomax survived through grant support, lectures, administrative work at Texas universities, and through the publication of song collections. In addition to his cowboy song collection, he cowrote, or more properly, edited, a series of classic books about American folk music. After the initial cowboy collection, John enlisted his son Alan to cowrite the books with him. *American Ballads and Folk Songs* appeared in 1934, *Negro Folk Songs as Sung by Lead Belly* in 1936, *Our Singing Country* in 1941, and *Folk Song U.S.A.* in 1947.

All of the books published after the cowboy anthology, with the single exception of the Leadbelly book, were unique in the sense that they included many genres of American folk music. There were Cajun songs, blues, many songs about work, prison songs, country ballads, and Anglo-American folk songs. The most significant area that Lomax omitted was foreign language songs of various immigrant groups. The only other anthology of this period that was so broad was Carl Sandburg's *American*

Songbag, published in 1927. Sandburg was a renowned poet and biographer of Abraham Lincoln, who also would perform folk songs while playing the lecture circuit.

To find these songs Lomax, at first alone, then later with his son, traveled to the most remote corners of the United States. They went to prisons, rice plantations, lumber camps, farms—any place that they heard or imagined there would be singers of folk songs. The Leadbelly book stemmed from the Lomax's meeting a chain gang prisoner named Huddie (Leadbelly) Ledbetter at the Angola Prison in Louisiana. After Leadbelly was released from prison, Lomax hired him as a chauffeur and for a brief period took on the management of his career. He was able to get Leadbelly hired in various schools and to perform for folklore societies.

Copyright and Folk Songs

John Lomax died in 1948, when the "old" copyright law was still in existence. This law provided for a term of copyright that lasted twenty-eight years, with a twenty-eight-year renewal period. If Lomax had not created his own versions of songs, most of the songs that he collected would have been considered to be in the public domain. This means that either the author was unknown, or the song had been composed over fifty-six years ago. Songs that *were* copyrighted received a payment of two cents per song, split between a music publisher and the songwriter. Other revenues were available from songs being printed in sheet music, or by the end of his life from performances on the radio.

With the exception of a few songs like "Home on the Range," during John's lifetime these copyrights were not of tremendous economic value. A year after Lomax's death, however, a vocal group called the Weavers had a big hit record of the song "Goodnight Irene," and the royalties were considerable. The Weavers were fortunate enough to have some other hit records, and during the 1950s, first Harry Belafonte and then the Kingston Trio and various other pop-folk acts had hits with single songs as well as albums. By the 1960s, inadvertently or by plan, Alan Lomax was sitting on a sizeable gold mine of copyrights.

There could have been an easy solution to the ethical questions involved in these copyrights if John Lomax had been working from a more sophisticated knowledge of the music industry. The obvious and equitable solution would have been for the Lomaxes to own the music publishing rights to the songs that they collected, and for the singers to receive the songwriter's half of the pie. (The royalties are generally split 50–50, between the songwriter and the music publisher.) But John Lomax was not working from this sort of knowledge base, and in farming out the music publishing rights he was left with a situation where the only way that he could receive any income from the songs was by cutting himself and/or Alan in on the song-writers' money. Another way that Lomax could have dealt with the situation would have been to assign the administration rights to the songs to a New York publishing house for a small percentage of the overall income. This is exactly what many songwriters do today. The administering publisher makes sure that the proper copyright forms are filed and fills requests for copies of the songs from recording artists or producers. The fee for this service varies from 10 to 20 percent, far less than the 50 percent fees that music publishers normally receive. Music publishers earn these fees by soliciting and obtaining new recordings for a songwriter. In the case of folk music, this is a much less vigorous activity than, say, soliciting a new recording of a Cole Porter song.

The point is that not dealing with these issues created a situation whereby the Lomaxes were taking money that in many cases did not belong to them. It should also be noted that Porterfield mentions a number of cases where John Lomax's lack of generosity involved minimal payments to performers; in Leadbelly's case, taking 50 percent of his concert fees. When Alan joined the team, the split became one-third each. This meant that Leadbelly was only receiving one-third of the income for his performances. Even by the rather convoluted financial standards of the music industry, these fees were excessive.

Cecil J. Sharp

Cecil J. Sharp was an English scholar who came to the United States in 1915. Sharp sought to rekindle interest in what he felt was the fast-disappearing English folk song, by rediscovering English songs and ancient customs in the southern Appalachian mountains. Sharp was enticed to visit the southern mountains by Mrs. Olive Dame Campbell, who had begun collecting songs herself in 1908. Dame felt that the task of collecting the tunes required the services of a trained musician, and Sharp, accompanied by Maud Karpeles, made three trips into the mountains. He and Karpeles published their collection in 1917 under the title *English Folk Songs from the Southern Appalachians.* Sharp's trips amounted to forty-six weeks of work and he collected 1,612 tunes. According to Wilgus, Sharp met with regional collectors and established rapport with them, eliminating the sorts of feuds that had erupted between John Lomax and Jack Tharp.

It was Sharp's view that the southern Appalachian mountains represented an area frozen in time because of their isolation. The modern reader needs to be reminded that in 1915 there were no radios, no television, and nothing comparable to the modern highway system that exists in today's America. Sharp believed that in order to facilitate a folk song revival in England, it would be necessary to make the singing of folk songs an everyday and commonplace event. He hoped to prove to the English that this could be done—that it was possible to resist the vulgar industrialization of daily life and, in effect, to return to a simpler time. He saw music as something to be practiced and transmitted from one family member to another. The isolation of the southern mountains represented a desirable trait that facilitated this process.

Because of his antipathy toward modern life, Sharp had no interest in collecting anything resembling the popular music of the day. Because he was eager for people to sing the songs that he collected, tunes were a more important part of his publications than texts. This set him in opposition to the promoters of Childe ballads, who had exactly the opposite focus. In order to make room in his publications for the tunes, Sharp often printed incomplete or partial texts, sometimes including as little as one verse of a song. Sharp also suggested that musicians accompany the songs by creating harmonies on the piano. In his later work he himself made such musical arrangements. He also saw folk music as fodder for classical composers, feeling that it could provide a source of inspiration that could then be taken to a higher cultural level.

Sharp thought of African Americans as part of the vulgarization of the Anglo-American culture. He considered them a culturally inferior group and ignored them in his collecting activities. Filene reports that the African American population of Appalachia was 13.4 percent of the total population, and more recent oral histories and biographies of mountain and bluegrass musicians certainly reveal considerable cultural interchange between white and black musicians.

Despite Sharp's focus on British ballads, he did turn up a few native American songs, like "John Hardy" or "The Lonesome Prairie." Because they carried the stigma of popular music, he avoided any sentimental songs, this being anathema to Sharp.

THE COLLECTORS: REGIONAL AND OTHERWISE

John Lomax is probably the most famous of the early collectors of American folk songs, but there were a number of other important efforts to preserve and publicize the music. There were scholars and inspired amateurs collecting songs all over the southeastern region of the United States. Other scholars were at work in other areas of the country, as well as in northeastern Canada. Some restricted their collections to a particular state, like the Frank C. Brown collection in North Carolina, Henry M. Belden's Missouri research, Phillips Barry's two books of songs from Maine, W. Roy MacKenzie's work in Nova Scotia, and Charles Lummis's little-known collection of almost four hundred California Spanish-American folk songs. Other collections were archived and/or published in Florida, Georgia, Indiana, Kentucky, Michigan, Pennsylvania, South Carolina, Virginia, and West Virginia. Many of these collectors worked for many years before publishing their findings. Belden, for example, began his collection in 1903. According to Wilgus, it was essentially completed by 1917, but it wasn't until 1940 that it was published as a book.

Other scholars preferred to group songs on a regional basis, like John H. Cox's *Folk-Songs of the South* (1925), Eloise Hubbard Linscott's *Folk Songs of Old New England* (1939), Vance Randolph's four-volume *Ozark Folk Songs* collection (1946–1950), or Dorothy Scarborough's *A Song Catcher in the Southern Mountains* (1925). Some authors compiled anthologies that represented large helpings of songs from many areas, such as Louise Pound's *American Ballads and Songs* (1922).

A number of other collectors became fascinated by songs that concerned specific occupations, lifestyles, or musical genres and they concentrated their efforts on these areas. Examples of such endeavors include Joanna C. Colcord's collections of sailor's songs (1924 and 1938), William M. Doerflinger's *Shantymen and Shantyboys* (1951), Charles J. Finger's *Frontier Ballads* (1927), George Pullen Jackson's collections of white spirituals (1917–1943), George Korson's three books of Pennsylvania coal mining songs, George Milburn's *The Hobo's Hornbook* (1930), Franz Rickaby's *Ballads and Songs of the Shanty-Boy* (1926), and Mary Wheeler's *Steamboatin' Days* (1944).

A few scholar–authors were generalists, concerned with songs of specific ethnic groups, especially African Americans. The collectors and compilers of African American songs included Howard W. Odum and his University of North Carolina colleague Guy Johnson (1925 and 1926), R. Nathaniel Dett's collections of Negro spirituals (1827 and 1936), Thomas P. Fenner's collections of plantation and religion songs (dating as far back as 1874), Dorothy Scarborough's *On the Trail of Negro Folk-Songs* (1925), James Weldon Johnson and J. Rosamund Johnson's two books of spirituals

(1925 and 1926), and Newman I. White's *American Negro Folk-Songs* (1928).

Meanwhile, a remarkable woman named Frances Densmore was compiling over a dozen books of American Indian songs, traveling all over the United States and into Canada through virtually the entire first half of the twentieth century. It is interesting to note that several other women—including Laura Boulton and Natalie Curtis—were also collecting the music of the American Indian.

The Strange Career of Lawrence Gellert

Lawrence Gellert was born in 1896, the son of a Hungarian refugee. He grew up in New York's Greenwich Village. His older brother, Hugo, was the art editor for the *New Masses,* a magazine that was a cultural organ associated with the Communist Party.

For health reasons, Lawrence's doctor recommended that Gellert leave New York and go south. He settled in Tryon, North Carolina, a town south of Asheville, where he lived with a black woman and edited a newspaper.

Because of Gellert's personal situation and his willingness to share the difficult economic straits of African Americans, he was able to collect over five hundred songs in Georgia, the Carolinas, Alabama, Louisiana, and Mississippi beginning around 1924. Over two hundred of these songs were protest songs. Gellert sent a few of these songs to his brother, who encouraged him to collect and record additional songs. One of the other ways that Gellert was able to gain the confidence of his informants was by never writing down their names or locations.

Although a handful of protest songs appear in books like the Odum and Johnson collections, no one had ever believed the dimensions of African American protest music to be so deep. As a result, Gellert was accused of making up the songs himself. Two collections of these songs appeared in 1936 and 1939. A small independent record company called Timely Records pressed about a hundred copies of an album of Gellert's material. But it wasn't until the early 1980s, and the Rounder Records release of two albums by Gellert, that it became apparent that the material in Gellert's collection was certainly authentic. Yet, outside of several pages in Bruce Bastin's *Red River Blues* and Lawrence Cohn's collection *Nothing but the Blues,* one would hardly notice that Gellert had ever even existed. Pete Seeger prints a single Gellert-collected song in his book *Where Have All the Flowers Gone?,* referring to Gellert's bringing the song back from a "trip" in the south. Apparently Seeger was not aware that Gellert spent a number of years in the south collecting these songs. But Seeger appears wildly generous compared to the treatment that Gellert gets at the hands of the Lomaxes, who simply mention one of his two publications in a bibliography. So why is more attention not paid to Gellert, or to the material that he collected?

Possibly the explanation lies in some of the controversies in which Gellert became embroiled. I have already mentioned the skepticism that other collectors had toward Gellert's work. He certainly did not follow the traditional folklore methodology of carefully citing each informant, or of keeping detailed records of the time and place that the songs were collected. Possibly more to the point, he found examples of resistance and hostility toward the prevailing white culture that were virtually inaudible and invisible to the bulk of folk song collectors. The very existence of his collection threatened the credibility of what other collectors had found. If Gellert's work was legitimate, then why could other collectors not duplicate it, or at least confirm it? This question could have opened up a whole can of worms about the relationship between the collector and the artist. How much of what the singer performs for the collector relates to the collector's approval or disapproval of the singer's repertoire? Just as Cecil Sharp was uninterested in, for example, parlor songs, collectors would not have expressed approval of, say, a black singer who sang white country songs. Yet many interviews have confirmed that African American musicians listened to country music on the *Grand Ole Opry* or other radio programs and they even occasionally played gigs with white musicians for white audiences. The white collectors existed in a sort of patronage relationship with their informants. It did not seem to occur to them that a black singer would be hesitant to sing a song about a lynching to a white middle-class informant in a southern venue.

But there were other elements at work in addition to the general skepticism about Gellert's work. Gellert was an outspoken individual, who insisted on "telling it like it is." The late Richard Reuss's pioneering *American Folk Music and Left Wing Politics 1927–1957*, edited by his wife JoAnne C. Reuss, discusses the controversy that developed in left-wing political circles when Gellert insisted on using the word "nigger" when it occurred in direct quotations and song lyrics. In a sort of harbinger of the notion of political correctness, Gellert's communist and neo-communist colleagues took him to task for this usage. Gellert did not back down, and he defended his using that term in direct quotes from his informants. So apparently even in the radical circles where his research should have been welcomed with open arms, he was something of a controversial figure.

As if Gellert hadn't irritated enough people, he proceeded to take on John Lomax in his treatment of Leadbelly. According to Nolan Porterfield's biography of Lomax, Gellert was "incensed that Lomax had taken up the cause of Leadbelly, a convicted murderer, but had shown no sympathy for the Scottsboro boys, who were widely held to have been railroaded into jail on false charges." He accused Lomax of having a slaveholder mentality, and charged that Lomax had "failed to get to the heart of contemporary Negro folk lore." In taking on a folkloristic icon like John Lomax, Gellert was opening the door to a further rift between himself and "legitimate" collectors.

Topping it all off, Gellert became involved in a law suit against blues artist–folksinger Josh White when White recorded an album called *Chain Gang*, which featured songs from Gellert's collection, arranged and partially rewritten by Josh White and choral conductor Leonard de Paur. Columbia Records producer–musical entrepreneur John Hammond produced White's *Chain Gang* album in 1940. Gellert demanded songwriting and music publishing credits, much as John and later Alan Lomax did for their efforts. White and de Paur fought back, declaring that the songs did not belong to Gellert, but were either traditional or belonged to their anonymous authors. According to Elijah Wald, White's biographer, it is unclear whether the lawsuit ever got to court but Columbia did indeed give Gellert coauthorship credit.

An odd sidelight of this controversy is that in 1964, when I was a member of the Journeymen, we recorded a song that I had learned from one of Gellert's books and he and I shared cowriting credits. In this case, I contacted him through a music publisher prior to the recording date and there were no difficulties. Of course there is a certain irony to a Marxist scholar recording powerful protest songs but not sharing the royalties with his informants. To be fair, it would have been difficult for Gellert to reconstruct the names of the song's real authors and, since White's recording was made as much as fifteen years after the songs had been collected, to contact the authors.

Gellert's final confrontation with the keepers of the folk legacy came with Irwin Silber, who edited *Sing Out!* for some years and served as a sort of cultural commissar and self-appointed conscience of the folk song movement. Gellert was involved in the supervision of the recording and distribution of a campaign song written in support of Henry Wallace and sung by Paul Robeson. According to Bruce Michael Harrah-Conforth's

M.A. thesis on Gellert and *Laughing Just to Keep from Crying*, Gellert had arranged for the pressing and distribution of 50,000 of these records, but Gellert and Silber became involved in a bitter argument about who was supposed to foot the bill for the records. The argument resulted in a lawsuit, and fifteen years later Silber wrote an article in which he accused Gellert of either writing all he songs in his collection himself, or having someone else do it.

My conclusion to the Gellert mystery is that he has remained a relatively obscure figure for a number of reasons. The songs that he collected contradicted the prevailing theories about the passivity of African American singers and songs. He antagonized some of his left-wing supporters by his unwillingness to accede to their notion of political correctness. He took on John Lomax, the most prominent collector of folk songs in the United States, and further antagonized Josh White, a prominent performer and one of the icons of the folk music revival. He topped that off by alienating Irwin Silber, who was one of the most important figures in left-wing song circles.

Whatever one thinks of these controversies, it is obvious that Gellert has not received proper recognition for his unique work. It is true that some three long-playing records from his collection have been released, although they are not currently available on CD. It is also true that left-wing choruses performed some of his songs in the 1930s, that modern dancer Helen Tamiris choreographed and performed some of these songs in dance performances in the 1930s, and that a few of the songs were printed in various radical songbooks. But the two slim volumes from Gellert's research, published in 1936 and 1939, are long out of print. The Bruce Michael Harrah-Conforth M.A. thesis on Gellert remains unpublished, and Gellert's collection is housed in relative obscurity at the University of Indiana. (One hundred and fifty of the lyrics of Gellert's collection are printed in Harrah-Conforth's thesis.) Alan Lomax, known to be something of a controversial figure himself, wrote a lengthy book about the blues, *The Land Where the Blues Began*, without so much as mentioning Gellert. Some other scholars have mentioned him in more detailed discussions of other collectors and collections, but many have ignored him entirely. Probably the most fair-minded and extensive treatment of Gellert is in Bruce Bastin's book, *Red River Blues*. (Bastin is British!) Gellert's extensive work has been essentially ignored. In fact, in all of the Lomax collections, Gellert appears in one brief bibliographical listing.

One would think, with the extensive research being done into the blues and African America music, that someone would publish a book devoted to Gellert's life and a collection of his songs. Similarly, his collection certainly deserves to be preserved with some CD reissues. If record companies can essentially reissue every recording of Alan Lomax's work, why can't we give Gellert's informants something resembling equal time? The bottom line is that Gellert's collection of over five hundred songs remains the largest collection of African American music prior to World War II. The over two hundred protest songs in the collection are far and away the best testimony to the fact that black songs of protest were present in profusion in the southern United States, whether or not the other folk song collectors were able to find them.

SONGBOOKS

In addition to the collectors and scholars who researched American folk music in a formal way, there were a number of early publications that were simply small songbooks designed for performers to use. Some of these books were written by performers, for whom songbooks represented another way of promoting their careers to the general public. Others were collections of songs compiled by musicians and song collectors who lacked formal folkloristic training. Benjamin Filene points out that some of the earliest of these collections were compiled by women. Josephine McGill was a New Yorker who spent her summers collecting songs in the Kentucky mountains, beginning in 1914. Two years later she enlisted a pair of classical musicians from New York to assist her. McGill compiled one music folio alone, and two with the assistance of her companions Loraine Wyman and Howard Brockway. Bascom Lamar Lunsford, a North Carolina lawyer and banjo player, coauthored another collection with composer Lamar Stringfield. John Jacob Niles, a performer-composer-collector, authored a series of folios and wrote a book called *Singing Soldiers* about songs sung by African American soldiers during World War I.

The difference between the songbooks and the work of the folklorists was that the songbooks almost invariably contained piano arrangements for middle-class parlor piano players. Usually, there were no scholarly notes concerning where the songs were collected or details about a song's history. They were designed for singers to use, rather than for scholars to study. The collectors' publications generally included extensive notes on the songs, referred to variants of the songs, and even listed other publications that contained other versions of the songs. Carl Sandburg and the Lomaxes straddled the line, listing information about the songs in such a way as to satisfy the more serious student of folk music, but they also included piano arrangements for the many piano players who bought the books. The early collectors didn't bother to include any information for guitarists, because the bulk of middle-class musicians before World War II were more apt to play these songs on the piano than on guitar.

EARLY COMMERCIAL RECORDINGS
AND AMERICAN FOLK MUSIC

Periodically there is some convergence between commercial record companies and the preservation of valuable historical and artistic performances. At the same time as John Lomax and Howard Odum were collecting folk music from (mostly) nonprofessional musicians, the major record companies discovered that there was a market for what we might call "roots-oriented music." After considerable pressure from New York–based musician–songwriter–entrepreneur Perry Bradford, in 1920 Mamie Smith became the first successful African American blues artist on record. When her second recording, "Crazy Blues," sold hundreds of thousands of copies, the record companies came to understand that there was a market out there for black music. The blues records released in the early 1920s were all of female blues artists who had one foot in vaudeville or cabaret music and the other in the blues. Ma Rainey and Bessie Smith, in particular, were able to transcend the limitations of the early recording process to bring a high level of emotion and artistry to most of their records. It was inevitable that record companies would discover an earthier variety of blues, and artists like Papa Charlie Jackson and Blind Jefferson were marketed almost exclusively to African Americans. Despite limited promotional efforts, these artists sold thousands of records.

A similar process occurred in country music. A Georgia fiddler named Fiddlin' John Carson recorded his first sides in 1923, at the insistence of Atlanta record salesman Polk Brockman. The producer was Ralph Peer, who disliked Carson's music and was astounded when the initial pressing of five hundred copies sold out almost instantly.

Peer is quite a story in himself. Originally employed by Okeh Records, he moved over to RCA, negotiating a deal for himself whereby RCA received his services free of charge, but he retained the music publishing rights of everything that he recorded. This resulted in Peer building a powerful publishing company, Southern Music, which still exists today, seventy years later.

Record producers (also known as A&R, for artist and repertoire, men) traveled all over the southern United States seeking artists to record. They played as important a role in the transmission of folk music as did the folk song collectors. The audience for the two groups, however, was entirely different. Most of the collectors primarily focused on ballads, with a particular fondness for unaccompanied ballads of British origin. To the extent that collectors published books of songs that included texts and music, the audience for the books were middle-class whites who could read music. The record company producers were interested in music that was salable. In country music, these early recordings focused on instrumental music featuring fiddle, banjo, guitar, and mandolin. It was a different story for the blues. After the fascination with the women divas of the early and mid-1920s wore off, hundreds of recordings were made with soloists who sang and played guitar. Other recordings featured duos or black string bands like the Mississippi Sheiks. The audience for these blues recordings consisted of black working-class people. In his book *The Old, Weird America*, Greil Marcus points out that many of the black consumers who bought these records did not own phonographs. He sees the ownership as a sort of cultural talisman, a purchase made to indicate a pride of cultural ownership. There may be some truth to this contention, but it doesn't seem to have occurred to him that the people might have played these records on phonographs owned by friends who *did* own record players. We know that this process occurred with radio broadcasts, where people would gather in the home of someone in the community who owned a radio.

Various writers have remarked on the fact that the recordings from this period, roughly 1920 to 1938, were very close to folk performances. Many of the songs recorded were traditional songs, or they were tradition-based songs, new songs rewritten around traditional verses and/or themes. In blues, and in some country songs of the period, the artists often used a device called floating verses. These verses are lyrics found in the folk tradition and known to many singers and their audiences. Many of the verses, especially in blues, might reappear in numerous other songs. For example, a common blues floating verse is:

> *You don't know, you don't know my mind,*
> *You don't know, you don't know my mind.*
> *When you see me laughing, I'm laughing just to keep from crying.*

Many of the blues yodels recorded by Jimmie Rodgers made use of floating blues verses. The blue yodels were blues tunes with yodeling, and the texts were free-form verses in the same way that many of Blind Lemon Jefferson's blues songs were groups of verses that did not necessarily tell a simple coherent story.

There is a sort of implied snobbism among folklorists that assumes that music collected by folklorists is of necessity purer and more authentic than anything recorded by a commercial record company. Even the Lomaxes, who went to great pains to go to remote or off-the-beaten-track locales like prisons to collect music, seemed to feel a certain superiority to material that was tainted by the evil hand of commercialism. Yet many of the musicians recorded by the collectors, such as Muddy Waters, David "Honeyboy" Edwards, or for that matter Woody Guthrie and Leadbelly, were later recorded by commercial record companies. Alan Lomax himself was responsible for some of these recordings and, in fact, at times produced records commercially for large companies.

Another interesting aspect of the commercial recordings was the way in which they revealed the strong influence of African American music on country artists. White country artists like Frank Hutchison and Dock Boggs had been strongly influenced by black blues musicians early in their careers. Some of the black string bands, like the many jug bands or the Mississippi Sheiks, performed music very similar to that of the white string bands. It is reasonable to assume that there was a certain amount of musical interchange between the two, despite the prevailing cultural and physical segregation between them.

Many of the root-oriented recordings of the 1920s and 1930s were recorded "in the field," similar to the methods used by the folk song collectors. Record companies would rent facilities at radio stations or set up shop in warehouses. Occasionally, A&R people like Peer would advertise in local newspapers a few weeks before they hit town. The ads invited artists to audition for record deals.

I mentioned earlier that Peer owned the publishing rights of everything that he recorded. ASCAP (American Society of Composers, Authors, and Publishers), which controlled the performance royalties of music, paid less in royalties for songs in the public domain. These were songs that either have unknown authors, or were composed more than fifty-six years ago. In the case of public domain songs, Peer copyrighted them as "adapted and arranged by _____" but he couldn't very well sue another artist who recorded a familiar song like "On Top of Old Smokey." What Peer did was to pressure his artists to come up with new, original material. Jimmie Rodgers was performing other people's songs when Peer first met him.

Peer sent him home to write his own songs, which Rodgers proceeded to do with the help of his sister.

Aside from the people who produced these recordings, there were others employed by record companies who were "talent finders." This was particularly true of African American music, whose purveyors were not apt to have contact with white record company personnel. The record companies relied on white southerners who lived near the blues singers who acted as talent filters, passing on the best of the local artists to the record companies. Henry C. Speir, a music-store owner in Jackson, Mississippi, recorded Charley Patton, Skip James, and Tommy Johnson, all of whom were significant figures in the story of the Delta blues. J. B. Long, in Durham, North Carolina, was responsible for recording Piedmont blues artists Blind Boy Fuller, Buddy Moss, Sonny Terry, and Brownie McGhee. Many of these talent brokers found white as well as black artists. Speir, for example, also was responsible for recordings by *Grand Ole Opry* star Uncle Dave Macon and old-time country string band the Leake County Revelers.

Folklorist D. K. Wilgus regards 1938 as the cut-off date when "race and hillbilly records were further removed from their folk roots." By that time, movie cowboys had infiltrated country music, and early rhythm and blues had begun to replace folk blues in the affection of African Americans.

THE AESTHETIC AND HISTORICAL IMPORTANCE OF EARLY COUNTRY AND RACE RECORDS

In 1952 a filmmaker named Harry Smith compiled six albums on Folkway Records containing reissues of the sort of recordings described above. He called the set the *Anthology of American Folk Music*. It included recordings by many of the artists discussed here, and others who were more obscure. These recordings, as we will see when we discuss the folk music revival of the 1950s and 1960s, had a powerful influence on the young urban revival singers. Subsequently, the set was reissued on three double compact discs in 1997. A fourth set, originally planned by Smith but never actually released, was issued soon afterward by Revenant Records.

Two chapters down the line we will discuss the influence of the *Anthology* in some detail. But since the recordings on these albums were all made in the 1920s and 1930s, some comment on the music itself is appropriate here.

Many of the country and blues artists of the 1920s and 1930s came from folk communities. Frank Hutchison and Dock Boggs were coal miners and many of the early blues singers worked on large southern plantations. So their backgrounds were quite similar to the people that John Lomax, for example, encountered on his collecting trips. One can argue that when someone becomes a professional musician who charges money for a performance, there is a different level of interaction between the performer and the audience than exists in a community where a group of people are sitting in a living room taking turns playing and singing music. For blues musicians this is a difficult distinction to make because so much of the music consisted of solo performances, and so many of the performing situations were informal gatherings, such as parties, picnics, or street singing. Does the singer passing around a hat or tin cup make that much of a difference in the nature of what he performs, or how it is received? At what point does professional stagecraft become part of the picture? So many of the artists of the period, like Mississippi John Hurt, made a handful of records but never gave up their "day jobs" to become full-time professionals.

In listening to the songs on the *Anthology*, what strikes the contemporary listener is the looseness, spontaneity, and emotion of so many of the performances. Many of the themes describe circumstances, locations, and events that are familiar to both the singer and his audience. Blues songster Furry Lewis sings about the fatal crash that killed Casey Jones, Mississippi John Hurt sings about John Henry, and there are ballads about murdered girls and bandits.

There is indeed a good deal of emotion transmitted in these early performances, and yet for the most part they follow the dictum of traditional folk-based performances: "It's the song and not the singer." The emotion transmitted is in the organic nature of the performances themselves. Clarence Ashley sings "The Coo Coo Bird" almost deadpan, and the banjo accompaniment doesn't vary from one verse to the next. But somehow we are transported to some remote mountain scene and story, even though we have never lived there and can scarcely imagine the ground rules that govern the scene.

Greil Marcus makes a great deal of many of the artists' concerns with the afterlife, and the contradictions between their actual day-to-day hard-edged lives and the lives of their artistic imaginations. But it isn't only exotic and strange elements that attract the urban listener, it is also the energy and lack of self-consciousness in the performances. We know a musician like Madonna in the way that she and her media people want us to know her. What we know about John Hurt or Dock Boggs is what their songs tell us, not what some identity that a PR person has fabricated. It is these stories and these imagined tales that have so attracted the urban revivalists. When some of these artists re-emerged in the sixties, some revivalists were able to develop more direct knowledge of the artists and their music.

OTHER OUTLETS

Besides the work of the collectors and the early blues and country music recordings, the music was also promoted through various mountain festivals, radio, and tours of early folk performers. Carl Sandburg delivered lectures on Abraham Lincoln, and part of the package was his songs, accompanied on guitar. Later the Lomaxes toured Leadbelly, bizarrely decked out in chain gang prison stripes. Presumably, John Lomax felt that this provided a touch of authenticity. Country music was presented live on the *Grand Ole Opry* in Nashville, on the *WLS Barn Dance* in Chicago, and on other radio stations. Artists in both country music and blues worked at radio stations for little or no money, but the stations allowed them to freely advertise their live performances, which were then attended by the radio audience.

The folk song collectors, commercial record companies, radio stations, and promoters of live musical events each played a role in creating a market for a music that previously had not been marketed.

chapter 2

Protest Music Before the Folk Revival of the Sixties

Protest music has engendered its own set of controversies in the world of American folk song. Since many folklorists in the United States were primarily looking for American versions of old English ballads, their level of enthusiasm for comparatively new songs that discussed social issues was low. When the Lomaxes, Dorothy Scarborough, and other collectors began to find many American songs that were not derived from British models, some of the songs they discovered concerned various social issues. Among these songs were songs about work, songs sung at work, and complaints about social conditions involving issues of gender, race, working conditions, etc. These songs took various musical forms, including work songs, blues, prison songs, and even ballads.

Generally when people mention protest songs today they are thinking of the music adopted by radical political causes during the 1930s through the 1950s, or they are thinking of the music of the civil rights movement, the protests against the war in Vietnam, or the work of singer–songwriters such as Bob Dylan and Phil Ochs and their associations with the New Left movements of the 1960s.

The tradition of songs of social complaint in this country go back to the times of the Revolutionary War and American conflicts with British rulers. There have also been songs associated with virtually every political cause, and most presidential elections—even down to Bill Clinton's use of the Fleetwood Mac song "Don't Stop Thinking About Tomorrow." Protest songs vary from complaints about personal situations to calls for mass action against corporations or governments. An example of the personal approach is the folk song "The Wagoner's Lad." In this song the singer complains:

> Hard is the fortunes of all woman kind,
> They're always controlled, they're always confined;

Controlled by their parents, until they are wives,
Then slaves to their husbands the rest of their lives.

This is a song about social class, as well as gender. The man in the song complains that the woman's parents don't like him because he is poor:

Your parents don't like me, they say I'm too poor,
They say I'm unworthy, to enter your door;
I work for my living, my money's my own,
And them as don't like me can leave me alone.

The mountain song "Single Girl" complains about the lot of a married woman and has a refrain, "Lord, I wish I was a single girl again."

Other folk songs discuss working conditions. In the song "The Farmer Is the Man," the singer complains that "the middleman's the one who gets it all," and describes the farmer's broken-down wagon.

The Hutchinson family toured widely in the 1840s, singing antislavery songs and popularizing the abolitionist cause. Other songs of social protest are found in labor song-poems and broadsides, single sheets of ballads that were sold by their composers. Clark D. Halker, writing in his book *For Democracy, Workers and God: Labor Song-Poems and Labor Protest 1865–1895,* points out that labor publications proliferated during the 1870s and 1880s and that these publications published virtually everything that was sent to them. Halker mentions two professional musicians who performed prolabor songs in Chicago and Saint Louis during this period. Historian Philip S. Foner compiled a large group of labor songs in *Labor Songs of the Nineteenth Century.* Almost all of the songs used existing tunes, and the subjects varied from many songs decrying the practices of bankers, songs about various presidential candidates or elections, antislavery songs, and even some racist labor songs that demanded an end to Chinese immigration. Other songs related to various early unions, such as the Knights of Labor, or the early years of the AFL (American Federation of Labor). Foner also reprints songs from the early days of socialist agitation in the United States, dating back to 1900. He also points out that there were many other songs in the German and Yiddish language, representing the mother tongues of American immigrants.

One of the most interesting things about the nineteenth century labor song–poets is that more than half of them actually were workers. This is a sharp contrast to the urban radical singers like the Almanac Singers, most of whom had seldom if ever actually been involved in working-class occupations.

One of the reasons that folklorists are generally indifferent to protest songs is that so many of the songs are about specific struggles, and when the struggles are over the songs do not pass into oral tradition, but are usually forgotten. It is the alteration of traditional songs that so interests the folklorist and songs about specific issues rarely meet this test of time. Another impediment is the problem of authorship. Although folklorists have generally accepted the notion that songs are not written communally, there is a certain cachet identified with the fact that the initial authorship is not specifically traceable. On the other hand, a few folklorists have studied such song-makers as Larry Gorman and Joe Scott, some of whose songs have passed into oral tradition. Still, there seems to be something appealing to scholars about the almost mystical way that folk songs are woven into the fabric of a culture without the footprint of individual authorship.

THE WOBBLIES (THE I.W.W.—INDUSTRIAL WORKERS OF THE WORLD)

The American labor unions of the nineteenth century were a relatively genteel group. The first major union federation in this country was National Labor, organized in 1866, which was soon surpassed by the Knights of Labor. Their vision of the workingman was really of skilled laborers, not the sort of industrial worker who labored in the American factory system. The I.W.W. came from a wholly different political and ideological place. They believed in the notion of a single big union that would take on all of the bosses on behalf of cotton mill workers, apple pickers, or migratory farm workers. The Wobblies welcomed them all, and they did it in the context of a sort of anarchist political orientation. They were militant agitators rather than pipe-smoking skilled workers, and one of their weapons was the general strike, a European tactic rarely practiced in the United States. In a general strike, all workers go out on strike in order to support whatever specific group is agitating for wage increases or better working conditions.

The Wobblies are an important part of protest music history. The way that they moved into music is typical of their type of improvisational-organizing methods. The Wobblies held many meetings on streetcorners in Seattle but were often drowned out by Salvation Army brass bands and hymn singers. It quickly occurred to the Wobblies that they ought to have their own songs. They put together their own songbook, known as *The*

Little Red Song Book, which appeared around 1909 and sold thousands of copies.

The Wobblies' songs generally had new words, but used the melodies of traditional hymns, many of which were the same songs that the Salvation Army was trumpeting. Some of the most famous of the Wobbly songwriters were Ralph Chaplin, Joe Hill, Harry (Mac) McClintock, and T-Bone Slim. Ralph Chaplin's song "Solidarity Forever" remains the most popular union song ever written in this country, with its stirring chorus of

> *Solidarity forever!*
> *Solidarity forever!*
> *Solidarity forever!*
> *For the union makes us strong.*

Chaplin wrote the song in 1915, and he used the tune of "John Brown's Body" for the music.

Mac McClintock was the only one of the group who had a career as a professional musician. He made records and appeared on the radio. His song "Hallelujah I'm a Bum" achieved great popularity, once again using an old gospel tune for the melody.

Joe Hill became a legendary figure in the union movement, idolized as a martyr to labor's cause or, in the view of others, despised as a common burglar. Hill was indicted and convicted on charges of killing a grocer in Salt Lake City in 1914, and despite pleas to pardon him coming from all over the world, Hill was executed in 1915.

The entire story remains very controversial today. No one ever identified Hill as actually being at the grocery store, and Hill's defense was quite mysterious, saying only that he was involved in a quarrel that resulted in his being shot. Part of the mythology of Joe Hill is that he refused to explain the situation because he was allegedly having a romantic liaison and didn't want to compromise the woman involved.

Like the other Wobblie songwriters, Hill mostly used existing melodies for his lyrics. Few of his songs are well-known today, but "The Preacher and the Slave" is still sung by protest singers today. The strangest thing about the saga of Joe Hill is that today he is best known because of a song written about him by poet Alfred Hayes and composer Earl Robinson in 1936. The song has been recorded by a number of artists, including Paul Robeson and Joan Baez, and so it is known today among musicians and fans of the 1960s folk revival.

The Wobblies opposed World War I, and a number of their leaders were sent to jail. Their demise was also hastened by the rise of the Communist movement in 1919. The communists were much more organized and methodical than the Wobblies had ever been, and some of the Wobblie leaders converted to communism. Factional disputes in the organization led to the loss of their Chicago building, and even their printing press. By 1929, the organization's treasury had dwindled to twenty-nine dollars. Although the I.W.W. still exists today, its importance and its songs are historical rather than contemporary.

COMMUNISM AND AMERICAN FOLK MUSIC

After the demise of the I.W.W., music was temporarily disenfranchised as a tool for social change. It wasn't long before the Communist Party more than filled the void, but in a very different way.

During the 1920s the membership of the Communist Party in America primarily consisted of foreign-born immigrants, according to R. Serge Denisoff, writing in his book *Great Day Coming: Folk Music and the American Left*. Until the late 1930s, only one-seventh of the approximately 20,000 members of the party spoke English. Denisoff gives no source for this startling and questionable statistic. These immigrants came from Eastern Europe and Germany, and consequently knew little or nothing about American music. The Soviet Union was attempting to utilize Russian folk music as a way of reaching the Russian peasants for whom folk music was the idiom that they knew and understood. In the United States, the Communist Party initially thought they could organize choruses of working men and women and teach them to sing new art songs with political lyrics.

In order to understand the importance of the radical movement in the United States, especially in the 1930s, it is necessary to reflect on social conditions during this era. The farm depression of the mid-1920s in the United States was followed by the Crash of 1929 and the Great Depression that followed. Unemployment approached catastrophic proportions, and when Franklin Roosevelt was elected president in 1932, the country was teetering on the edge of utter economic disaster.

Meanwhile, the Soviet Union had managed to fight off invasions by various foreign forces and to pursue a whole new vision of the future. This Marxist vision was ultimately supposed to lead to a world of absolute economic equality, "from each according to his ability, to each according to his needs." The political state itself would supposedly wither away, leading to a world of political and economic equality, free of any sort of exploitation. This egalitarian fantasy was enormously appealing to intellectuals and artists in an America where unemployed workers were selling apples on the street, stockbrokers were jumping from buildings, banks were going out of business, and no one seemed to know what the future might hold. Consequently, artists of all sorts—painters, writers, musicians, dancers— were attracted to this utopian vision of the future. Quite a few of them were attracted to the Communist Party, and quite a few joined it. Many subscribed to writer Lincoln Steffens's opinion of the U.S.S.R.: "I have seen the future and it works."

The party encouraged the formation of the Workers Musicians Club. It contained a group called the Composer's Collective, which was a part of the Pierre Degeyter Club. The two dozen members of this collective included such prestigious names as Aaron Copland, Henry Cowell, Wallingford Riegger, Charles Seeger (Pete's father), Elie Siegmeister, and Marc Blitzstein.

The goal of these classically trained musicians was to create a new proletarian music that would expand the musical consciousness of the American working class. To achieve this end they taught classes, created a chorus and orchestra, and experimented by marrying politically radical song lyrics to modern compositional techniques. Their role model was Hans Eisler, a German communist composer who fled Hitler's Germany and immigrated to the United States in 1933. Eisler scorned folk music, which he regarded as trivial and old-fashioned, and championed the use of more radical musical techniques involving twelve-tone scales and atonal music. Initially this notion was attractive to the members of the club, but several factors made many of them change their mind.

There was an active singing tradition in the southern United States, where many textile mills and coal mines were located. The Communist Party became involved in organizing alternative radical unions during the 1920s, especially among the textile workers and coal miners. Out of this political agitation several authentic "labor minstrels" emerged. One was a woman named Ella Mae Wiggins, who was murdered in Gastonia, North Carolina, while organizing textile workers. She was a singer and songwriter, and a New York radical named Margaret Larkin carried Wiggins's song, "Mill Mother's Lament," back to New York, sang it at various rallies supporting the textile workers, and published an article about Wiggins in *The Nation,* a noncommunist magazine that was sympathetic to radical politics, as well as in the communist newspaper the *Daily Worker.* A recent book, *The Voice of Southern Labor: Radio, Music and Textile Strikes,* written by Vincent J. Roscigno and William F. Danaher cites a number of performers, recordings, and radio exposure of prolabor songs, all of which supported the struggles of the textile workers during the 1930s. Among the performers mentioned is Dave McCarn, who wrote and recorded the songs "Cotton Mill Colic" and "Rich Man/Poor Man." McCarn was a textile worker himself. His record sold thousands of copies in mill towns and his songs were actually sung by striking workers from the backs of trucks. The Dixon Brothers sang their "Weave Room Blues" on the radio in 1933 and 1934 and they also recorded a number of other songs about mill life. J. E. Mainer sang his song, "Hard Times in the Cotton Mill," inspired by his witnessing the mistreatment of children working in the cotton mills. Homer "Pappy" Sherrill, a fiddler and singer, quit the mills for a full-time career as a musician. Roscigno and Danaher also mention that many of the cotton mills spawned bands consisting of mill workers. An unusual union technique was the development of flying squadrons, which would go from factory to factory, singing and turning the power off before the plant managers could figure out what was happening. Mill hands also danced on the picket line as an expression of solidarity.

A number of the lyrics printed in the Roscigno and Danaher book complain about unfair bosses and call for union unity. One difference between the textile songs and coal mining songs is that most of the people singing the textile songs were rank-and-file workers, not union organizers, with the exception of Ella Mae Wiggins. Another difference was that the songs were played on the radio and appeared on records. By the time the coal miners' songs appeared on record, they were being sung either by professional folksingers like Pete Seeger or organizers or prounion advocates such as Aunt Molly Jackson and Sarah Ogan Gunning, who had moved away from coal mining country.

The person responsible for a shift in the avant-garde emphasis of the Degeyter Club was a coal miner's wife named Aunt Molly Jackson. Jackson was a strong and prickly character who was a ballad maker and organizer for the communist-led National Miners Union. Like the Wobblie songwriters, she set her lyrics to existing melodies. Unlike them, however, the tunes that she utilized were southern mountain tunes. In 1931 a radical committee investigating mining conditions in Harlan County, Kentucky, including important American novelists John Dos Passos, Theodore Dreiser, and Sherwood Anderson, "discovered" Aunt Molly. She and her stepbrother Jim Garland spoke to the committee, and she sang her song "Ragged, Hungry Blues."

The resulting publicity in the communist press brought Jackson and Garland to New York, where they remained. Jackson's performance for the Workers Collective profoundly influenced Charles Seeger, who after an initial assessment of folk music as primitive and musically uninteresting began to envision a new radical music movement built around traditional American folk music, rather than classical art song.

Another step in utilizing folk songs for radical causes was the emergence of two singer–songwriters named Ray and Lida Auville. The Auvilles, like Aunt Molly, were actually from the southern mountains and had a repertoire of traditional music. They moved to Cleveland and began to write songs in both folk and popular musical styles, performing them on fiddle or guitar. In 1934, a collection of twelve of their songs was published by the John Reed Club in Cleveland. *Daily Worker* columnist Mike Gold endorsed their efforts, even comparing their songs to Joe Hill's work. The Composers Collective was somewhat less enthusiastic. According to Richard and Joanne Reuss's *American Folk Music and Radical Politics, 1927–1957,* Charles Seeger and Elie Siegmeister, writing in communist periodicals in 1935, found the Auville's music "banal and artificial in the texts and melodies." (Seeger was writing under the pseudonym Carl Sands in order to protect himself against any charges of communist involvement.) Mike Gold fought back, defending the Auvilles' work.

CHARLES SEEGER AND ALAN LOMAX AS THE CULTURAL COMMISARS OF AMERICAN FOLK MUSIC

Between Aunt Molly Jackson's presence in New York and the controversy over the work of the Auvilles, Charles Seeger began to reconsider his attitude about folk songs as a tool for social change. A battle ensued within the Degeyter Club between the avant-garde faction and the composers who thought they saw a new musical direction for class-conscious composers. The Composers Collective withdrew from the Degeyter Club in 1935 and Seeger's vision prevailed in the movement. Although there was some communist sponsorship of choral groups that were closer to an art music model, even these groups began to do arrangements of folk material. Some of the black protest songs that Lawrence Gellert had collected were arranged for choruses, and songbooks were published that mixed American and international folk songs. At the same time, through various government cultural programs, Charles Seeger became friendly with Alan Lomax and the two of them created a vision of using folk songs as a tool for radical change.

Somewhere along the way, the Auvilles seem to have disappeared from the scene. None of the various books about folk music and radical politics refer to anything about the Auvilles after 1936, when a couple of their songs about the Spanish Civil War were printed in mimeographed songbooks. Apparently, like Lawrence Gellert, they were in effect "written out" of the "approved" history of the radical song movement. Since no recordings of the Auvilles exist, it is difficult to speculate on whether the short lifespan of their musical influence reflected a lack of musical and songwriting talent or some other internal conflict in the radical movement.

R. Serge Denisoff has pointed out that the Seeger–Lomax vision of utilizing folk songs as a tool to "liberate" the American working class was almost as crazy as Eisler's idea of transforming the American worker into a singer of difficult art songs. The fact is that outside of the southern United States, factory workers and union members in general had no background or interest in the American folk song. They were consumers of popular music, like most urban Americans.

Lomax must have had some insight into this problem; through his contacts in radio, records, and the presentation of live performances he quickly grasped that singers like Aunt Molly Jackson or even his friend Huddie (Leadbelly) Ledbetter were too raw for the average American. Lomax saw Woody Guthrie as a magnificent folksinger who epitomized his vision of the radical songwriter, but he also understood that Pete Seeger, Josh White, and Burl Ives were musicians who had a smoother and more polished sound and could appeal to the average American.

It is important to understand just how powerful an influence Lomax and Charles Seeger exercised on the development not only of protest music, but on the folk music revival that was to follow. The two were a somewhat unlikely pair, equally opinionated and sure of themselves, extremely judgmental on musical matters. Once Charles Seeger was "converted" to the cause of using folk music as a platform for social change, he and Alan Lomax shared a vision of the power that the music could exert. Seeger attempted to use his various positions as a government employee working for the Theater Project to bring folk musicians into small towns, hoping to revive the average person's dormant interest in roots music. This notion of community organizing was a very idealistic one, years ahead of the notion of community organizing pioneered by such activists as Saul Alinsky. Seeger's community program was a dismal failure, but it was an interesting approach to reviving folk music.

Even more than Seeger, Lomax had the ability to advance the careers of the folk musicians who he felt were worthy and talented. He did this by helping them get recording contracts, sometimes with major record companies; by hiring them for radio shows that he was directly or indirectly involved in; by helping musicians get work in nightclubs; and by writing about them in books, magazines, or album notes. Lomax also acted as a mentor for a number of folksingers, employing Charles Seeger's son Pete as his assistant at the Archive of American Folk Song in the Library of Congress, teaching him some of the many songs that he and his father had collected, and greatly expanding Pete's notion of the scope and history of American folk music. Alan also managed to maintain a relationship with Leadbelly, even after his father and Huddie had a series of bitter disagreements resulting in some ugly legal actions.

A less pleasant part of Lomax's character was his need to control the history and direction of American folk music. Both Lomax and his father were relentless once they developed a grudge, in John's case against Cowboy Jack Tharp and in Alan's case against Lawrence Gellert. John was a conservative southerner who never made any secret of his distaste for radical causes and who was constantly hustling to advance his finances—whether by writing books, getting grants, or copyrighting songs that he may have edited but certainly did not write. Much the same could be said about Alan, whose copyrighting of folk songs was certainly a contradiction to his radical political views. And for both Lomaxes, they were loath to recognize that there were other people working in the field of folk songs and folklore who were doing important and serious work.

THE DEVELOPMENT OF RADICAL FOLK SONGS

For many years New York City was the center for the production of American music. Anyone who wanted a recording contract would ultimately go there and it was also the key marketplace for the production of network radio shows. Within a few years of one another Woody Guthrie, Leadbelly, Josh White, Pete Seeger, Lee Hays, and many other folksingers gravitated to Manhattan. Lee Hays, Pete Seeger, and Millard Lampell began singing together in early 1941. Pete Seeger and Milland Lampell moved into a house Peter Hawes had rented. Hawes soon moved out and Woody Guthrie, Bess Lomax, Gordon Freisen, and Sis Cunningham moved in. The group was known as the Almanac Singers. A whole other group of musicians and singers, including Hawes's brother Butch, Gordon Freisen, Sis Cunningham, Arthur Stern, Charles Palachek, Cisco Houston, composer Earl Robinson, Woody Guthrie, as well as blues singers Josh White, Sonny Terry, and Brownie McGhee, were at times involved with the group.

The Almanacs functioned like an early hippie commune; they shared expenses and when they accepted performing jobs, they did not disclose to their employers exactly who was going to show up. As a result, their performances were extremely ragged and unpredictable. Pete Seeger developed into the best performer in the group, and when he didn't appear on particular jobs there were often complaints from the clients.

Most of these singers had a radical background. Hays had learned his politics under radical preacher Claude Williams at Commonwealth College in Arkansas, Woody Guthrie had written a column for the West Coast communist daily *People's World,* and Freisen and Cunningham had been involved in radical causes in Oklahoma. Robinson was a long-time Communist Party member, and many of the other performers frequently performed for political causes. Josh White recorded a number of the protest songs that Lawrence Gellert had collected and later coauthored other protest songs with poet Waring Cuney. Leadbelly, partly through the influence of Alan Lomax, began to write some protest songs, like "The Bourgeois Blues," a song built around an incident where Leadbelly and his wife, Martha, and Alan Lomax and his wife could not find a restaurant to eat in or a place to stay that would accept both black and white patrons.

The Almanacs sang for many radical causes. During the 1930s and up until shortly after World War II, a number of the unions in the C.I.O. (Congress of Industrial Organizations) were either influenced or dominated by the Communist Party. The party itself was gravely shaken by an event that took place in August 1939. Hitler and Stalin agreed on a non-aggression pact, guaranteeing that the two countries would not attack one another. In 1937 the Communist Party had been heavily involved in the Spanish Civil War, which pitted a loose coalition of socialists, anarchists, and communists against the fascists led by Francisco Franco. American communists enlisted in the Abraham Lincoln Brigade, which went to Spain to support the radical government. During this time communist propaganda was strongly antifascist and, in fact, suggested the formation of a united front against fascism. When Hitler and Stalin came to their agreement, suddenly the American Communist Party switched over to opposition against any involvement in European politics. The focus went from antifascism to a hands-off policy. During this period Russia and Germany carved up Poland between them and Russia invaded Finland. These actions were rationalized by the party as necessary in order to build buffer zones for the Russians against any future conflict with Germany. Initially the British and Americans had hoped that Hitler and Stalin might kill each other off, leaving the world, so to speak, safe for capitalism. This was part of the reason that party members swallowed the Hitler-Stalin pact.

This was possibly the first situation that was relatively obvious of the Marxist view, that the end justifies the means. In other words, individual actions must sometimes be taken that are unpleasant or undesirable in order to achieve a positive ultimate result. The aim in this case being the survival of the "socialist" state.

On a musical front, the result was that the Almanacs recorded an album called *The Death of John Doe* in April of 1941. It included six antiwar songs that strongly attacked President Roosevelt with lines such as "I hate war / And so does Eleanor." The Party had decreed that the United States should not support the British or French, even though World War II had actually begun by this time. The U.S. had also passed the Selective Service Act in October 1940, which required men between the ages of twenty-one and thirty-five to register for the draft. This was done because Roosevelt and Congress anticipated that we would soon join the British and French at war. The Almanacs' album was so incendiary that the radical owner of the label, Eric Bernay, issued the record under the name of an entirely different company.

Unfortunately for the Almanacs, the album was a bit late in the game. It was issued in spring 1941. On June 22, 1942, Germany attacked Russia and the album was withdrawn from circulation. But the implications of the record for the careers of Pete Seeger, Josh White, and Millard Lampell went much deeper than embarrassment.

Although the antiwar album was not widely circulated, in addition to the almost obligatory laudatory reviews in the communist press, it was also reviewed by *Time Magazine,* the *New York Post,* and the *World Telegram.* None of these mass-media publications were favorably impressed by the Almanacs' antiwar posture, and the groundwork was laid for most of the artists above, among others, to be subpoenaed by various congressional committees searching for Reds in the post-war years.

The Almanacs' next project after the *John Doe* album was a set of union songs. The *Talking Union* album was released just before the German invasion of Russia in June 1941. Among the songs included were Florence Reece's Kentucky mining song, "Which Side Are You On?," Woody Guthrie's "Union Maid," and "Talking Union," written by Lee Hays, Millard Lampell, and Pete Seeger.

The Almanacs did perform for union meetings, although with mixed results. Some of their songs were welcomed on the picket line, but in many cases the workers were puzzled by the way the performers dressed and by the folk style of performance, instrumentation, and the repertoire of the singers.

SOME KEY FIGURES AND THE EVOLUTION
OF THE ALMANACS

All of the existing accounts, whether histories of the folk song movement or biographies or autobiographies of its various participants, discuss the internal difficulties and conflicts between the various members and partial members of the Almanacs. By "partial members" I am referring to such musicians as Tom Glazer and Burl Ives, who were on the fringes of the group and who recorded with various Almanacs, although never with the entire group. Although Alan Lomax was much better known as a folklorist, he was also a sometime songwriter and a creditable singer who occasionally would perform or write with various Almanacs.

The two most difficult Almanacs seem to have been Lee Hays and Woody Guthrie. Hays was actually fired from the group when seven members pressured Pete Seeger to dismiss him. His various neuroses—ranging from hypochondria to excessive consumption of alcohol and his general ornery nature—became too much for them to handle. As anarchistic as the group might have appeared on the surface, Seeger seemed to be the one person who constantly sought to promote and improve the artistry of the Almanacs.

Guthrie was an entirely different story. He was a sort of harbinger of the beatnik ethos—he rarely acknowledged any level of personal responsibility. He had no qualms about sponging off anyone who could offer him bed and breakfast. He was an incorrigible womanizer with girlfriends, wives, and children scattered all over the country. He was also a person who had strong opinions and even stronger inconsistencies. It is interesting that Guthrie's persona seems to have captivated many aspects of American popular music to this day. Bob Dylan modeled himself after Woody early in his career, and even before that, "Rambling" Jack Elliott imitated Guthrie's speech, his stories, and his style of singing and playing. Guthrie's son, Arlo, carried the banner to another generation of urban folksingers, and Billy Bragg and others have written melodies to long-buried Guthrie lyrics that resurfaced through the Woody Guthrie Foundation, run by Nora Guthrie, one of his daughters. The more I read about Guthrie, the more I wondered about the seeming longevity of his appeal while so many of his contemporaries remain virtually unknown today. Pete Seeger describes Woody's long-term appeal as "the genius of simplicity."

It seems to be a combination of image and songwriting. When it comes to the songs, the truth is that most of Woody's are *not* sung to any great degree in the twenty-first century. But then there were hundreds of songs. A half dozen of them have become standards, songs that virtually every folksinger and country–folk-oriented singer–songwriter knows. "This Land Is Your Land" is probably his most famous song of all, but "Roll on Columbia," a song written as part of a twenty-six-song outpouring commissioned by the Bonneville Power Authority in Washington, is practically the state song in Washington. Other Guthrie songs that are often performed include the romantic "Pastures of Plenty" and "Deportees," a song that commemorates an airplane crash involving migratory farm workers. Like traditional folk performers, Woody allowed the song to tell a story without imparting theatrical devices in his performance style. This is a lesson many of today's revivalists have not learned.

"This Land" and "Deportees" are at the heart of what I will call the "Woody Guthrie problem." "This Land" began its life as Woody's response to Irving Berlin's treacly opus "God Bless America." The original "This Land" had a chorus with the line, "God blessed America for me." It was obviously intended as a critique to the vague political sentiments in Berlin's song. In addition to the verses that are sung today, there was also a verse about hungry people at the relief office and a wall marked with the sign "private property." What happened to this song?

There are four books currently in print that discuss Woody Guthrie. None of them explains why the chorus was changed or the radical words omitted. In a written communication, Pete Seeger pointed out that the song's initial popularity came from printings in school songbooks, which undoubtedly preferred the lyrical verses over the political ones. I believe that it is fair to say that Guthrie was in his own peculiar way an opportunist, just as apt to "sell out" as to stand on principle. Surely, the song in its common form has nothing in it that even the most confirmed conservative would object to hearing. It is a series of romantic images of fogs, highways, the shining sun, and other attractive images. It is not clear how the changes in the song's lyrics evolved. Did Guthrie edit it himself? Was it one or another folksinger who saw the commercial potential of the song? (A similar editing job was done on Woody's dust bowl ballad "So Long It's Been Good to Know You," although in that instance Guthrie himself did the editing for the Weavers, two of whom had been his friends since the days of the Almanacs.)

"The Song of the Deportees" raises another aspect of Guthrie's talent (or limitations). He didn't write the melody; it was written by Marty Hoffman. In fact, Guthrie seems seldom to have ever written an original melody. All of his tunes were derived from country songs, blues, gospel songs, and whatever else he had encountered in his years of travel. Of course, the Wobblies' songs seldom used original melodies either. On the other hand, they didn't write hundreds of songs. Another musical problem is that Guthrie was an adequate musician who played fiddle, mandolin, harmonica, and guitar, but none of them particularly well. He was exactly the opposite of Pete Seeger, who was always seeking to improve his instrumental technique through practice, study, and by keeping an open ear to whatever musical styles he encountered. An interesting sidelight is that Seeger recorded "Woody's Rag," a nice mandolin solo Guthrie had concocted. Guthrie also wrote some wonderful children's songs.

Another interesting aspect of Guthrie's legacy is that virtually all of his protest songs have been forgotten. Some of his best songs were the *Dust Bowl Ballads*, recorded by Victor in 1940, after Woody had seen the movie of *Grapes of Wrath*. Woody also recorded an album called *Struggle* for Disc, the predecessor of Folkways Records, which included two excellent long ballads, "The Ludlow Massacre" and "1913." Both songs describe mining strikes, one in Colorado and the other in Michigan. "1913" has been recorded by others, but it is not often performed. Both songs are rather long and do not have choruses, which may account for their limited circulation. Many of these Folkways records found their way into libraries and schools, providing another impetus for the folk revival.

On balance, more than anything else, Guthrie could have used an editor for his lyrics and a collaborator to write melodies. Part of what makes many of the songs sound so dated is that the melodies are tunes that were already venerable when Guthrie transplanted them onto his lyrics. In fact, I would have to say that Guthrie was a musical pirate. Virtually all of his melodies were borrowed whole from other sources. "This Land Is Your Land" comes from the Carter Family's "Darling Pal of Mine," which itself was derived from "My Loving Brother," a gospel song. "Rambling Round" was borrowed from Leadbelly's "Goodnight Irene." Guthrie liked that tune so well that he also used it for "Roll on Columbia." "Jackhammer John" was the Delmore Brothers' "Browns Ferry Blues," and "Pastures of Plenty" uses the tune of the folk ballad "Pretty Polly." These are such obvious adaptations that it is difficult to imagine anyone claiming ownership to these songs with a straight face.

Folklorist Ellen Stekert is one of the few people in the folk song movement who has taken on the Guthrie legend. In a review of a book of his collected essays and poems in *Western Folklore,* Stekert wrote, "The sad fact is that Guthrie produced reams of abominable prose and ditties, only the smallest fraction of which is aesthetically worth anything either in the folk culture from which he came or the urban culture to which he wanted at times to belong." This judgment is a bit harsh for my taste, but it is a necessary corrective to the endless worship of a sadly shortened career and life.

In all ways, Guthrie was the original beatnik. His novels, newspaper columns, and many of his songs read like quick outpourings rather than considered work. This sort of volubility, incidentally, appears to be one of the symptoms associated with Huntington's Chorea. Woody delighted in portraying a proletarian image, sleeping with his clothes on, trashing Burl Ives's sheets by sleeping with his boots on, walking away from his various wives for extended trips, abusing the hospitality of his friends, cheating on his various wives, and portraying a principled radical while doing whatever pleased him. Woody's horrible and extended decline and painful death from a mysterious disease only added to the romantic imagery of a brief candle that burned out in multicolored flames. We will never really know how much of Woody's idiosyncratic behavior can be attributed to his character as opposed to his periodic drinking sprees or Huntington's Chorea, the disease that took his life in 1967.

The legend of Woody Guthrie has been carefully nurtured by his Almanacs associates, and through the trust fund that has attempted to bring new life to his songs. In my opinion, a recent biography by Ed Cray covers much of the same ground revealed by Joe Klein twenty-five years ago. In many ways, Woody's life and work are a perfect expression of the left wing's inability to promote its own ideology to a mass audience and its unwillingness to either ignore or come to terms with the music industry. In his book *Working Class Blues*, William Malone has made the point that several country artists, notably Hank Williams Sr., actually had much more of a connection to the working-class American than Woody ever was able to make. Malone points out that Woody's politics greatly appealed to Alan Lomax, while many of the country singers were either conservative or had no interest in politics. Malone feels that it was Guthrie's politics rather than his accomplishments that made him so appealing to left-wing folklorists.

Lee Hays probably was the closest to "having it right," in regard to Guthrie's appeal. He pointed out in his collected writings, edited by Robert S. Koppelman, that Woody represented absolute freedom, devoid of any responsibility to "any living soul." As Hays put it, for an eighteen-year-old this is an incredibly appealing ideology. My own view is that Hays may have set that age limit way too low, when it came to the more privileged American post-teenagers and young adults of the 1950s and 1960s. For the beatnik and hippie generations, those DON'T TRUST ANYONE OVER THIRTY folks, Guthrie's ideology represented real maturity, rather than obeisance to the middle-class values of parents, teachers, or the culture at large.

There are several recent recordings of Guthrie material by other artists. British folk-punk-rocker Billy Bragg recorded two albums with the alternative country-rock band Wilco, and Ani DiFranco's Righteous Babe label put together a series of songs by Woody and reminiscences about him by a number of artists, including DiFranco herself, Bruce Springsteen, Arlo Guthrie, and Jack Elliott. The Bragg–Wilco albums consist of songs for which Woody had written lyrics but had never crafted melodies to fit them. Bragg's performances tend toward vocal overkill, in my opinion, although some of the songs where members of Wilco sing without him work fairly well. As with most group projects, the Righteous Babe performances vary in quality and interest. To paraphrase Sonny and Cher, the legend goes on.

JOSH WHITE

Josh White had a long and interesting career. As a young boy he was a lead man for various blind streetsingers in South Carolina, notably Blind Man Arnold. Josh started his own recording career at the age of sixteen, recording blues under the name Pinewood Tom and religious songs using the name the Singing Christian. Josh was handsome and articulate, and he quickly became a major figure on the New York scene during the late 1930s and '40s. Josh moved to New York in 1932 and recorded numerous songs before an accident hurt his hand and temporarily ended his music career in 1936. After three years working at various jobs outside of music, a chance meeting with choral conductor Leonard De Paur led to a role in the play *John Henry,* which starred Paul Robeson. Josh played the role of Blind Lemon Jefferson, for whom he had performed the role of lead boy in real life.

Josh went on to work with a trio called The Carolinians. De Paur and White arranged and rewrote a half-dozen songs from Lawrence Gellert's published collections. When fabled Columbia Records producer and talent scout John Hammond heard them he was able to persuade Goddard Leiberson, president of the label, to sign them. The songs were very strong antiracist statements, especially for 1940, and unlike the Almanacs' work were issued by a major record label. During the same year, Josh was featured on a CBS radio show produced by Alan Lomax and Nicholas Ray called *Back Where I Came From.* The show brought Josh national exposure and he enjoyed nightclub engagements at Café Society, first with Leadbelly, then with cabaret singer Libby Holman. He then recorded another album of protest songs, called *Southern Exposure*. These newly composed songs were cowritten by a Harlem poet named Waring Cuney.

Josh White did not appear with the Almanac Singers as such, but he played guitar on the controversial *Songs for of John Doe* album, even doing a bit of singing on it. He also recorded with some of the Almanacs in another group called the Union Boys.

A bit later I will discuss how Josh's activities on behalf of left-wing causes would seriously impair his performing career. He also had an odd relationship with the Almanacs as a whole. Most of the Almanacs were striving to present a "folkie" image in terms of dress, speech, and repertoire. For some of them this was an affectation, given their college education and sophisticated background. Josh White, on the other hand, was becoming an increasingly sophisticated and professional entertainer and musician. His guitar style was rooted in the blues, but he had modified it in order to play a broad repertoire that ranged from show tunes to jazz-influenced ballads. By 1947, Josh White began to cut his ties to the radical movement and move his career in another direction. Many of these developments are described in detail in Elijah Wald's excellent biography, *Josh White Society Blues*.

Leadbelly's relationship to the Almanac Singers was much more tenuous than Josh White's situation was. Leadbelly was a "songster," rather than a blues singer; a human repository of ballads, reels, work songs, prison songs, blues, and what-have-you. He had been discovered by the Lomaxes during his second prison term in Louisiana, and John and Alan had briefly functioned as his personal managers. John took him to folklore meetings and schools and wrote a combination biography-songbook about him. It was a short-lived relationship, because Leadbelly came to the conclusion that John Lomax was taking advantage of him. There was also some inevitable conflict between the two of them, based upon John's southern conservative nature and Leadbelly's lifestyle and desire to be independent of his "white boss."

Initially, Leadbelly lived in Connecticut and served as a driver and sort of general butler for John Lomax between tours. After their disagreement surfaced, Leadbelly returned to New York and found an apartment for himself and his wife, Martha. Leadbelly appeared in the early folk gatherings sponsored by the Almanacs, but he did not record or travel with them. He recorded a number of albums, particularly for Moe Asch's Asch and Disc labels. Although Leadbelly sang some topical songs, such as his "Bourgeois Blues," "We're Gonna Tear Old Hitler Down," and "National Defense Blues," his normal repertoire moved in many other directions.

Leadbelly's main influence on the folk music revival came through some of his songs and arrangements such as "Goodnight Irene," "Cottonfields," and "The Rock Island Line," all of which became major hit songs after his death in 1949. Leadbelly was an imposing and powerful figure, but his diction was difficult for white urban audiences to follow. In an effort to remedy this, Alan Lomax encouraged Huddie to construct introductory stories around many of his songs. Some of these introductions were virtually as long as the song themselves, but unfortunately they too were difficult for white audiences to readily understand. Leadbelly's primary instrument was the twelve-string guitar, and Pete Seeger absorbed some of his guitar style, along with many of the songs.

Pete Seeger was the heart and soul of the Almanac Singers. It was his enthusiasm and hard work that gave the group any semblance of an identity. Pete's father, Charles, introduced him to American folk music through his own government work. His musical background had included playing tenor (four-string) banjo in a jazz band. By spending time with southern mountain musicians he learned how to play the five-string instrument. The five-string banjo is tuned and played very differently from its four-string cousin, but through his father and Alan Lomax Pete had access to many musicians and to recordings in the Library of Congress collection. Soon Pete had mastered the banjo and invented many of his own playing techniques.

Pete shared his father's and Alan Lomax's politics, and he threw himself into the Almanacs with great enthusiasm. By all accounts it was Pete who always could be counted upon and whose performances and energy often saved the day. Like the rest of the Almanacs, he concentrated on using folk melodies and grafting leftist political messages on to them. In addition to their politically oriented works, the Almanacs recorded two albums of folk songs. It is in these 1941 recordings, made for General Records, that Seeger's banjo playing and singing begin to reveal the style that he utilizes to this day. They are also, by the way, some of the best recordings of a young and relatively healthy Woody Guthrie.

The other members of the Almanacs included, from time to time, Millard Lampell, later a Hollywood screenwriter, and Bess Lomax Hawes, who later became an important figure in the folk song revival—first as a guitar teacher who organized large classes and later as the Folk Arts Chair of the National Endowment for the Arts. Still other Almanacs included Sis Cunningham, who with her husband Gordon Freisen later started *Broadside;* Arthur Stern; and Peter "Butch" Hawes. Other offshoots or recording partners of the Almanacs included Tom Glazer, who later established a long and successful career in children's music, and Burl Ives, who became famous first as a ballad singer in his wayfaring stranger persona, and later as an actor and country singer.

WORLD WAR II AND THE ALMANACS

When Germany attacked Russia in June 1941, the Communist Party lost interest in the peace movement and wanted all of its adherents to make common cause with the Soviet Union. The United States in turn was attacked by Japan on December 7, 1941. It was then that the Almanacs totally transformed their attitude toward the war. Peace songs had already been eliminated from their repertoire and the emphasis moved to writing songs to encourage the war effort.

For the most part the pro-war songs weren't as interesting as the anti-war songs were. Virtually none of them have survived, with the exception of Woody Guthrie's song about the sinking of the ship the *Reuben James*. The war presented the Almanacs with a bit of a dilemma. The Communist Party had decreed that all efforts should be directed toward winning the war and that workers should temporarily delay making a stir about working conditions or wages as long as the fascist menace existed. This put the Almanacs in a bit of a bind because Josh White, for one, was writing songs that pointed out that African Americans were sacrificing their lives without any guarantee that things would be better after the war. The other Almanacs were still singing union songs, but the emphasis was on supporting the war effort and strikes and divisive social issues were not mentioned in any of these songs. Listening to the songs on the twelve-CD reissue *Songs for Political Action*, painstakingly compiled by Ron Cohen and Dave Samuelson, there are occasional complaints about war profiteering and the cost of living, but mostly the songs praise the C.I.O. and talk about the impending defeat of Hitler.

Pete Seeger was drafted in 1942 and Woody Guthrie went on periodic tours of duty with the Merchant Marine before he too was drafted near the end of World War II. The Almanacs and other groups made up of Almanacs and friends continued to record during the war. Possibly the most impassioned recording that the Almanacs ever made was their 1943 album of Spanish Civil War songs, *Songs of the Lincoln Battalion*, recorded for Asch-Stinson Records. The Abraham Lincoln Brigade was the name given to the unit of three-thousand American volunteers who fought in Spain. Over half of them died. The performers on the recording were a

modified Almanac group, including Pete Seeger, on a weekend pass from
the Army; Baldwin and Bess Lomax Hawes; and Tom Glazer.

This album was a sort of sequel to an earlier album called *Six Songs for
Democracy,* released by Eric Bernay in 1938 on the Timely label. The earlier album featured the singing of Ernst Busch, a German tenor, and it
followed the Hans Eisler model of formally arranged art songs. It is odd
that the Almanacs recorded their album so long after the Spanish Civil
War had ended, but to the American left the Spanish Civil War was one
of the most critical events of the century. There was also a great deal of
bitterness about the war, because Franklin Roosevelt promoted an em-
bargo on weapons, while the Germans were generously supplying Francisco Franco's army. (None of the Almanacs, by the way, fought in Spain.)
Like most of the Almanac Singers' protest songs, one rarely hears any of
the songs of the Lincoln Battalion today, although there is a current,
though not widely distributed, album of songs and reminiscences of
the Lincoln Battalion that features folksinger Tony Saletan and a group of
several other artists, some of whom are children of battlion member
George Watt.

There were Almanac offshoots in Washington, D.C., and Detroit during World War II. The Detroit group initially played for quite a few union
rallies, especially for the autoworkers union, but the work dried up fairly
quickly. Without the dynamic presence of Pete Seeger, there really wasn't
a core group, and even when he had been around the group had barely
survived economically. Alan Lomax and his sister Bess worked for the Office of War Information. As always, Lomax created radio shows featuring
various members of the Almanacs and put together a songbook. Lomax
and his wife, Elizabeth, also wrote two radio shows built around American
legends—cowboys and mountain feuds. In the latter case, Lomax had the
Martins and Coys uniting to fight the Nazis! During the program, Lomax
combined a bunch of the Almanacs with traditional fiddler Arthur Smith
and the mountain string band the Coon Creek Girls. Oddly, these shows
were never broadcast in the United States but appeared on the BBC in
England. It is quite possible that they inspired a series of later radio ballads
by Ewan McColl.

A number of other performers were on the scene in World War II, including Richard Dyer Bennet, Burl Ives, Earl Robinson, and Will Geer.
Josh White became quite friendly with Eleanor Roosevelt and often performed at the White House. Dyer Bennet was an art singer and classical
guitarist, a left-wing sympathizer whose songs were essentially apolitical.
Robinson was a songwriter and composer whose most famous song was

"Joe Hill," cowritten with Alfred Hayes. He wrote a cantata called "The Lonesome Train" about the death of Abraham Lincoln. The cantata was written in 1942 with Lyricist Millard Lampell. When Roosevelt died in 1945, Robinson's cantata and another choral work written by Tom Glazer called "The Ballad of Franklin D" were widely performed.

By the time the war had ended, the Almanacs had received some unwanted publicity in the form of newspaper articles reminding readers that the Almanacs were the same folks who had record antiwar songs shortly before America had entered the war. They were also cited in several congressional reports on communist entertainers and artists. Meanwhile, Pete Seeger returned home with a brand-new vision. He wanted to start a new organization, a sort of super–Almanacs that would have branches all over the country and lead a new fight for social change and a radical America. The name of the organization was People's Songs.

PEOPLE'S SONGS AND PEOPLE'S ARTISTS

The Almanac Singers were not the first group to sing protest songs, but they were certainly an important force in bringing music and politics into close alignment. In 1946, Pete Seeger spearheaded a meeting that led to the formation of two organizations. People's Songs was an organization designed to encourage the writing and transmission of radical protest songs, and People's Artists was essentially a booking agency that sought to find jobs for radical performing musicians. The organization published a bulletin and put together a songbook consisting of protest songs from all over the world called *The People's Song Book*.

There were a number of differences in the vision behind this organization as opposed to the way the Almanacs had functioned. People's Songs was envisaged as an organization, not a collective, of a half-dozen or so singers. The new organization formed a satellite chapter in Los Angeles and there were members, and a less formal organizational scheme, in San Francisco and Chicago. The original Almanacs were all folksingers, but the new group was designed to be more inclusive and it included Broadway and cabaret composers, folklorists, and even record producer John Hammond.

There was tremendous enthusiasm at the beginning, and many of the Almancs and neo-Almanacs such as Lee Hays, Alan Lomax, Earl Robnson, Woody Guthrie, Millard Lampell, and Tom Glazer were on the national board of directors. Pete Seeger was elected as the national director and Boots Casetta was chosen to run the Los Angeles branch. Paul Robeson, the well-known black activist, singer, and actor, later joined the board of directors.

During this same period, important political changes were taking place in the United States. It became clear that the United States and the Soviets were locked in a struggle for political and economic control of the world. Western Europe was aligned with the United States, the Eastern European countries were controlled by communist regimes, and the rest of the world was eventually, and often reluctantly, forced to choose sides between one ideology or the other. The stage was set for the cold war, a mostly nonshooting, ideological conflict between the superpowers.

Given these developments, it was inevitable that left-wing sentiment in the United States would become identified with communism and disloyalty. Communism, in particular, became unacceptable to the majority of the American people and Russia became regarded as a threat to the American way of life.

The initial enthusiasm of 1946 began to give way to financial difficulties and internal disagreements. At first, a combination of a series of successful Town Hall concerts presented by Alan Lomax, the success of the organization's songbook, and some positive interactions with the C.I.O. seemed to indicate that the organization would take off. Certain elements of the Hans Eisler ideology were even incorporated into the organization in the form of a few workers' choruses. Broadway composers who joined the organization included some well-known songwriters, including Harold Rome, lyricist E. Y. "Yip" Harburg, and hit songwriter Bob Russell.

As he had done in the Almanacs, Seeger was handed the unenviable task of asking Lee Hays to resign as Executive Secretary of the organization. Alan Lomax had many other projects besides People's Songs going and did not take a strong hand in the organization. Leonard Jacobson worked as the booking agent for People's Artists. At first he was able to bring in performing jobs, and regular hootenannies—group performances in New York—brought in fairly consistent revenue to the organization. A series of Town hall concerts in 1947–48 did not prove financially viable, and by 1949 the organization fell apart.

HENRY WALLACE AND THE ELECTION OF 1948

Henry Wallace had been Roosevelt's Secretary of Agriculture, and later was vice president during FDR's third term (1940–1944). When Roosevelt ran for his fourth term, Wallace was replaced by Harry Truman, who became president when Roosevelt died in 1945. Wallace did not believe in the cold war anti–Soviet ideology, and he proceeded to run for president in 1948 on the independent Progressive Party ticket. People's Songs became closely involved in the Wallace campaign. Many of the members, including Alan Lomax, wrote songs denouncing the major political parties and advocating Wallace's candidacy. Pete Seeger toured nationally with Wallace and many of the People's Songs artists performed at rallies in support of the Wallace candidacy. Among them were Paul Robeson and Earl Robinson.

Although there is no question that Henry Wallace was not a communist, the Communist Party was closely involved in his campaign and heavily supported him. The C.I.O., which had been a major ally of the Almanacs and was involved in the early organization of People's Songs as well, began to expel left-wing unions from the organization. Some C.I.O. affiliates such as the National Maritime Union, which had been friendly to radical causes, began to purge their leadership of communists and left-wingers. The organization, whose very fiber had been the support of the union movement, was now having to deal with a union movement that didn't want anything to do with it. Unions began to compile their own songbooks without the help of People's Songs, and the only unions that continued to hire radical folksingers were the handful of relatively weak unions that had been expelled from the C.I.O., such as the U.E. (United Electrical Workers) and the Mine, Mill, and Smelter Workers.

The Wallace campaign proved to be something of a disaster. The goal had been to get at least five million votes, but the party managed only slightly over one million. J. Strom Thurmond, who ran on the segregationist Dixiecrat Party ticket, actually polled more votes than Wallace. Despite the fact that his support had been eroded from both the left and the right, Truman was reelected president. This surprised almost everyone. The *Chicago Tribune* published a headline giving the election to republican Thomas E. Dewey. It is quite probable that Truman himself was surprised by his victory. Comedian Bob Hope sent Truman a one-word telegram: UNPACK!

THE DEMISE OF PEOPLE'S SONGS, THE COMMUNIST INFLUENCE, AND THE BEGINNINGS OF FRAGMENTATION

By March 1949, People's Songs was in a desperate financial situation. An unsuccessful concert at Carnegie Hall featuring some major jazz and folk figures failed to raise any money, and the organization disbanded. It was succeeded by a similar organization called People's Artists, the same name that the booking wing of People's Songs had used.

By this time, a number of important artists who had been supporters of People's Songs withdrew or became inactive in the organization and in radical politics. Tom Glazer, Burl Ives, and Oscar Brand had all been involved from Almanac days, but they were noncommunist liberals. Josh White had briefly been a communist, but according to Elijah Wald's biography, essentially only because it provided him with the opportunity to make romantic conquests and to get gigs. The more that People's Songs were tied in to communist causes, the less useful the organization would be for performers seeking gigs. Essentially, the radical movement had developed a symbiotic relationship with this group of singers. The singers used the organization to get gigs, and the organization used the singers to promote radical causes. If the singers didn't entirely agree with the causes they could write the whole thing off as just another economic opportunity. After all, most musicians have played for organizations from the Republican Party to the Elks Club. This doesn't necessarily mean that they agreed with the politics of their employers.

As the cold war heated up, a number of developments occurred. The U.S. Congress became increasingly interested in rooting out communists who had been involved in the entertainment business, and a communist-led coup overthrew the Czech government in February 1948. Czechoslovakia was the last democratically elected government in Eastern Europe. The noncommunists who had been involved in political music began to question the connections between People's Songs, the Communist Party, and the Soviet Union. After all, it was possible to be a political radical and to disagree with communist ideology.

Richard Reuss has written what is still the best analysis of the relationship between left-wing politics and folk music preceding 1960. In his book, *America Folk Music and Left Wing Politics, 1927–1957,* edited by his wife Joanne, he writes: "Was People's Songs, Inc. really a subunit of the American Communist Party? At the risk of begging the question, it is fair to say no. But there is no doubt that the goals and even the identity of People's Songs, and later People's Artists, were substantially influenced by the worldview of the Communist Party in the post war era."

Reuss goes on to maintain that the Communist Party exercised little direct control over the organization, although many of its members were communists. He then quotes Irwin Silber, who became the driving organizational force in People's Artists. Silber says that there was a subgroup of folksingers in the party who met to discuss the overall direction of the role of People's Songs and People's Artists. According to Silber, this club had some twenty members from 1946 to 1949, and "ten or twelve" during the People's Artists era, 1950–52. Silber does not mention who these key members were, although almost without question, he was one of them. It would certainly be interesting to know whether Alan Lomax, or Pete Seeger, for example, were among the members. By 1950, Seeger had moved to the country, and he drifted out of the party. How much attention did the artists pay to formal Marxist theory in their thinking? The general tack that Seeger and Earl Robinson have taken in their writings is that they were naive in regard to Communist Party practices in Russia. According to Silber, this communist folk club did not attempt to micromanage the direction of the artists' organizations, but was more involved in general ideological discussions. He added that there were often ideological disagreements within this group itself. Silber himself seemed to have no hesitation assuming a sort of commissar role. As noted, he feuded with Lawrence Gellert, and in the mid-sixties attacked Bob Dylan as a sell-out.

PEOPLE'S SONGS AND THE COMMUNIST PARTY

It is always easier to question political positions years after they occurred. Still, there are a number of questions about the relationship between radical folksingers and the Communist Party that are persistently difficult to answer. The radical folksinging movement started as a support group for left-wing causes, in particular the communist movement in Russia. The original communist movement presented a utopian image of the future, where poverty would be eliminated and equality for all would prevail. From the time of the Russian Revolution in 1919, the United States, England, and France tried to depose the communists through support of anticommunist groups in Russia and by sending military assistance and even troops to try to depose the communist regime to invade the U.S.S.R.

Given the alleged idealism of the communist movement and its position as the David in a David versus Goliath confrontation with the West, it is not too surprising that the American left wing initially supported the Russian Revolution. It would seem that an intelligent person would have viewed the movement with increasing suspicion as various developments emerged.

When Stalin succeeded Lenin, the former's persecution and eventual murder of Trotzky, his elimination of seemingly loyal rivals in the Moscow Trials of the late 1930s, the 1939 pact with Hitler, and the invasions of

Poland and Finland all seemed to pass without any serious reservations on the part of communists in the United States. The Moscow Trials were particularly problematic, with many old Bolshevik comrades confessing to plotting against the government in ways that certainly appear to be peculiar if not suspicious. This caused some party members, including Charles Seeger, to drop out. The antifascist struggle in Spain also had its share of subterfuge and controversy. The communists engaging in all sorts of skullduggery against noncommunist radicals, including murder, in their efforts to control the Spanish Republican government.

Many radical writers left the League of American Writers when the communist leadership of the organization refused to deal with any of these issues. Among these writers were novelist John Dos Passos and critic Granville Hicks. There is no record of folksingers expressing any public opposition to what was going on in Spain or Russia during this period. Although some left the party in response to these actions, they made no public statements. Was this because of slavish devotion to communist doctrine, or political naivete? Certainly many of the young idealists were attracted by the martyrdom of such union leaders as Harry Sims and Ella Mae Wiggins.

If this wasn't enough to disturb American party members and loyalists, shouldn't they have been shaken up by the Czech coup of 1948, the Hungarian invasion of 1956, and the Czech invasion of 1968? Then of course there were the persistent rumors, later shown to be accurate, of the imprisonment and even killing of political opponents of the regime, many of whom were themselves politically progressive. Quite a few Americans did leave the party, especially during the post–World War II events described above.

To this day, an intelligent and thoughtful man like Pete Seeger only expresses regrets that he did not properly comprehend Stalin's cruelty. Earl Robinson's reactions to post-war communism are similarly vague, and many of the important figures who were party members or supporters, like Alan Lomax, have simply avoided the subject entirely.

If these issues were not sufficient to induce a certain level of skepticism about the goals of the Communist Party, it would seen that the party's position on the "Negro question" would have caused some concern. During World War II, party leader Earl Browder reconfigured the Communist Party as the Communist Political Association. This was part of the notion of all factions of the left uniting against the Nazis. At the end of the war Earl Browder was denounced as a "revisionist" by French communist czar

Jacques Duclos. Browder was then replaced by long-time party stalwart William Z. Foster.

Adopting the Soviet model of creating national states for various Asian minority groups, such as the Kazakhs, Foster believed that the solution to what he called "the national question"—the situation of African Americans in the United States—was to create a separate black state in the American South that would consist entirely of African Americans. It doesn't appear that anyone took this notion seriously.

Keep in mind that People's Songs was attempting to go out of its way to involve blacks in all of its events. The group promoted economic and social integration and its members often wrote songs promoting these programs. Wouldn't it be natural to assume that communist folksingers would at the very least question Foster's policies? I have never seen any mention of the national question or the creation of a black belt southern independent nation in any books or journals written or published by radical folksingers. It would appear that if a communist doctrine didn't work for these folks, they simply ignored it, rather than opposing it.

WHO OWNS AND EDITS THE LEGACY OF RADICAL FOLK MUSIC?

If we read any of the books about the relationship between radical politics and folk music, we get the impression that the communists entirely dominated political folk music, although there were a handful of noncommunist liberals or radicals such as Rox Berkeley, Joe Glaser, and Dave Van Ronk. The various small left-wing Trotskyite splinter groups in New York also wrote and sang songs making fun of communism. This leaves aside the actual folk aspects of the music, such as the recordings and performances of the textile workers described earlier in this chapter. Some of the music that was in effect coopted by the communist movement, such as the songs of Sarah Ogun Gunning (Aunt Molly Jackson's half sister), really did not belong there. Although Gunning wrote a song entitled "I Hate the Capitalist System" that included the line, "I hate the capitalist system," not only was she not a communist but upon her rediscovery she asserted that she did not approve of communism or communists. Josh White continued to perform some of the strongest political songs of any of the Almanacs long after he repudiated any semblance of communist ideology. Although Lawrence Gellert was himself a communist, the protest songs that he collected were written and sung by "the folk."

Brookwood Labor College, which dates from 1921, had a politically mixed bag of students that gathered for a two-year course of study in a small town north of New York City. It was founded by Norman Thomas, the leader of the Socialist Party, and A. J. Muste, a pacifist leader. Tom Tippitt, an official of the United Mine Workers, introduced mining songs to the students in an attempt to use the songs to agitate for workers' rights. Due to internal disagreements, the school fell apart in 1933. Another socialist-supported group was the Southern Tenant Farmers Union, organized in Arkansas. Among its leaders were A. B. Brookins and John Handcox, both black preachers and song leaders. Handcox was an excellent songwriter, and his "Raggedy" and "Roll the Union On" became well known in the union movement. Handcox had to flee the South in fear of his life, and he became marginalized as an obscure figure in the history of radical folk music until he was rediscovered many years later. Charles Seeger had recorded Handcox in Washington, D.C. in 1938.

The Highlander Folk School in Monteagle, Tennessee, seems to have included members of both the Communist Party and the noncommunist left. Zilphia Horton, wife of founder Miles Horton, collected hundreds of songs. It was at Highlander that "We Shall Overcome" was transformed into what later became the anthem of the civil rights movement.

By the 1960s, the role of the Communist Party in radical folk music had moved from a dominant position to a presence barely on the margins of the radar of the New Left. The radical right also began to exert a musical presence, both in the writing and recording of segregationist songs.

*　　*　　*

In 1948, I attended the Progressive Party convention in my hometown of Philadelphia. I was thirteen years old at the time, and there I had my first taste of the five-string banjo, when Pete Seeger performed at the convention. As an urban kid whose musical education consisted of seven years of classical piano lessons and a few concerts by the Philadelphia Orchestra, I was sympathetic to radical politics, but had no idea that music could be enlisted in the cause of politics. As a matter of fact, I knew next to nothing about music. As my friend the brilliant musician Frank Hamilton once said to me, "I wonder how many middle-class kids had their lives ruined by listening to the pied piper of folk music, and then proceeded to pick up banjos and guitars, and ride freight trains or hitchhike on highways."

chapter 3

People's Artists, the Weavers, the Blacklist, and the Beginning of the Folk-Pop Revival 1949–1952

During the summer of 1949, a scheduled performance by Paul Robeson in Peekskill, New York, led to a Ku Klux Klan attack, a rescheduling of the performance, and yet another attack. The cold war was on in earnest, and anyone suspected of being a communist or being sympathetic with communism was fair game for congressional investigations, blacklisted from film, television, or radio work, and lambasted in the press. Alan Lomax fled to England in 1950, safe from intrusion into his political beliefs.

PETE SEEGER AND THE WEAVERS

The Weavers were formed at the end of the Wallace campaign in 1948. Besides Pete Seeger, the other members were Pete's old friend Lee Hays and the younger singers Ronnie Gilbert and Fred Hellerman, who, like the senior members of the group, had a radical folksinging background from their days as camp counselors at Camp Wo-Chi-Ca.

Initially the Weavers sang at People's Songs hootenannies and for radical causes. Hays and Seeger started to collaborate on songs, and their "If I Had a Hammer" eventually became one of the best-known American political folk songs. "Kisses Sweeter than Wine," another eventual hit song, also evolved out of this collaboration. When People's Songs folded, the four turned professional and secured an engagement at the Village Vanguard club in New York's Greenwich Village. The gig was actually supposed to be a solo Pete Seeger performance, but the four of them agreed to work for the $200 that Seeger would have been paid to perform alone.

Unlike the Almanacs, the Weavers were well-rehearsed and their engagements were easy to listen to, yet the material still retained some of the elements of the traditional folk song. Their Vanguard engagement lasted for six months, and they were signed to Decca Records in 1950. In September 1949, the group recorded two songs for the Hootenanny record label formed by People's Artists members Irwin Silber and singer Ernie Lieberman. The two songs recorded were Hays and Seeger's "The Hammer Song" and an extremely political song called "The Banks of Marble," written by Les Rice. Rice's song refers to "the banks of marble, with a guard at every door," and "the vaults of silver" that various working folks have sweated for. During the next two years, Decca sold over four million Weavers records and they became the first hit pop-folk group.

It is important to understand what aspects of folk song that the Weavers retained and to what extent they were influenced and even controlled by the commercial music establishment. The Weavers' recordings featured large orchestras and even background singers. Seeger's banjo playing and Hellerman's guitar work were retained, but in many cases they were subordinated to Gordon Jenkins's orchestral arrangements. In their hit song "On Top of Old Smokey," West Coast folksinger Terry Gilkyson was added to the ensemble. Seeger lined out the words to the song, which were then repeated by the Weavers. With no offense to Gilkyson, who was an excellent songwriter, it remains a mystery why the group or Decca Records felt that his presence was necessary. What seems so odd in retrospect is that less than ten years later the Kingston Trio, who were an avowedly commercial group of college friends, did their recordings with banjos and guitars, without the use of orchestrations. Never mind that the Weavers' instrumental abilities were head and shoulders above the Trio, the point is that coming from a position of specifically wanting to commercialize and popularize American folk songs, the Trio presented them in a much more "authentic" arrangement, at least instrumentally, than the Weavers. This is peculiar when one considers that it was the Weavers, especially Pete Seeger, who had extensive grounding in the instrumental styles of American folk song. An interesting sidelight to the Weavers' "commerciality" is that Hays has acknowledged that he enjoyed singing with large orchestras; in fact, he even claimed, "I'd been wanting to sing with a big orchestra all my life."

The Weavers were comanaged by Harold Leventhal, an old radical friend of theirs, and a more typical music-business hustler named Pete Kameron. Kameron put considerable pressure on the group to stay away from their radical friends and not perform for radical causes. Richard Reuss even quotes Seeger as acknowledging that the group was not allowed to sing at People's Artists hootenannies. According to Lee Hays, though, Kameron should not be depicted as the heavy. The group had agreed that they should avoid left-wing associations in order to keep their high commercial profile going for as long as possible. They knew that, inevitably, their prior left-wing affiliations would be revealed by the media. Robert Koppelman also mentions that apparently Seeger would occasionally sneak out to attend left-wing meetings in cities where the group was appearing. Of the four, Seeger seems to have been the least comfortable with mass popularity, Decca's orchestrations, or the need to avoid any sort of associations with radical political groups.

People's Artists was formed out of the wreckage of People's Songs in July 1949. Initially Pete Seeger and Irwin Silber were elected to the steering committee. It was People's Artists that had organized the Robeson concerts at Peekskill and Pete Seeger opened the show, and his family was one of the many who were attacked with stones thrown at their car windows at the conclusion of the concert.

With Alan Lomax gone and with Seeger reduced to an inactive role, it was Irwin Silber who became the cultural commisar of the organization. Silber was not a musician, but a square-dance caller who had been a member of the American Folksay dance group. He was the first person connected with the radical folk song movement who could be described as an administrator, rather than a performer. For Silber and for People's Artists, the success of the Weavers represented a difficult dilemma. On the one hand, the organization was happy to see their colleagues taste commercial success and access to large nationwide audience. This was something that none of the Almanacs had ever been able to achieve. On the other hand, there was some bitterness about the Weavers removing themselves from the political arena. There were also attacks on the group for performing African American music, and some criticisms that there were no black artists represented in the group.

People's Artists even organized another quartet to perform at hootenanies, since the Weavers were no longer available. The group consisted of two women and two men, and included a black woman and a black man, as though to taunt the Weavers' white-bread appearance.

It is interesting that the left-wing critiques of the Weavers, outside of the racial ones, don't relate very much to the music of the group. One exception was the *Little Sandy Review,* a little-known folk magazine in Minneapolis. Editors Paul Nelson and Jon Pankake, perhaps the first of the so-called "folk nazis," railed against the Weavers' "folkum," blaming the Weavers for the entire pop direction of the folk revival. It is interesting to note that *Little Sandy* only dates from 1960; apparently even the revived Weavers group, sans strings and choruses, was too commercial for the Minneapolitans.

Listening to the original Decca recordings some fifty years later, an uncomfortable resemblance to Muzak emerges. Some of the background vocals on "Goodnight Irene," for example, bears more resemblance to the Norman Luboff Choir or the Roger Wagner Chorale than a folk group. Despite their avoidance of political material, there were some respects in which the Weavers broke new musical ground. Their recording of "Wimoweh" was an inspired attempt to bring South African music and the political struggles in that nation to the attention of Americans. And their recording of "A Trip Around the World" is possibly the first example of world music being recorded by American folksingers outside of the relatively tame South African recordings of Marais and Miranda.

The Weavers and Copyright

I have already pointed out that it was customary for folklorists to copyright songs that they collected. The Lomaxes and Lawrence Gellert, who had little in common with one another, both followed this practice. To explain the significance of copyright, it is necessary to briefly explain the various royalties that songs earn.

The two primary sources of income for songs are through the royalties paid for recorded performances by the record company and the income that derives from airplay on the radio or television. During the heyday of the Weavers, the publisher and songwriter equally shared royalties of two cents a record. Performance rights income is, and was, much more complicated because it depends on how many times a song is performed on either radio or television. Radio is sampled in a way that is similar to the polling of voters regarding their choice of political candidates. In other words, performance income for radio play represents an intelligent guesstimate of airplay rather than a precise count.

The two major performing rights groups, ASCAP and BMI, both pay less money for new arrangements of songs that are in the public domain than they do for original songs. To be more specific, no one knows who wrote a chestnut like "On Top of Old Smokey." By copyrighting their new arrangement, usually under the rubric "Arranged and Adapted By _____," the Weavers were able to receive these royalties. In this example it is difficult to fault the Weavers for wanting to accept this income, which otherwise would have been retained by the record company. The

Weavers used a collective name, "Paul Campbell," for these credits. However, the Weavers also recorded a number of songs that the Lomaxes had collected, in many cases from the Weavers' friend Leadbelly. These songs were credited to "Joel Newman," who was actually a combination of Leadbelly and John and Alan Lomax. Irwin Silber criticized the Weavers for this "callous approach to the musical heritage of the Negro people." Perhaps it would have been more accurate to criticize them for not attacking the Lomax approach to copyright, but that is another issue.

The Blacklisting of the Weavers and Its Effects

Given the intensification of the cold war and the past history of the Weavers, especially Hays and Seeger, it was inevitable that the group would run into trouble with the various groups seeking to out communists in the arts. The magazines *Counterattack* and *Red Channels* listed a number of People's Songs stalwarts as communists. By 1951 the Weavers had lost their Decca recording contract, had a number of gigs terminated, and were denied television work. An ex-employee of People's Songs named Harvey (Matt) Matusow appeared before the House Un-American Activities Committee and named the Weavers and other artists as being communists. He later recanted his testimony, but by then the damage had been done.

In perspective, the oddest thing about the censorship of the Weavers is that the group themselves had done a superb job of removing their politics from their music. What frightened the Red hunters about the group was not what they were doing currently (1950–52), but what they had done in previous years. Seeger and Hayes were called to testify before the House Un-American Activities Committee to testify about their relationship to the Communist Party, and asked to name "other communists." Like most of the other entertainment business figures who testified, Lee Hays took the Fifth Amendment, refusing to testify because he might incriminate himself. Seeger took the First Amendment, which questioned the right of the committee to inquire into his political beliefs. Thus began an almost ten-year odyssey with government trials, eventually backing down in 1962 on a technicality. Others who refused to cooperate included singer–actor Tony Kraber, Earl Robinson, and Irwin Silber.

The practical effects of blacklisting were that the people who were on the lists became pariahs in the entertainment industry. They were only hired by radical causes; they couldn't get record deals, movie contracts, TV shows, or any decent gigs. Burl Ives not only testified before the McCarran Committee in the Senate, but even named names of people whom he accused of being communists. Some other folksingers, such as Tom Glazer and Oscar Brand, had never been communists and they simply separated themselves from the People's Artists performers. Josh White voluntarily appeared before the House Committee, and even had three prior meetings with FBI agents. He portrayed himself as a dupe of radicals, but he did not name names.

Irwin Silber attacked Burl Ives, Josh White, and Tom Glazer as stool pigeons, either because of their denunciations of the communist influence in songwriting or their testimony before the U.S. Congress. Silber later feuded with the New Left when he denounced Bob Dylan's pop-folk sensibilities. Always quick to question the motives and politics of artists, he was less forthcoming about his own errors or motives.

A little-known aspect of the left was the blacklisting done by the left itself. Seeger, the other Weavers, and performers still active in People's Artists still were able to get some work through the radical movement, especially in New York. Radical groups no longer would hire Brand, Glazer, Ives, or White. Because Ives had named names, he did resurrect his career, although more in the field of film than music. Later, he reappeared as a successful country singer. Brand describes himself as being blacklisted from both the left and the right—unable to get nonpolitical gigs since of his past radical associations, and unable to get gigs through People's Artists because he was considered to have "left the fold." The same strictures applied to Glazer and White, although Glazer subsequently transformed himself into a children's artist and author, and Josh managed to make some inroads on the college concert circuit and also continued to make records.

The Weavers reunited in 1955 for a Carnegie Hall concert promoted by their original comanager Harold Leventhal. By that time, some new artists had appeared in the folk-pop genre. On the East Coast Harry Belafonte, Vince Martin, and the Tarriers became successful recording artists, and on the West Coast the Easy Riders and the Gateway Singers took up the pop-folk torch. The story of the pop-folk revival is the subject of the next chapter of this book.

*   *   *

I was a student at Goddard College in 1954. An indication of the financial havoc that the blacklist exerted on the career of blacklisted artists—several other students and I hired Pete Seeger to do a performance for which the fee was thirty-five dollars and a ride to his next gig in Montreal. Just two years before, Seeger and the Weavers were making hit records and touring nationally for "big bucks." He did a great performance, by the way.

During the early and mid-1990s, I did a series of performances at senior centers and residential facilities in northeastern Colorado and southeastern and south-central Kansas. None of these facilities was located anywhere near a large city. I would usually close the show with the song "Goodnight Irene." I don't think I ever did a performance where the seniors didn't at least sing along on the chorus. This indicates how pervasive the Weavers' songs were in an area of middle-America where performances of American folk songs were a relatively rare event.

chapter 4

The Pop-Folk Revival, 1955–64

When the Weavers were blacklisted and thus effectively removed from any national exposure as either performers or recording artists, many Americans identified folk music with radical, "un-American" causes. Nevertheless, folk music did not disappear from the American popular musical scene. In 1951, a young African American of Jamaican origin named Harry Belafonte began a series of successful nightclub performances at the Village Vanguard in New York. Belafonte had previously sung both jazz and pop, but now he switched over to folk and calypso music. In 1954, Belafonte landed a recording contract with RCA Records. His first album was a pop-folk album, but in 1956 he started to record calypso songs and had a number of hit recordings, including "The Banana Boat Song" and "Jamaica Farewell." Belafonte was a sexy, light-skinned man who wore his shirts partially unbuttoned, exposing a good deal of skin. He represented a very different image than the other "folksingers," who generally presented themselves in a less flamboyant way.

Belafonte was based in New York, but quite a bit of the continued impetus for the folk song revival was coming from the West Coast. In 1952, singer–songwriter Terry Gilkyson joined forces with People's Songs veterans Rich Dehr and Frank Miller to form the group the Easy Riders. Between 1952 and 1959, the group recorded six albums for Columbia Records, finally hitting paydirt with their 1957 record "Marianne." Gilkyson has become a somewhat neglected figure in the folk song revival, but he was a fine songwriter. He wrote the folk-pop hits "The Cry of the Wild Goose," successfully recorded by Frankie Laine, "Fast Freight," later recorded by the Kingston Trio, and some fine lesser-know songs such as "The Girl in the Wood" and "The Solitary Singer." His daughter, Eliza, is currently an active and well-respected singer–songwriter.

Another West Coast folk-pop act was the Gateway Singers, founded by bassist Lou Gottlieb with Jerry Walter, Jimmy Wood, and Barbara Dane. In Gottlieb's chapter in the book *Wasn't That a Time,* edited by Ronald Cohen, Lou says that the Communist Party told the group that they needed to get rid of Barbara Dane because her then-husband, Rolf Cahn, had been expelled from the Communist Party. Dane was replaced by a black singer named Elmerlee Thomas, which I suppose gratified the party hacks, who at one time had criticized the Weavers for not having any black members. When Wood quit the Gateways he was replaced by Travis Edmundson, who later achieved some fame (and riches) teaming up with Bud de Sheel in the group Bud and Travis. Gottlieb himself left the group to return to graduate school for his PhD in musicology, and he was in turn replaced by Ernie Leiberman, who used the name Ernie Sheldon for fear that his connections with People's Songs and the radical movement would be revealed.

The interesting thing about all of the artists mentioned so far in the present chapter is that, like the Weavers, virtually all of them had radical associations. Gottlieb was a party member, Dehr and Miller were in People's Songs, and Belafonte had gotten in some difficulties because of some benefit performances he gave for left-wing organizations. Ironically, the Gateway Singers recorded for Decca, the same company that had axed the Weavers because of their associations with radical groups. Did the label not know about the skeletons in the Gateway's closet, or did they not care, as long as these associations were not publicized? The Easy Riders recorded for Columbia, and Belafonte for RCA. Apparently, as long as radical singers were able to avoid any publicity about their political activities, the major labels, sensing that they could make money on folk music, were willing to record them.

A few months before Belafonte recorded "The Banana Boat Song," a New York trio called the Tarriers had a hit with it. This may seem unusual to the modern reader, but up until the mid-1960s it was not unusual for one group to record a song that was already popular, or becoming popular, in a version by another artist. This was referred to as a cover record. The Tarriers included guitar and banjo virtuoso Erik Darling; Alan Arkin, who later became a well-known actor; and singer-guitarist Bob Carey. Since Carey was black, this was one of the first integrated pop performing groups. The Tarriers virtually had two hit records on the market at the same time. They backed a singer named Vince Martin recording a song called "Cindy, Oh Cindy," a rewrite of an old work song called "Pay Me My Money Down." The Tarriers and Vince Martin differed from all of the other acts in the sense that except for Alan Arkin, who soon left the group, they were not especially identified with radical politics or causes. Arkin's father, David, had been active in the West Coast branch of People's Songs.

A few other artists emerged during this period performing music in a folk-pop vein. British guitarist Lonnie Donegan recorded Leadbelly's version of the song "Rock Island Line," which became a big hit record in both the United States and the United Kingdom. In England, it led to the "skiffle" movement—a sort of jug band–style music with homemade instruments that influenced many of the (then) very young British rockers like the Beatles. Donegan's stay on the American popular music scene was more like Andy Warhol's "everyone becomes famous for fifteen minutes" dictum. (Dave Van Ronk once told me a wonderful story about Donegan coming up to Moe Asch's Folkways Records office in New York attempting to collect royalties from Asch's Leadbelly reissue recording of the "Rock Island Line." According to Dave, Asch threw Donegan down the stairs.)

Another folk-pop entry into the hit parade was Tennessee Ernie Ford's recording of the song "Sixteen Tons," a song written by Merle Travis. Travis came from a Kentucky coal mining family but then moved out to Los Angeles, becoming an extremely influential guitarist and a successful songwriter. Although Travis's song, with its chorus ending with the line, "I owe my soul to the company store," represented a higher level of social commentary than any of the Weavers' songs, Travis had no radical associations and Ford was in fact quite conservative.

In addition to these successful recordings, there was other folk activity during the early 1950s, particularly on the West Coast. San Franciscan Stan Wilson became a regionally popular nightclub singer and recording artist, and a young singer named Odetta left the world of musical theater and art song to become a folk singer. Initially, she partnered with banjo picker Larry Mohr before going out on her own.

THE KINGSTON TRIO

The beginning of the real folk-pop boom came with the performances and recordings of the Kingston Trio. The original trio (there's still a Kingston Trio out there today, but with none of the original members) consisted of Dave Guard, Nick Reynolds, and Bob Shane. The trio set the standard for the many pop-folk groups that would appear during the next four years. They wore peppermint-striped button-down shirts, they ran onto the stage, they had a certain comedic sense (depending on your taste), and they were extremely enthusiastic. Guard had attended a Weavers concert in 1957 and went on to learn to play the banjo from Pete Seeger's instruction book, followed by some lessons with banjo virtuoso Billy Faier. They were all college students in the San Francisco Bay area, although Guard and Shane were originally from Hawai'i.

The group started to perform in San Francisco and picked up a personal manager named Frank Werber. They cut a demonstration record, which led to a Capitol Records recording contract. Their first single, "Scarlet Ribbons," didn't make too many waves, but when the trio's album came out in 1958, a disc jockey in Salt Lake City picked up on the song "Tom Dooley," a traditional southern mountain murder ballad, and by playing it repeatedly got Capitol to release the song as a single. It became an enormous hit and it is still obligatory for the group to perform it at concerts almost fifty years later.

The Kingston Trio went on to become one of the pioneers to perform on the college concert circuit, and they made a half-dozen major hit albums in short order. They toured incessantly and were enormously popular. In 1962, Dave Guard left the group to pursue his own musical direction and allegedly also because he was extremely angry at what he believed to be financial mismanagement of the Trio's publishing income by a legendary music-business character, the late Artie Mogull. Different people were floated as replacements for Dave, including John Phillips, the leader of my group, the Journeymen. Eventually, John Stewart was selected. He had been performing with a group called the Cumberland Three. John was not the world's greatest singer, but he brought a whole new dimension to the group: he was a top-flight songwriter. Prior to his joining the group the Trio had always needed to look to other writers for material or dip into the traditional folk repertoire. John was one of the first singer–songwriters to make his way into the folk movement. By 1967, he found that the Trio was becoming a boring experience. Over the years he recorded several dozen solo albums, had a hit single with his song "The Power of Gold," and wrote the song "Daydream Believer," which became a huge hit for the Monkees, and again for Anne Murray.

SELLING OUT

While the pop-folk boom was percolating, a different sort of revival was happening in some of the major American cities, especially New York, Chicago, and San Francisco. Most of this movement will be covered in the next chapter, but the point here is that a sort of oppositional culture developed between the pop-folk stars and the urban revivalists. The latter group had very strong feelings about the alleged purity of their music, and they found the pop-folk groups distasteful and downright threatening. It wasn't just the music, it was that the pop-folk acts told jokes on stage (many of which were bought from professional gagsters); it was the style of dress, the running on stage, and, to be honest, that the pop-folk people were making huge amounts of money.

The Kingston Trio was followed by a large group of people who were essentially imitators of their style and repertoire. Each of them had a somewhat different approach, designed to distinguish them from the Kingston Trio. The Brothers Four were a group of four fraternity brothers from the University of Washington. They signed with Columbia Records and, like the Trio, they were able to come up with some hit singles, especially "Greenfields," released in 1959, and later "The Green Fields of Summer." They had a sort of barbershop vocal sound, and like the Trio were young and enthusiastic.

A big part of the folk-pop movement's impetus came through one particular booking agency, International Talent Associates. ITA, as it was called, booked the pop-folk acts all over America's colleges during the school year and found work for the groups during the summer at state fairs, nightclubs, and other venues. If the group one particular college wanted wasn't available, or if the school's budget was too low, the agency would quickly convince the school to take one of the lesser-known groups at a lower price.

The Limeliters were a different breed of cat. Each of them was a professional musician, not a college student. The reader has already met Lou Gottlieb through his work with the Gateway Singers. In 1959, he hooked up with tenor-lead vocalist Glenn Yarbrough and Alex Hassilev, a classical guitarist who performed in a variety of languages. Alex took up the banjo to give the group a pop-folk sound that was in vogue at the time. Gottlieb was an extremely clever fellow, perfectly capable of doing high-quality stand-up comedy. Yarbrough was probably the first of the pop-folk singers to have an outstanding solo voice, and Hassilev had solid instrumental and vocal abilities. The Limeliters show was pitched to a more sophisticated audience than any of the other pop-folk groups.

The other hit pop-folk groups during the next couple of years were the Highwaymen, the New Christy Minstrels, and the Serendipity Singers. The Highwaymen consisted of a five-person group that more or less combined elements of the Kingston Trio and the Brothers Four. They had two giant hit records, "Michael Row the Boat Ashore" and their version of Leadbelly's "Cottonfields." Like the Brothers Four, they had met at college, in their case, Wesleyan College in Connecticut. The New Christy Minstrels was a nine-person group of professional musicians put together by Randy Sparks. The original group featured a number of musicians who went on to pursue music careers in other contexts. Barry McGuire became a solo artist, Dolan Ellis was a talented singer from Phoenix, Larry Ramos later joined the Association, and Kenny Rogers became a huge country star. The group was named after a nineteenth century touring minstrel show. It became almost a revolving-door musical group with people constantly leaving and being replaced by other musicians. The Serendipity Singers also included nine singers and musicians. Seven of them met while attending the University of Colorado. Dickie and Tommy Smothers were two comedic musicians who formed a duo and gently satirized pop-folk music. Finally, the Rooftop Singers, formed by Erik Darling, an original Tarrier and Pete Seeger's replacement in the Weavers, had a huge hit record in 1963 with "Walk Right In," an old jug-band song. The song featured two twelve-string guitars and anticipated the folk-rock movement that developed a few years later. The expert guitar playing of Erik Darling and Bill Svanoe was much closer to a sound rooted in the blues and African American music in general than any of their contemporaries were able to achieve.

A whole series of other groups were also quite successful in doing college concerts, but never had any hit records. Among the best known of these were Bud and Travis, the Chad Mitchell Trio, the Journeymen, the later version of the Tarriers, and the Modern Folk Quartet. Others included the Cumberland Three, with a young John Stewart, later to replace Dave Guard in the Kingston Trio, the Halifax Three with future Papa (of the Mamas and Papas) Denny Doherty, and the Travelers Three.

Bud and Travis were probably the first Anglo pop-folk group to perform a repertoire that included a substantial number of Mexican songs, sung in Spanish. The Chad Mitchell group featured clever topical-political songs, including some written by Tom Paxton. Right around the end of the pop-folk boom, in 1965 future country-folk superstar John Denver replaced Chad Mitchell in the Chad Mitchell Trio. The Journeymen featured lead singer Scott McKenzie, who later struck paydirt as a soloist with fellow-Journeyman John Phillips's song, "If You Go to San Francisco." John Phillips soldiered on with a new cast of Journeyman in autumn 1964, which included his wife, Michelle, Marshall Brickman, and a few months later Denny Doherty. That group evolved into the Mamas and Papas.

There were also many pop-folk groups that got to record and tour but never really were very successful. Many of the groups were modeled after the Christies, between seven and ten members. Among the lineup was the Christy Minstrels' "farm team" group; the Back Porch Majority; Les Baxters's Balladeers, with David Crosby; the Café Au-Go-Go Singers, including Stephen Stills and Richie Furay; and America's Children.

BUYING IN AND SELLING OUT

In 1991, I attended a conference on the folk music revival at Bloomington, Indiana, where keynote speaker John Cohen described playing on *Hootenanny* in 1963. One of the members of the audience at this academic presentation was Lou Gottlieb. The producers of *Hootenanny* had asked Lou—by that time the leader of the pop-folk group the Limeliters—to listen to the group John performed with, the New Lost City Ramblers, play a few songs. In the middle of the third song, Bob Gibson, another performer, entered the room and Lou got up in the middle of the rehearsal to hug Bob and talk to him. Apparently, John regarded this as one of the most insulting experiences he had ever had in the music business. Even describing it some thirty years later, his face flushed beet-red with anger. When Lou got up to speak, he explained that it was because of *his* recommendation to the producers that not only the New Lost City Ramblers, but also Lester Flatt and Earl Scruggs, among the founding fathers of bluegrass, as well as Maybelle Carter of the Carter Family were chosen to appear on the show. Lou also pointed out that he doubted that John Cohen had *ever* deigned to listen to a Limeliters album, while Lou's musical taste was much more eclectic, spanning everything from folk music to jazz and classical music. Since John had no response to this comment, I tend to think that it was probably accurate.

For me, this exchange encapsulated the culture clashes that persisted between the "purist" revivalists and the pop-folk singers. The purists dressed in jeans or what they thought were the sort of clothes that old-time country music might affect in the 1920s, while the pop-folk people wore the styles of the day. The pop-folk musicians and the more anarchistic of the urban revivalists referred to the purists as the "folk Nazis." The folk Nazis seemed to feel that they had a monopoly on truth and authenticity. In Cohen's keynote speech, he refers to his promotion of traditional music as a "crusade," and there certainly was an almost religious feeling to the purists' war against the pop stars.

Looking back at it all, there are certain aspects of the evolution of the music that the purists could not bear to acknowledge. Most of the people in the urban folk revival were "Pete Seeger's children." They bought banjos in pawnshops, learned traditional songs, and followed Pete's directions to go to the people who originated the music. Pete constantly begged his audiences to listen to one or another traditional musician whose music he was playing during his concerts. And many of us did exactly that. By the same token, many of the people who later became entranced with traditional music heard their first banjo picking from Dave Guard, and their first folk songs from the Kingston Trio. I am thinking here of someone like Michael Cooney, who became one of the most dyed-in-the-wool traditionalists, but who as a teenager was inspired by pop-folk artists.

Then, too, there is that nagging little matter of Pete Seeger himself being, in a sense, the first folkie to "sell out." The Weavers' Decca recordings, as I have already pointed out, were as much pop as folk. Yes, there was the banjo and the guitar, but they tended to be overwhelmed by the string sections and the big choral arrangements with additional singers. It is true that *Sing Out!* occasionally chided Seeger and the Weavers for watering down their music, but the criticism Seeger received was mild compared to the rantings of John Cohen and Ron Radosh (later a conservative cold-warrior historian) in *Sing Out!* Radosh railed against the musical arrangements that the pop groups used, he blasted them for telling corny jokes, and he even accused them of pandering to racist stereotypes in some of their spoken commentaries. The truth is that we were all inspired by Seeger, so all of the folk music aficionados were reluctant to criticize his musical compromises.

Then there is the ugly little matter of money. When the folk revivalists were learning about the music, none of us comprehended the notion that we could make a living, much less a good living, as professional musicians. We didn't imagine that college concerts would pay $2,000 or more in 1963, and we didn't envisage careers as songwriters or studio musicians. We didn't know that songwriting royalties for a hit song could sustain a person's musical career for a lifetime. Most of the purists did not attempt to sustain lifelong careers as professional musicians. Some of them taught college, enabling them to tour on weekends and during the summer, others had full-time jobs in other fields. For the pop-folk musician, music was a career that he or she chose. And in popular music, playing music requires a number of things that are difficult for the part-time musician to grasp. First of all, to the general public, pop musicians are regarded as entertainers. This means that they are expected to be funny and energetic. If they perform music that is thoughtful or difficult to understand, they do so at the risk of not having an audience, or losing the audience that they do have. But beyond this, the professional musician tends to accept that unless you are extremely successful, when work comes in you simply do it. The full-timer finds herself playing in bars, in noisy venues, and in places where the audience resents hearing anything that they are not already familiar with. So the full-time professional finds that anachronistic situations are often the norm.

PETER, PAUL & MARY AND SIMON AND GARFUNKEL

This brings us to two folk-pop groups that may not have satisfied the ultrapurists, but who managed to achieve some credibility with the urban revivalists as well as the collegiate folk fans. Apparently, Albert Grossman had entertained the idea of creating a "hipper" version of the Kingston Trio and had unsuccessfully experimented with various combinations of singers, including Bob Gibson and Carolyn Hester. Peter Yarrow was a folksinger who hooked up with manager Grossman. Together they expanded this notion of putting together a folk-pop trio that was intended to be the sort of anti–Kingston Trio. They recruited Mary Travers, who had attended the Little Red Schoolhouse elementary school where Pete Seeger performed on a regular basis. At Mary's suggestion they added Paul (Noel) Stookey, who had been doing solo performances mixed with stand-up comedy at coffeehouses in New York's Greenwich Village. Noel adopted the stage name *Paul*, because Peter, Paul & Mary rolled off the tongue much more trippingly than would Peter, Noel and Mary or Noel, Peter and Mary. A deliberate contrast in appearance was created within the act, where Peter and Paul were in ultracool mode with well-trimmed beards, and Mary was the "wild chick," with long blond hair that rolled all over the microphone and around her face.

If the Kingston Trio was designed for middle America, PP&M had an element of bohemianism in their appearance and presentation. Peter's role was to play the somewhat intellectual, serious folksinger, Paul was the hip humorist with his amusing car imitations and one-liners, and Mary was supposed to appeal to the lustful inclinations of the college students.

The group made their debut in 1961, and their first album, released in 1962, sold over two million copies. Their opening salvo was a two sided-hit, "Lemon Tree," a sophisticated folk tune by folk-art singer Will Holt, and "If I Had a Hammer." The album also included Pete Seeger's antiwar song "Where Have All the Flowers Gone?" Mary was the only member of the group with a certified radical political background, having sung in a group called the Song Swappers who recorded with Pete Seeger. There were three things that differentiated Peter, Paul & Mary from the folk groups of that particular time. First, they took on the mantle of political folksingers, which either didn't interest the other folk-pop groups, or was something they avoided out of fear of being blacklisted. PP&M performed for the civil rights movement, against apartheid in South Africa, and for other progressive causes. The second aspect of their career that made them stand out from the other pop-folkers was that a woman was in the group. Since the Weavers, the pop-folk groups were an all-male enclave, although the Rooftop Singers, who came on the scene a year later, also included a woman in their lineup. Possibly the most significant difference of all was that PP&M had a string of hit singles. None of the other groups had more than a couple of hit singles, although the Kingston Trio and the Limeliters did release a number of hit albums. After their initial double-sided hit, PP&M's hits included John Denver's "Leaving on a Jet Plane," Peter's own "Puff the Magic Dragon," and two songs by a (then) obscure young singer–songwriter named Bob Dylan. These songs were "Blowing in the Wind" and "Don't Think Twice." Dylan was also managed by Albert Grossman, so he was simultaneously reinforcing PP&M's fame while introducing his "new kid" to the American public (not to mention collecting money from his share of his various clients' royalties). PP&M managed to survive the onslaught of rock 'n' roll with the song "I Dig Rock and Roll Music," written by record producer Jim Mason and Paul. Six of the band's singles made the Top Ten mark on the American musical charts, and the trio released eight albums that went gold (sales of 500,000 or more) before 1970. PP&M still play about fifty concerts a year, and they are the only one of the folk-pop groups where all of the group members are the original people involved.

Another aspect of Peter, Paul & Mary's success was that, unlike the other groups that I have covered so far, they were somehow able to retain some credibility in the urban-revivalist community, while at the same time enjoying tremendous success in the pop world. There were some folk purists who referred to PP&M as "two rabbis and a hooker," a sort of nasty parody of the men's Hassidic-looking beards and the wild-girl bohemian image that Mary presented. Nevertheless, the band's popularity seemed to cross over into all of the areas of folk fans, and their taste in material showed more courage in terms of their political commitment than the other folk-pop artists demonstrated. In this sense, as artists, PP&M formed a sort of bridge between the pop-folk fans and the more tradition-oriented urban revivalists. In the next chapter, I will talk about some of the other artists who for one reason or another were also able to bridge this gap. Among them I would include Odetta, Joan Baez, Ian and Sylvia, and Judy Collins. It is arguable whether this was a matter of image or politics as opposed to matters of musical style, taste, and artistic presentation of the music.

The final major folk-pop group is (Paul) Simon and (Art) Garfunkel. Oddly, they are barely mentioned in existing books about the folk revival—just three almost-incidental references in Ronald Cohen's book, for example. It could be a combination of their tremendous commercial success and their odd early history in the music business. Recording under the names Tom and Jerry, the duo had a hit pop record in 1957, when both of them were sixteen years old. It wasn't a folk record, but a piece of pop fluff called "Hey Schoolgirl." The two were childhood friends, and they made various attempts to record again, culminating in their 1964 album for Columbia, *Wednesday Morning, 3 A.M.* The record was initially a failure, and Simon took off to play in England. Meanwhile, a disc jockey in Miami became enamored of the song "The Sounds of Silence." It was originally simply one of the songs on the album, but the DJ pestered Columbia to put it out as a single. Columbia producer Tom Wilson added electric guitar, bass, and drums to the existing track without consulting Simon or Garfunkel, and Paul found himself living in England with a hit in the U.S. It became their first big song as Simon and Garfunkel, and resulted in their reuniting to tour and record.

This was the beginning of the duo's long and successful career in the music business, a career marked by break-ups, patch-ups, further break-ups, and another recent reunion tour. Simon wrote all of the songs, but although Simon has had some success as a soloist, notably with his *Graceland* album, and Garfunkel has had some hit singles on his own, the two seem to be a classic example of the whole being greater than the sum of its parts. This is evidenced by their massively successful Central Park concerts in New York and a recent gig playing before 600,000 people in Italy.

Simon is a bit of an idiosyncratic character; according to his biographer Laura Jackson, while he was roaming through England just prior to his Simon and Garfunkel hits, he told people that if he didn't become a millionaire before the age of thirty he would consider himself a failure. On the other hand, Simon definitely sees himself as an artist, and he labors mightily over his recordings and songs, making notes on dozens of legal pads and rewriting his songs constantly. Sometimes Simon's ambitions exceed his artistic grasp. His movie, *One Trick Pony*, was a minor disaster, but it was exceeded in futility by his more recent Broadway musical, *The*

Capeman, which went through directors like a thirsty kid wolfing down ice-cream cones on a hot summer day.

Simon was in effect one of the first of the breed that we now refer to as singer–songwriters, performers who write their own songs. A student of English literature and poetry, Simon's songs abound in literary symbols and references to popular culture heroes like Joe DiMaggio and Elvis. As a duo, the two enjoyed a string of hit singles with their songs "Homeward Bound," "The 59th Street Bridge Song," "Mrs. Robinson" (from the movie *The Graduate*), and one of their all-time classics, "Bridge over Troubled Waters," brilliantly performed in a wildly different version by soul singer Aretha Franklin. As a soloist, Simon had his biggest success with *Graceland,* where he performed with a number of South African musicians. In a sense *Graceland* continued the work of the Weavers in bringing international music to the attention of the American public. Garfunkel has also had some success as a solo artist, particularly with songwriter Jim Webb's "For All We Know" and Van Morrison's song "I Shall Sing."

It puzzles me why Simon in particular doesn't seem to be acknowledged by the folk establishment. He plays acoustic guitar quite well, as a songwriter he is one of the few that is even roughly comparable to Bob Dylan— who despite it all seems to have maintained his "folk credentials"—and with Garfunkel he even recorded the old folk song "Scarborough Fair" in a musically interesting way. Possibly it is his desire to be regarded as a sort of literary genius, something Dylan has achieved but which he at least does not appear to be striving for. It may also be that Simon doesn't seem to have retained many folky associations; he tours with New York studio musicians and for the most part he avoids the sort of interactions that Dylan still maintains with important figures in the folk mafia. And, once again, there may be some jealousy involved. Certainly, Simon is more than a millionaire due not only to the success of his recordings but also the extensive songwriting royalties that he receives from the airplay and record sales of his many successful songs. Nevertheless, I do not feel that it is logical or fair to ignore Simon's role in the general appreciation of pop-folk music.

LAURA NYRO

Laura Nyro was possibly the first "organic" singer–songwriter—not a Tin Pan Alley–contracted songwriting hack who wrote three songs a day, but a young Bronx native who had a certain genius for playing with words and phrases, either making them up or recontextualizing them. Because she played piano, was a bit of a recluse, and her records tended to be (unsuccessfully) a bit more commercial than what was considered "folky," Nyro has never clearly fit into a single musical category. Moreover, the hit recordings of her songs were usually done by pop groups or singers such as the Fifth Dimension or Barbra Streisand. Consequently, her name rarely appears in books about the folk revival, although a number of other artists, like Joni Mitchell, have acknowledged her influence.

BEGINNINGS AND ENDINGS

In 1960, I met a talented songwriter-arranger named John Phillips through my old friend Izzy Young, proprietor of the Folklore Center. John had wandered into Izzy's store looking for someone to play banjo and guitar on a recording by his pop group the Smoothies. The group had been singing jazz-flavored pop music in the vein of a sort of pop Four Freshmen. I played on their Decca recording sessions, and John and I started to hang out together. At the time I was living with Karen Dalton, a talented singer originally from Enid, Oklahoma. I had met Karen in Denver at a music party and we came back to New York with her sister and my close friend Art Benjamin in a tiny 4CV Renault that I had bought. That is indeed a story of its own, but I'll stick to the musical aspects of the tale.

John told me that he and the Smoothies' lead singer, Scott McKenzie, wanted to quit and start a folk group. He asked if I would be interested in joining them. At the time I was about to leave a truly grim folk-pop group called the Citizens that had been recording an album for Laurie Records. I told John that it sounded good, and I wanted to include Karen in the group. I had a five-room railroad flat apartment on West 106th Street between Amsterdam and Columbus Avenue, an area of New York in a low-rent district below Columbia University. John was considerably more worldly and sophisticated than I was, and he intuited quickly that Karen and I would not stay together for long. We did two rehearsals, which mostly consisted of Karen and John arguing about vocal parts, which John seemed to be able to invent with the ease of squeezing a tube of toothpaste.

At any rate, Karen and I did break up, and the three of us rehearsed for six weeks, six days a week, ten hours a day, until we had an album's worth of material. The songs were a blend of traditional songs that I brought into the group, some things John wrote, and another song that I had written. In a matter of a couple of months we acquired a manager, a booking agent, turned down an offer from MGM Records, and signed a deal with Capitol. We did three and a half years on the road, playing college concerts, a few nightclubs, TV shows, and we did Schlitz Beer commercials. Sometime in our third year, Scott and I decided that we'd had enough.

People often wonder why groups break up. Anyone who has been in a touring musical group knows that constant touring tends to make minor personality disputes into major annoyances. In the Journeymen, John Phillips and Scott McKenzie were very close friends, almost like brothers. After two and a half years on the road together, the two of them got so irritated with one another that they literally did not speak to each other. They communicated through me (e.g., "Dick, will you tell Scott to tie his shoes"). Forty years later it seems totally ridiculous, but we often rented two different cars so that they would have only minimal contact with one another. Not all groups dissipate exactly in this way, but I remember reading that the Budapest String Quartet, who played together for many years, would never sit together on an airplane or in a restaurant. Maybe that's why they were able to stay together! About the time we broke up, the Tarriers and the Highwaymen also called it a day. The Beatles were starting to shake up the world of popular music, and a young man named Bob Dylan was about to make his own revolutionary forays into the American music scene.

chapter 5

The Urban Revivalists: The New York Scene, 1950–64

MOE ASCH AND FOLKWAYS RECORDS

The pioneer folk label was Asch-Stinson Records, originally formed as a partnership between Moe Asch and Herbert Harris. The partners split up and Harris started Stinson Records and Asch issued his recordings under the Disc label.

The Germans had developed tape recorders during World War II, and tape quickly replaced discs as the major recording format in use in professional studios. When the long playing 33 1/3 RPM unbreakable records were introduced in 1949, suddenly songs could be longer than three minutes, and the notion of recording albums became commonplace rather than something to be reserved for only the most famous or popular artists.

Disc went into bankruptcy and was replaced by Asch's new company, Folkways. Folkways and Stinson both started to issue long-playing records of such artists as Leadbelly, Brownie McGhee, Josh White, and Woody Guthrie. Occasionally, the larger record companies issued folk song compilations such as Alan Lomax's two albums for a subsidiary of Decca Records, *Mountain Frolic* and *Listen to Our Story*. Lomax's records were anthologies of old-time country-folk songs by artists of the 1920s and 1930s, like Uncle Dave Macon. They came with extensive notes written by Lomax and were a revelation to some of the early urban revival singers. These albums were not widely circulated, but they became known to some of the fans of artists such as the Weavers, who had influenced many of their fans to develop a deeper interest in folk music.

Twelve-inch LPs were also available, but they were generally reserved for lengthy works such as symphonies. By the early 1950s, the record companies had eliminated the ten-inch long-playing record and replaced that format with twelve-inch records. Originally, the ten-inch LPs had four songs on each side of the album and twelve-inch records had eight songs. Because record companies didn't want to pay songwriting royalties for sixteen songs per album, gradually the number of songs on a twelve-inch record was reduced to ten, five songs on each side.

Moe Asch was a colorful individual and also a visionary. It was his desire to document the music of the entire world. He was not interested in competing with major record companies, but he wanted to archive music that he personally felt was of historical interest. The Folkways label started to issue recordings of ethnic music from all over the world, usually including scholarly notes by ethnomusicologists.

Most of this recording activity was centered in New York City, which was also the home, or close to the residences, of most of the early revivalists such as Burl Ives, Susan Reed, and various Weavers. Small rock 'n' roll record companies were springing up all over the United States but they were not involved in recording folk music, with the exception of some recordings by blues artists or what came to be known as bluegrass musicians. In 1952, Asch issued a series of six twelve-inch LPs, *The Anthology of American Folk Music.* These recordings, as noted, were put together by the eccentric filmmaker Harry Smith, who lived on the Bowery in Manhattan. He had amassed a collection of thousands of 78 RPM records, and he chose eighty-seven of these songs for the six albums.

There were a number of peculiar aspects of this recording. They were blatantly illegal in the sense that they were recordings by country and blues artists of the 1920s and 1930s that had been made by various record labels. Folkways issued them without the permission of the record companies, and with no payments to the artists. Illegal reissues were not entirely unprecedented; several tiny labels had already reissued recordings of traditional jazz that were owned by major labels. The most amusing of these was a label called Jolly Roger, which reissued albums of such artists as Louis Armstrong and King Oliver, pirated from old Columbia and RCA Victor 78s. The custom record pressing division of RCA was supposedly pressing these records, illegally taken from the company's own vaults.

A number of the artists on the *Anthology* reissues were the same ones that Lomax had used on his two reissue albums. We could debate the ethical issues involved in marketing these recordings without anyone's permission, but in effect Asch was saying that since the original owners of the records had no interest in continuing to market their products, he was going to do so on the grounds that the recordings were of artistic importance. (Oddly, this is an argument that has resurfaced fifty years later in respect to violations of the copyright act in the area of file-sharing of out-of-print records and books.) In any case, the records came out with little or no fanfare, and none of the owners of the songs made any demands for payment initially. They probably either did not even notice that the records were on the market, or they felt that pursuing legal remedies wasn't worthwhile because there was very little money to be made.

Another odd feature of the *Anthology* recordings was that the records also came with a booklet that included Smith's peculiar impressionistic summaries of the song lyrics along with information about the songs themselves and rather odd, almost surrealistic drawings. The whole thing was designed to appear like a crazed surrealistic version of an old farmer's almanac.

Asch had taken some heavy risks in releasing these recordings. Aside from the possibility of lawsuits, issuing six albums of relatively obscure material was certainly a financial risk for the company. From an aesthetic and historical viewpoint, the risk certainly paid off. No one has ever written about the sales figures of the records, but anyone active in the revival, then or later, was heavily influenced by these albums. They included blues, country, folk, and cajun music—virtually an encyclopedia of American folk music. The only music that wasn't covered was the music of immigrant groups recorded in foreign languages. The *Anthology* mixed the black and white musical styles without any sort of musical or racial separation. It is interesting that many of the young urban performers did not follow this pattern, but focused either on African American music or Anglo–American music.

In addition to interest in the music itself, many future urban performers were introduced to such figures as Mississippi John Hurt, Furry Lewis, and Clarence Ashley. In the following ten years, the young revivalists found that all of these artists, and a number of others who had recorded during the 1920s and 1930s, were still alive. Most folklorists were not interested in these artists, feeling that they were not real folksingers, but had been seduced or reduced by the taint of making commercial records.

Asch was a political radical who maintained his independence from the prevailing communist ideology of the Old Left. When the Weavers were blacklisted, Asch recorded an extensive series of albums by Pete Seeger. Asch was notorious for not paying royalties to any of his artists. Dave Van Ronk once told me that he never made any attempts to collect royalties from Moe, but in place of what was owed him he would simply go up to the Folkways offices in midtown Manhattan and get copies of his own records and whatever other albums he was curious about. Moe also had a humane and ethical side of his personality, and he paid Seeger a $15 weekly retainer in lieu of royalties. This small sum helped Pete survive the darkest years of the blacklist.

ELEKTRA RECORDS

In 1950, a young college student named Jac Holzman started a record label while he was attending St. John's College in Maryland. One of his first recordings was of a fellow student named Glenn Yarbrough. Holzman moved up to New York and rented a loft in the western part of Greenwich Village. The loft served as a retail record store as well as the headquarters for the young Elektra label. Some of Holzman's early recordings included an album of Jean Ritchie and another by Tom Paley. Jean Ritchie was one of the few authentic folksingers on the New York scene. She grew up in Viper County, Kentucky and learned songs from her family in the manner favored by folklorists. She sang and played the dulcimer and guitar. Paley was a mathematics professor at Yale who was a renowned guitar and banjo player.

Both of these records were important in the folk revival. Ritchie's record reminded urban revivalists that there was indeed an actual folk community where songs were learned within families and communities. Paley was an excellent musician who was steeped in traditional music, but was also not afraid to add some of his own variations to these tunes. He was typical of many young revivalists in the sense that his singing was secondary to his extraordinary instrumental abilities.

Some other early Elektra recordings, issued on ten-inch LPs, included recordings of international folk music by Cynthia Gooding, a blues album by harmonica great Sonny Terry, and recordings made by filmmaker and radio personality Oscar Brand. Although Moe Asch did record some of young revivalists such as Dave Van Ronk and Mark Spoelstra, he made many more recordings of the older generation of singers such as Woody Guthrie, Leadbelly, and Pete Seeger. It was Elektra that opened up the possibility of recording for the young revivalists. By the 1960s, Elektra had also expanded its focus into international folk music, especially through the recordings of actor–singer Theodore Bikel.

Yet another arrow in the plentiful Elektra bow were the series of bawdy albums, *When Dalliance Was in Flower and Maidens Lost Their Heads*. These albums were a series of Elizabethan ballads with some wonderful creative musical accompaniments by Erik Darling simulating the lute with his banjo. The concept was developed by Elektra chief, Holzman, together with Canadian singer Ed McCurdy. The albums, complete with risqué covers, were a big success from the time of their first appearance in 1956. McCurdy went on to compose one of the classic antiwar songs of all time,

"Last Night I Had the Strangest Dream," which was performed and recorded by artists ranging from Johnny Cash to Simon and Garfunkel.

Holzman also recorded a bit of pop-folk music, issuing albums by the Travelers Three and by West Coast folksinger Bob Grossman.

VANGUARD RECORDS

Vanguard was a small independent label started by two brothers, Seymour and Maynard Solomon. The company started out by issuing classical music records. In 1955, the Weavers and their old manager, Harold Leventhal, decided to test the murky waters of the blacklist by doing a Christmas concert at Carnegie Hall. Vanguard had already issued ten-inch LPs of gospel-blues singer Brother John Sellers, and an album of Russian folk songs. Leventhal persuaded Maynard Solomon, who was politically sympathetic to the Weavers' dilemma, to record the concert. The concert quickly sold out, and it was clear that a market remained for the work of the Weavers. In 1957, Vanguard released a live LP of the concert. The album was a roaring success, the Weavers resumed a somewhat reduced touring schedule, and Vanguard was launched in the folk music business. The label later enjoyed a long and remunerative relationship with a young singer from Boston named Joan Baez.

THE ROLE OF KENNETH GOLDSTEIN

Relatively little attention has been paid to the important role of Kenneth Goldstein in the folk revival. Kenny, as everyone called him, was a journalist who started out in the world of folk music writing liner notes and producing albums for Stinson Records in 1951. He was the first to introduce some of the British folksingers to the American record scene, including A. L. Lloyd, Ewan MacColl, and Irish singer Patrick Galvin.

In 1955, Kenny persuaded Riverside Records to jump into the production of folk music. Riverside was a strong independent jazz label that introduced a number of important jazz musicians, such as guitarist Wes Montgomery and saxophonist Cannonball Adderly, on records. For Riverside, Kenny recorded a large number of records ranging from such relatively esoteric fare as the Childe ballads sung without accompaniment by Lloyd and MacColl to recordings by such artists as Oscar Brand, a young revival folksinger named Bob Gibson, and a banjo record featuring Billy Faier, a very young Eric Weissberg, and the author.

By 1960, Goldstein had moved over to Prestige where he produced or supervised another group of albums, including blues recordings by Gary Davis and Pink Anderson. Goldstein then turned to the academic world and for years was a professor of folklore at the University of Pennsylvania. What he brought to the folk revival was an honest appreciation and enthusiasm for all sorts of folk music ranging from old blues singers to unaccompanied ballad singers and young urban singers and instrumentalists. More than any other single record producer, he was open to the entire spectrum of American folk music styles.

SOME OF THE OTHERS

Another fixture of the New York folk scene in the mid-1950s was the Irish group the Clancy Brothers and Tommy Makem. In 1956, they formed a label called Tradition Records with the financial help of Guggenheim heiress Diane Hamilton. The label issued albums by the group and also by their friends Paul Clayton and Jean Ritchie as well as some fine field recordings of instrumental music that Clayton had made. The instrumental recordings featured the work of a fine guitarist named Etta Baker, who provided some of the young female urban revivalists with a model who was a fine guitarist.

Occasionally, other labels would issue folk recordings. One of these, discussed briefly at the end of this chapter, was called Esoteric Records. They issued a number of recordings of international folk music in the mid-'50s, as well as an entire album of talking blues songs.

THE NEW YORK SCENE AND THE FOLKLORE CENTER

It is impossible in a book of this scope to discuss how the revival evolved in every American city. I have therefore chosen to focus on New York, with some attention to what was going on in other cities, especially Chicago, Los Angeles, and Denver. A more encyclopedic work would have to include virtually every city where there was one or more large colleges or that had a large enough population for folk enthusiasts to emerge.

Since New York was the center of the revival movement, I look at the various styles that were part of the revival in separate paragraphs. This includes the protest singers, the early singer–songwriters, bluegrass, the old-time music scene, world music, and instrumental music. When I turn to the folk scene in other cities, the folk revival will be treated as a whole.

I have already devoted some attention to the New York folk scene because it was also the headquarters of the topical folksingers. Several developments crystallized simultaneously that spread the popularity and influence of folk music in the Big Apple.

One of the people who had been active in folk music in the late 1940s and into the 1950s was a young would-be bookseller named Israel G. Young, known to everyone in Greenwich Village as Izzy. He was a dancer and a dance enthusiast who had participated in Margot Mayo's American Square Dance Group. He developed an interest in folk music through the dance group and through a series of friendships that he made while hanging out in Greenwich Village. He became friendly with John Cohen and Tom Paley, two tradition-oriented musicians who later founded a string band called the New Lost City Ramblers along with Mike Seeger. During the mid-'50s Izzy met record producer–folklorist Kenneth Goldstein, who encouraged him to develop a catalog of books about folk music. This led to Izzy's renting a space on MacDougal Street in Greenwich Village in 1957. He called his store the Folklore Center.

In every city where the folk revival assumed some importance there seems to have been one or two central places where the impetus for the revival was funneled. In New York that place was definitely the Folklore Center. All of New York's folk musicians and fans could be found hanging out at the store. Some used it as a mail drop; some of the pop-folk singers bought books of folk songs in search of material for their performances and recordings. Record-company personnel dropped by the shop to see "what was happening," and Izzy himself became a concert promoter and one of the founders of the Friends of Old Time Folk Music. Some nights, Izzy would tire of the endless parade of tourists thronging MacDougal Street. He would lock the doors and the singers inside would pass around guitars and banjos and play new additions to their repertoire.

Izzy was not involved with the protest music group. Although his politics were progressive enough, he had no ties to any existing political viewpoints. Rather, he was a music, dance, and book junkie with great energy and enthusiasm for what he thought was honest and musical. As such, he was part of the counterculture that existed in opposition to the pop-folk music of the day. In 1960, he operated a sort of music concession at Gerde's, a bar just east of Greenwich Village. He brought in artists such as Brownie McGhee and Sonny Terry, and folk fans began to hang out at the club. Never a brilliant businessman, largely because he was never that interested in the business aspect of *anything*, Izzy was soon squeezed out of the club when Mike Porco, the owner, realized that he was onto something that could be a money-maker. Izzy and his partner, advertising man Tom Pendergast, were forced out and Mike took over the music as well as the bar.

A young performer who called himself Bob Dylan started to hang out at Gerde's and Mike got him a card in the New York Musician's Union, hiring him to play at the club. Even though Izzy was bitter about losing his foot in the venue, he immediately understood that Dylan was an unusual talent. Izzy championed him, and even presented him in a poorly attended concert at New York's Carnegie Chapter Hall.

Another role Izzy played was to recommend musicians for jobs and even record deals. Some of the revivalists started to give guitar lessons, and Izzy would give their phone numbers to prospective students. He was scrupulously fair and never asked for, nor received, any commissions from the musicians whose services he recommended.

Izzy's shop was also a center for gossip, personal musical, or otherwise, and he wrote a column in *Sing Out!* that varied between what he felt and what he had been told. Izzy was also quite outspoken about everything from music to politics to literature, and this sometimes irritated both his friends and enemies. He was even known to throw people out of his store either because they were obnoxious or simply because they irritated him.

By 1965, rents on MacDougal Street had soared and Izzy realized that he needed to sell musical instruments on a more consistent basis to make a living. He moved several blocks away, to a space on Sixth Avenue. The store was up a steep flight of stairs and the proprietor himself lived in an apartment above the store. An adjacent space was taken up by Marc Silber's Fretted Instruments, a shop that sold and repaired guitars, banjos, and mandolins. The two men, both opinionated, but each with a reputation for fair dealing, became partners. Marc was originally from Detroit and worked in Jon Lundberg's Berkeley, California store. Lundberg was a legendary repair person, especially adept at reworking Martin guitars, and in many ways his shop played a role in the Berkeley folk community that was similar to the influence of the Folklore Center. After he left Gerde's Folk City, Izzy continued to present concerts both in midtown and downtown, as well as in his own store.

Lou Gordon, another local entrepreneur, presented folk concerts in the early and mid-1950s at the Cherry Lane Theater in Greenwich Village,

and later at the Circle in the Square. Gordon also produced the Woody
Guthrie tribute concert at the larger Pythan Hall in 1956. The concert was
scripted by Millard Lampell of the Almanacs, and its success led to the
founding of the Woody Guthrie Children's Foundation.

Another center for urban folk revivalists was the fountain at Washington
Square Park, across from New York University in Greenwich Village. It all
started out accidentally when a guitarist named George Margolin brought
his guitar to the square and played songs for a few friends. On Sunday
afternoons, starting around 1950, singers and musicians would gather and
play music on summer afternoons. The city required a permit for playing
music in public. Initially, Pete Seeger and his wife Toshi got the permit,
and later George Sprung took over this role. George's brother Roger was
one of the earliest of these players. Roger Sprung was probably New York's
first bluegrass banjoist. A very young Eric Weissberg was playing in the
square while attending Music and Art High School. By the mid-1950s,
such musicians as John Cohen, Mike Seeger, Barry Kornfeld, Dave Van
Ronk, Happy Traum and Jack Elliott, Paul Prestopino, Dick Rosmini, and
Marshall Brickman would gather in the square and sing for most of the
day. Many of these musicians were better instrumentalists than singers, but
they generated enough excitement and enthusiasm to interest and amuse
the crowd of onlookers who gathered around the fountain. Other colorful
characters would appear in the square from time to time, including a self-
styled black cowboy named Lightnin' who did tricks with a long rope.

There were other places where the New York folksingers also gathered.
Once a week Tiny Ledbetter, Leadbelly's niece, hosted evening jam sessions featuring Reverend Gary Davis, a fantastic guitarist and gospel singer
who had come up to New York from South Carolina. Gary himself taught
guitar, informally or formally, to a host of urban revivalists, including
Barry Kornfeld, Dave Van Ronk, and Stefan Grossman. From time to
time, any of these musicians and many others, including Erik Darling,
Woody Guthrie, and others, would drift into the apartment to play with
Gary. These sessions sometimes included John Gibbon, an excellent guitarist who went on to become a psychologist, and Fred Gerlach. Fred was
one of the few musicians at the time who specialized in twelve-string guitar. He had an encyclopedic knowledge of Leadbelly's style on the instrument, and also threw in variations of his own. Fred went on to record a
couple of relatively obscure albums, moving out to the West Coast where
he was an influence on his nephew, a young guitarist named Jesse Kincaid.
Fred also recorded Gary Davis not only singing and playing, but also

preaching in a small church in the Bronx. Stefan Grossman also made many recordings of Davis and transcribed a number of his songs and instrumental pieces.

The old-time music players gathered at Alan Block's sandal shop in the West Village and they would play old fiddle and square-dance tunes. Alan's daughter Rory grew up around this beehive of old-time string-band music and she would later become a well-known blues artist.

The American Youth Hostel on West 8th Street in Greenwich Village had open-microphone nights on Sundays and often the Washington Square people wandered over there to perform, or they went to an apartment downtown, at 190 Spring Street, where first Paul Clayton and later Roger Abrahams lived. Both of them were folklorists and collectors as well as performers, and the Spring Street sessions tended to be more traditional than the other gatherings. Some of the people who played informally at Spring Street were Gina Glaser; Ellen Alder; Susie Shahn, the daughter of artist Ben Shahn; and an excellent banjo player named Luke Faust. The twin Kossoy Sisters, who recorded an album for Tradition Records, could sometimes be found at Spring Street or at the AYH jams. Other sessions occasionally took place, after 1958, at Alan Lomax's downtown loft when he returned from his voluntary exile in England. Still another scene developed around Theodore Bikel, who sang songs in a number of foreign languages. He held occasional sessions at his apartment and his Elektra recordings spurred interest in the music of various cultures. Other artists who contributed to this aspect of the revival included Israeli performers Geula Gill and Ron and Nama, who also recorded for Elektra. Martha Schlamme was another important influence in this direction. Her work was a blend of international music and cabaret songs, especially those of Bertold Brecht and Kurt Weill. In effect, she anticipated the direction that Judy Collins would move in more than twenty years later.

In addition to the various gatherings listed above, there seemed to be a constant round of parties where people would jam and sing. Some of these gatherings took place uptown. Three young musicians named Art Rosenbaum, Tam Gibbs, and Robby Robinson were in various stages of their academic careers at Columbia University. Robinson was a painter who had a graduate fellowship, Gibbs was a blues fanatic, and Rosenbaum was a young banjo player who later became an art professor at the University of Georgia while continuing his musical career—both as a live performer as well as by issuing recordings of traditional musicians that he recorded on location.

Hootenannies

"Hootenanny" was a word that Woody Guthrie and Pete Seeger brought back from a Seattle sojourn in 1941. In New York, the idiom was transformed by the Almanac Singers into a medium that featured group performances involving multiple performers and often utilizing vocal participation by the audience. People's Songs presented hootenannies three or four times a year in New York, starting after World War II. After the demise of People's Songs, People's Artists, and then *Sing Out!* magazine assumed sponsorship. A number of performers, including Leon Bibb, Laura Duncan, Betty Sanders, Pete Seeger, and Jerry Silverman, were regular participants.

Hoots continued into the 1960s, but just as *Sing Out!* itself became depoliticized, the word and the events became removed from their original radical connotations. Gerde's Folk City, in New York, for example had Monday night hoots that had no connection to politics. By the time of the *Hootenanny* TV show, in 1963, the word had lost its original connotations, although occasionally it is still used today in that older context.

Radio Shows and Journalists

Oscar Brand had a weekly radio show that featured many of the New York performers as well as touring professionals. Other radio shows were run by George Lorrie, Skip Weshner, international folksinger Cynthia Gooding, Bob Fasse, Henrietta Yurchenko, and banjo virtuoso Billy Faier. Although these shows were consigned to such relatively minor radio stations as WNYC and WBAI, they did provide a forum for folk music and folk musicians.

The *Village Voice* sporadically covered the folk scene, but when Robert Shelton began to write reviews for the *New York Times* in the late '50s, it became apparent that the audience for the music was expanding beyond Greenwich Village. Shelton was part booster, part fan, part music critic. He became a great advocate for Bob Dylan, who hit town in 1961. Shelton was a stringer—paid by the *Times* on a space basis—rather than a regular music critic. He supplemented his income by writing liner notes, using assumed names, because he sometimes later reviewed the same albums for which he had written the notes. Later, Shelton became the editor for the short-lived *Hootenanny* magazine.

Another sort of journalism was coming from a folk fan magazine called *Caravan,* founded by a folk music fan named Lee (Hoffman) Shaw in

1957. *Caravan* was a combination folk gossip column and cheerleader headquarters. It generally favored traditional music and the young revivalists and was skeptical of the pop-folk artists. Shaw eventually tired of putting out the magazine, a time-consuming labor of love, and for a while banjo virtuoso Billy Faier took over the editing tasks. By 1960, the magazine had folded. Shaw found that she missed having a journalistic outlet, and she edited and published a few issues of a mimeographed journal called *Gardy Loo,* a kind of less formal version of *Caravan,* which had become more of a serious journal.

"Us and Them"

Although the urban revivalists did not view themselves as beatniks, they shared the beatniks' contempt for American mass culture. Most of the revivalists were either living in cheap apartments in the Village, or in various low-rent sections of Manhattan. The urban-folk male uniform was jeans and a flannel shirt; women wore baggy sweaters or plaids and jeans, they grew their hair long, and they didn't wear makeup. There was a certain amount of antipathy toward anyone who was making money. Naturally, folksingers who made money were anathema to those of us who felt we were pursuing the Holy Grail of artistry.

The pop-folk musicians wore button-down shirts with candy-colored stripes, or they dressed in suits. They often literally ran onto stage and utilized quite a bit of scripted humor in their shows. The revivalists were often funny, but a premium was placed on spontaneity and maintaining an "honest" approach to the music. It was never entirely clear exactly what this meant, but it included such things as always mentioning the original sources of the songs that you performed; not using "modern" chords, but rather sticking to the sort of chord progressions that traditional blues or country musicians played; and a certain nondramatic dryness of performance styles.

The kings of the traditional music revival scene were the New Lost City Ramblers and attending their concerts was kind of a wild cross between going to a party and a college folklore lecture. There was an incessant amount of tuning, partly because the three artists played a raft of instruments. Every time the musicians switched off, a new volley of tuning erupted. To the general public, Rambler performances were virtually incoherent and dull, but their fans loved the puns, the references to obscure records, and even the tuning with the attendant humorous interplay between the musicians. Out of these performances, many younger revivalists were inspired to form their own string bands, some of which, like the Highwoods String Bands and the Red Clay Ramblers, went on to record and tour on their own.

Although the Ramblers were never a top-selling recording act, their influence went far beyond record sales. Mike Seeger and John Cohen were dedicated to collecting and preserving traditional music, as much or more than interpreting or performing it. Mike recorded a number of important albums, including several collections of bluegrass music, tracing the evolution of the style, and covering both the older generation of pickers and some very young ones.

Among the artists Mike recorded was Elizabeth Cotton, one of the stranger stories in the annals of the folk revival. Elizabeth Cotton helped Ruth Crawford Seeger find her young daughter, Peggy, who somehow got lost in a department store in Washington, D.C. Ruth then hired Elizabeth as her maid. One day, Elizabeth picked up Peggy's guitar, playing it left-handed and upside-down. The family was astonished to discover that without their knowledge they were harboring an original and excellent instrumentalist and composer in their own household. Mike proceeded to record Cotton, and her tune "Freight Train" ended up being a hit record in England by Nancy Whiskey. It also became a staple among urban revivalists.

John Cohen is a photographer as well as a musician. He recorded a previously unknown traditional singer and instrumentalist named Roscoe Holcomb, and made a movie called *The High Lonesome Sound* about Holcomb's hard life. Cohen went on to make other movies of traditional musicians, as well as eventually publishing his pictures of a young Bob Dylan. Dylan seemed to fascinate Cohen, who also interviewed him at some length for *Sing Out!* This was rather peculiar given Cohen's negative attitude about commercial music, but I suppose it indicates that attitudes about the arts are more complex than mere opinions would indicate.

The other original Rambler, Tom Paley, was not an archivist, but an original instrumental stylist who was not as dedicated to re-creating traditional music styles as the other members of the group. After the band recorded several albums, Paley left the group and was replaced by another multi-instrumentalist, Tracy Schwarz. The group continued to record and tour for years, although some of their activities were limited by Cohen's day job as a professor in the fine arts department of SUNY–Putnam.

One of the significant aspects of the Ramblers' work was that although Mike Seeger, for one, was fully capable of playing bluegrass music, the group itself focused on the music that preceded bluegrass. This is often referred to as old-time music, or mountain music, to distinguish it from the bluegrass music that was pioneered by Bill Monroe. Old-time music had its origin in the southern mountains and many of the bands had only three members, who played fiddle or mandolin, banjo, and guitar. Much of the impetus for this music was that it was used for square dancing. Bluegrass was a sort of modernized style of music, using an entirely different style of banjo picking synthesized by Earl Scruggs. The lead parts were almost always played on banjo or fiddle, except that in Monroe's band, since Monroe played mandolin, the lead parts were often played by the mandolin. Bluegrass also featured much more intense vocal harmony, and usually the singing was upper-register tenor. The melody was sung in the tenor register and another harmony part floated *above* the melody line. Bluegrass also added string bass and often dobro to the instrumental lineup.

By the end of the 1960s, bluegrass and old-time musicians separated themselves into different camps, and there was relatively little interaction between them. This factionalism even persists today, where banjo instructional camps offer instruction in both styles, with different instructors teaching each style. The prevailing mode is that you either play bluegrass or you play old-time music!

Another interesting musician who came to New York from her native Georgia was Hedy West, the daughter of radical poet and union organizer Don West. Hedy was probably the only other person in New York during the mid-'50s besides Jean Ritchie who had learned music in her family and from other traditional musicians. She was in New York attending graduate school in theater at Columbia, but she began to perform at concerts and coffee houses. She went on to record two albums for Vanguard. Her song "500 Miles," which she had originally learned from her grandmother but had rearranged (partly because she hadn't remembered the exact original melody), went on to become one of the most poplar songs in the folk revival. Hedy was a friend of mine, and my band the Journeymen made the first commercial recording of the song. Most people learned the song from Peter, Paul & Mary's recording. Their version was on an album that sold several million copies. Many other recorded versions of the song also exist, including a hit country version by Bobby Bare, who added a recitation and rewrote some of the lyrics. Hedy was one of the few people in the entire folk revival with a legitimate claim to the copyright of a traditional song.

Robin Roberts was a singer of English and Irish ballads. She did some recording for Tradition and Stinson Records and performed in the New York area. The folk revival was not particularly kind to ballad singers, emphasizing performers who presented themselves in a more dramatic instrumental or vocal context. Consequently, Roberts's influence was not commensurate with her vocal talents.

Carolyn Hester was a beautiful folksinger who came to New York from Texas. She got a major label recording deal with Columbia, but two unlucky circumstances intervened. Bob Dylan played harmonica on her recording and Carolyn generously talked him up to John Hammond, who ended up recording Dylan and devoting much more attention to him than to Carolyn. Her other piece of bad luck, career-wise, was her marriage to Dick Fariña. Fariña will be discussed in more detail in the section on Bob Dylan. A talented songwriter and vocalist, Fariña, like Dylan, tended to invent his identity in accordance with his own fantasies. Fariña essentially lost interest in Hester when he encountered the beautiful Mimi Baez, Joan's sister.

Hally Wood (Faulk) was a Texas-born singer active in the early days of People's Songs. She recorded two solo ten-inch LPs, one for Elektra and the other for Stinson. Hally had a harsh but very expressive voice and on the Elektra album she recorded unaccompanied songs that were a bit outside of what was popular in the folk revival. The Stinson album featured the superb banjo and guitar playing of Joe Jaffe, one of the early but little-known New York folk instrumentalists. A skilled musician, Wood also transcribed the music for the New Lost City Ramblers' songbook.

Bonnie Dobson was a Canadian artist, a native of Toronto, who lived in New York from 1964 to 1965. Like her fellow Canadian Ed McCurdy, Dobson was not a prolific composer. But her song "Morning Dew," which described the aftermath of an atomic explosion, became a widely performed and recorded anthem of the folk revivalists. Dobson wrote the song in 1961 and it was recorded by a wide variety of artists, including the Allman Brothers, Fred Neil, British bluesman Long John Baldry, the Jeff Beck Group with Rod Stewart, Lulu, and the Grateful Dead. Singer Tim Rose also recorded it and managed to cut himself in on the copyright. This was an unpleasant but not untypical aspect of the business part of the revival. Dobson recorded three albums for Prestige Records and, after returning to Toronto in 1965, moved to England in 1970 where she is the head administrator of the philosophy department at the University of London's Berwood College.

Happy Traum and his brother Artie were active participants on the scene, and are discussed in the next chapter when I look at the music scene that developed in Woodstock, a town about two hours north of New York City.

THE REVIVALISTS TURN PRO

By the late 1950s, a number of the urban revivalists realized that they had become full-time professional musicians. I remember meeting Dave Van Ronk in Washington Square around 1958. He had been a merchant marine, and had just come off a ship. He was astounded at the number of musicians and fans gathering in the square, and asked me whether it was actually possible to make a living "doing this." I responded that it was, sort of, if you combined some guitar instruction, performance, and recording.

Erik Darling was highly respected as a guitarist, banjoist, and singer–vocal arranger. He was also one of the few artists who seemed to move back and forth between the commercial and more tradition-oriented folk worlds. In addition to his hit recordings with the Tarriers and the Rooftop Singers, he replaced Pete Seeger in the Weavers when Seeger left the group in 1957. Erik was also one of the first of the revivalists to do studio work, recording on a number of albums by Ed McCurdy, a formally trained singer who moved from Canada to New York City in the early 1950s

Other revivalists who made their way into the world of studio work included Dick Rosmini; Bruce Langhorne, a very creative young black guitarist; guitarist-banjoist Barry Kornfeld; and myself. Eric Weissberg is the premier folkie studio musician of us all. A bass student at Juilliard, Eric quit to replace Darling in the Tarriers. Weissberg, Kornfeld, and I all played on a number of folk-pop records recorded under the names of other artists, including the Brothers Four, New Christy Minstrels, and Peter, Paul & Mary, usually without credits in the liner notes.

Another musician who had one foot firmly in the pop world but still seemed to be able to command the respect of all but the most moth-eaten traditionalists was Bob Gibson. Gibson made his mark playing at Chicago's Gate of Horn nightclub. He paired with singer–actor Bob Horn and the two of them influenced many later folk-pop musicians and revivalists. Originally a banjo player, Gibson moved to the twelve-string guitar and became renowned as a songwriter, and even more as a musician who rearranged traditional songs with modern harmonies.

Always a good musical hustler, Gibson performed in many venues that previously had never featured folk music, and he recorded for Riverside and Elektra Records. He also formed a booking agency and in general was active in the business end of folk music. His career was crippled by drug dependency, and he never really achieved the heights for which he appeared to be headed. Late in his career, he experimented with playwriting and became a children's-music artist before his death in 1996.

THE FOLKSINGER'S GUILD

You may assume that given the radical-political ideology of many of the urban revivalists, they would be actively involved in the American Federation of Musicians, the union that covers instrumental musicians. In fact, many of the folksingers were either not union members, or were only involved because their record company contracts required them to join. (All of the major labels required their artists to join either the AFM or AFTRA, the union for singers. This wasn't because the labels were pro-union, but because their agreements with the unions specified that all artists join the union.) Pete Seeger was a member of the New York union, Local 802, but had some problems when he was asked to sign a loyalty oath. All of the musicians who did extensive studio work were union members and received union wages for playing on recording sessions.

The union ostensibly covered all nightclub and concert work, as well as recording and television. However, the recording agreements were easier to police than concert performances in, for example, Kearney, Nebraska. As more of the young revivalists became professionals, they began to feel that they really had no organization to protect their interest. The AFM focused most of its energies on bands—symphonies and swing bands—and on recording and television and movie work. Many of the local unions also didn't feel that folk performers were competent musicians because they did not develop formal musical skills, for example, learning how to read and write musical notation. One of the more amusing examples of this happened to a topical singer–songwriter named Charley Brown. The union used to require live auditions and Charley auditioned in Massachusetts, where he was living. The musician had the option of either sight-reading dance-band charts or telling the union official that "I just sing and accompany myself."

Charlie opted for the latter and decided to sing a topical song that he had written about two labor heroes named Sacco and Vanzetti, who had been framed and executed on trumped-up charges, but in reality because of their anarchistic and pro-union views. This had happened in Massachusetts, so Charlie felt that the official would probably be familiar with the particulars of the case. Charley performed the song, deep into the lyrics, mostly staring at his guitar. Midway into the song, he looked over and saw that the union official was fast asleep, and loudly snoring. So much for progressive labor causes!

Dave Van Ronk, Roy Berkeley, Dick Greenhaus, and several other New York revivalists sponsored several meetings to organize a sort of Folksinger's Union. They called it the Folksinger's Guild. The organization tried to get folksingers to avoid free performances, and itself sponsored concerts by its own members, including Roger Abrahams, Luke Faust, Gina Glaser, and Happy Traum. Their efforts helped to guarantee a minimum fee of five dollars at the Village's coffeehouses. This seems laughable, but it was better than nothing.

Not all of the urban revivalists pursued music as a full-time profession. A number of the people loosely connected to the Guild, the scene at 190 Spring Street, and Washington Square were often found at parties and jam sessions, and even did the occasional gig, but they turned to other professions for their life work. Lee Haring was a talented banjoist, singer, and arranger who published some instructional materials and rehearsed various vocal groups. He went on to become an English professor at Brooklyn College. Robin Christianson was a singer with a large musical repertoire who opted to become a book salesman.

THE VILLAGE MUSIC SCENE

Folk City was probably the most attractive club for the folk revivalists. But there were also a variety of other performing opportunities to be had. MacDougal and Bleecker Streets were festooned with a number of coffeehouses and small bars. The best of these was probably the Gaslight, where Dave Van Ronk often held forth. The coffeehouses were known as "basket houses." The performers were paid ridiculously small fees and were instructed to pass a basket and to tell the customers that their pay was based upon the customer's generosity. These clubs included the Commons, Café Wha, the Bizarre, and a bunch of others. The Wha was open all day and had wall-to-wall music, often spearheaded by Oklahoma blues and country singer Karen Dalton and (later to be) hit songwriter Fred Neil. Many of these venues operated on a "seat of their pants" business model, and they would open, operate for a few months to a year or two, and then close. From a musician's point of view, any kind of job security in this environment would have been a complete delusion, but since most of the revivalists were young enthusiasts used to living on nothing, this wasn't necessarily a problem. The goal of the performers was to have a place to develop your craft and to build an audience.

EARLY SINGER–SONGWRITERS,
POLITICAL AND OTHERWISE

Although it's a bit of an oversimplification, the singer–songwriters could be divided into two groups: the politically oriented writers and another group who specialized in writing songs that were either more personal or oriented more toward commercial success.

If you remember the section "Protest Music," by the time of the urban revival, People's Songs had essentially gone under. The *People's Songs Bulletin* had evolved into *Sing Out!* magazine, and *Sing Out!* became increasingly less political, eventually leading to Irwin Silber giving up his position as editor. A series of other editors took over the job, including Houston performer Ed Badeaux, *Little Sandy Review* cofounder Paul Nelson, music critic Josh Dunson, New York folksinger Happy Traum, Bob Norman, and Alan Senauke. The emphasis of the magazine was much less on politics and more on covering the many aspects and musical styles of the folk music revival.

On a trip to England, Pete Seeger observed a number of young singer–songwriters who were writing topical songs on political issues. Seeger felt that *Sing Out!* was obviously no longer interested in focusing on topical songs, and he discussed this problem with Agnes "Sis" Cuningham and her husband, Gordon Freisen, old friends of his who had been involved in the radical political folksinging movement for years. Sis has even been a member and songwriter with the Almanac Singers. Since Gordon was a published writer, he could be counted on for editing and proofreading chores.

Broadside started out in 1962 as a rough mimeographed publication with a printing of several hundred copies. It was put together in Cunningham and Freisen's small public-housing apartment. It is interesting that the initial major support came from Izzy Young, a person not especially involved in topical folk music. He bought a large number of copies of the first issue for sale in his Folklore Center.

Freisen and Cunningham continued to publish *Broadside* for twenty-six years. The magazine barely survived financially; it was a labor of love. The importance of *Broadside* was that it provided a forum for a group of young singer–songwriters who had no other real outlet for their work. Gil Turner was one of the early strong supporters of the magazine. Since he was an MC at Gerde's open-mic night, he then brought many of his friends to the uptown "office" of the magazine. Some of the early performers whose songs appeared in *Broadside* were Bob Dylan (in his political phase), Malvina Reynolds, a San Francisco–area songwriter-performer, Phil Ochs, Tom Paxton, Len Chandler, Bonnie Dobson, Peter La Farge, and Mark Spoelstra. Other songs came from the pens of Eric Anderson, Peggy Seeger, Julius Lester, Jim Page, Charlie Brown, Janis Ian, Buffy Sainte-Marie, Nina Simone, Ernie Marrs, and Lucinda Williams. The songs were recorded in the office-apartment and then transcribed for the magazine.

Some of the songs that saw their first appearance in Broadside included Dylan's "Blowing in the Wind," Peter La Farge's "The Ballad of Ira Hayes," later to become a major hit recording by Johnny Cash, and Malvina Reynolds's "Little Boxes," a song about suburban tract housing. *Broadside* also issued an LP, and Folkways recorded other albums of the songs printed in the magazine. Oak Publications also issued several songbooks of *Broadside* songs.

Freisen and Cunningham were always broke, and not in good health. Somehow they managed to keep the magazine going for twenty-six years, except for a couple of years when a New York businessman named Norman Ross temporarily took it over. Folkways has issued an excellent set of recordings with detailed information about the songs that provides a history of the magazine, and eighty-nine recordings of the songs.

There were a number of outstanding singer–songwriters in Greenwich Village. Fred Neil, who held forth at the Café Wha, wrote "Everybody's Talking," "The Other Side of This Life," "Blues on the Ceiling and the Dolphin." He also cowrote the hit song "The Candyman," with an uptown pop writer named Beverly Ross. Tim Hardin, originally from Eugene, Oregon, lived variously in New York City and Woodstock and wrote Bobby Darin's hit song "If I Were a Carpenter," as well as "The Reason to Believe," "Don't Make Promises," and "The Lady Came from Baltimore."

Although Eric Anderson had some involvement with *Broadside*, most of his songs were romantic fantasies, like "Violets of Dawn." Anderson toured and recorded for Vanguard. Other singer–songwriters on the scene were David Blue, advertised as "the *most authentic*" [author's italics] Dylan imitator, and Paul Seibel. Tim Buckley was a spectacular-voiced singer–songwriter whose career fell victim to his drug habit, a problem which also cut down Tim Hardin and plagued Fred Neil. There were also artists like Karen Dalton, who were primarily interpreters of songs written by others.

The artists listed above do not provide a comprehensive listing of what was going on in New York City during the 1960s. Some artists, like John Sebastian and Gram Parsons, will be discussed in the folk-rock chapter of this book. A very young Emmy Lou Harris was living in New York in the late 1950s, but she was raising a child, and apart from a single album, was not especially active on the scene.

There were a handful of American Indian artists on the scene. Peter La Farge, adopted son of novelist Oliver La Farge, was probably the first one. Peter recorded several albums for Folkways and one for Columbia. Not especially talented as a singer, his major impact was through his songs, which described the plight of Native Americans. When Johnny Cash recorded La Farge's song about Ira Hayes, a Marine Corps hero of Iwo Jima who died drunk in a ditch, the songs reached a national audience. Cash went on to record an album consisting mostly of La Farge's songs, *Bitter Tears*, but the album was not nearly as commercially successful as the "Ira Hayes" song had been. Two other American Indian artists on the scene were Buffy Sainte-Marie and Patrick Sky. Sainte-Marie recorded for Vanguard and went on to write a number of influential songs and even some successful movie theme songs. She also appeared for over five years on the children's television program *Sesame Street*. Sky had several careers—as a performer, songwriter, instrument builder, and folklorist.

BLUEGRASS

The first bluegrass band in New York was a trio called the Shantyboys, formed in 1957. Roger Sprung was the enthusiastic banjo picker, Mike Cohen (John's brother) played guitar and sang, and Lionel Kilberg played a washtub bass. Sprung had also done some recording with Bob Carey and Erik Darling for Stinson Records in the mid-1950s. Sprung's aggressive banjo playing enabled the group to pull it off, particularly since hardly anyone in New York had ever heard anything like it. The Shantyboys were omnipresent in Washington Square, at jams, and at whatever gigs they could scare up. They were never a full-time band, but they certainly introduced much of the New York crowd to bluegrass, particularly bluegrass banjo. Roger was one of the first New Yorkers to go south to the various festivals and conventions that featured bluegrass, such as the one in Union Grove, North Carolina.

The Greenbriar Boys formed when Eric Weissberg, banjoist Bob Yellin, and lead singer Johnny Herald were all students attending the University of Wisconsin in 1958. Weissberg left the group by 1959 because Yellin was doing the lion's share of the banjo work, and although Eric enjoyed playing the mandolin, he had already developed a strong reputation as a banjo picker. Yellin came from a very musical family, and he had studied violin, voice, piano, and trumpet as a child. His older brother, Peter, became a renowned jazz saxophone player. Eric's replacement was Ralph Rinzler, and that trio performed together from 1959 to 1964. They recorded three influential albums for Vanguard. Herald was an excellent lead singer, in the vein of the bluegrass "high lonesome sound"; Yellin was a crisp and fast banjo player who won several banjo contests at Union Grove; and Rinzler was a steady anchor with his mandolin playing, backup singing, and extensive knowledge of folk music. The group also performed and recorded with a female lead singer, Diane Edmondson, during the height of the folk-pop boom and also appeared on the ABC *Hootenanny* television show.

In 1964, Rinzler left the band and went on to pursue various roles in the folk music industry, briefly managing Bill Monroe and Doc Watson, coordinating talent for the Newport Folk Foundation, and moving on to direct the music festivals of the Smithsonian Institute in Washington, D.C. By introducing Watson, Monroe, and others to urban audiences, Rinzler played a seminal role in spreading the influence of traditional music. When Rinzler left, he was replaced by the spectacular and idiosyncratic mandolinist Frank Wakefield and fiddler Jim Buchanan. Wakefield was a native of North Carolina, and this may have been the first band to combine urban revivalists with an "authentic" traditional player.

Because the Shantyboys and the Greenbriar Boys were highly visible on the New York scene, more and more urban products became interested in bluegrass. Other New Yorker pickers in the sixties were Steve Arkin, who later played with Bill Monroe, and Roger Lass, who did not pursue a career in music. An excellent fiddler named Tex Logan lived in New Jersey and had a day job as an engineer. He would show up from time to time at jam sessions. Another fiddler player was Gene Lowinger, who sometimes played in the square and at jam sessions. Mandolinist Andy Statman was a fiery presence on the scene before turning to a career in klezmer music. Banjoist Marc Horowitz has drifted in and out of a performing career and guitarist (and banjoist) Steve Mandell was the guitar player on the *Dueling Banjos* album. Paul Prestopino was a multi-instrumentalist who toured with the Chad Mitchell Trio and still travels with Peter, Paul & Mary. Most of his professional career has been spent as a maintenance engineer at the renowned Record Plant recording studio.

The oddest thing about the New York bluegrass bands is that the two primary bands, at least for most of the Greenbriar Boys' career, had only three members. Southern bluegrass bands had a lineup consisting of fiddle, mandolin, guitar, banjo, and bass. Some included dobro in place of the mandolin. Since a good deal of the bluegrass musical style is defined by harmony singing, the New York bands were at something of a disadvantage compared to their southern competitors.

Bluegrass scholar and performer Neil Rosenberg has pointed out that bluegrass was more of a modern theatrical style than old-time mountain music in the sense that bluegrass was a style that evolved on stage with the use of microphones, rather than a homemade musical genre that was developed in rural communities. For this reason it was perhaps better suited to the skills and backgrounds of the urban revivalists than to old-time music.

BLUES IN THE CITY

Although there were very few traditional white country musicians in New York and those who did migrate there were college educated, there were a handful of authentic blues musicians on the New York scene. Although Josh White became a sophisticated cabaret artist and concert performer, no one could question his musical apprenticeship with a variety of blind blues singers in the Carolinas. Brownie McGhee and Sonny Terry came from North Carolina and Tennessee, and both had been influenced by the legendary Blind Boy Fuller. Gary Davis was not a blues man per se but he had played on some blues recordings, and even though he sang religious songs, the accompaniments that he played represented blues and ragtime guitar styles. All of these musicians were resources for the young revivalists, and both Davis and McGhee gave guitar lessons to a number of the young urban revivalists.

Dave Van Ronk was one of the first white blues singers in New York. Through his regular performances at the Gaslight, his numerous recordings over the years, his friendships and mentor relationships with such notables as Bob Dylan as well as his work as a guitar teacher, he influenced many of the urban wannabe blues artists. Van Ronk was only an occasional (although excellent) composer, but he was a skilled interpreter of other people's songs, even recording some probing emotional versions of Joni Mitchell songs. Possessed of a harsh, rather growly voice, on the surface Van Ronk would not have seemed suited to such a role, but in fact he performed it with subtlety and grace. John Hammond Jr. was the son of the famous record producer, and through his early Vanguard recordings, beginning in 1962, he also influenced many blues wannabes. Hammond is not a composer but he interpreted many blues classics, at first as a soloist, and from time to time with blues bands. He initially played acoustic guitar, but later played electric guitar as well. Happy Traum, who studied with Brownie McGhee, performed a broad repertoire but always included blues in his performances. As with folk music in general, there were other excellent artists on the scene who did not choose to go into music as a career. We have already mentioned John Gibbon, one of Gary Davis's first students, and Ian Buchanan was an excellent guitarist and singer whose career was cut short by personal problems.

New York foreshadowed what turned out to be the future of the blues during the 1970s and '80s in the sense that there were very few young black musicians who took an interest in the blues. An exception to this rule was an artist named Larry Johnson, another student of Gary Davis. Johnson made a few albums, and has performed and recorded sporadically over the years. Guy Davis, who later became part of the black blues revival of the mid-'90s, also recorded several albums for Folkways.

Another group of blues musicians was spearheaded by a young Stefan Grossman. Stefan began his intense survey of the blues as a teenager. He is probably the most prolific author of blues instructional material anywhere, and he has transcribed several dozen books of guitar instructional materials, also recording a blues instruction album for Elektra with a very young Rory Block.

Danny Kalb was an aggressive blues guitarist who did a bit of session work, and later formed the Blues Project, a blues-rock band. John Sebastian was a young blues harmonica player in the Village. His father was a famous classical music harmonica virtuoso, and John studied classical piano as a child. During the early sixties, he spent a great deal of time in Greenwich Village, taking in the music scene, hanging out, and informally studying some of the guitar techniques of such important "rediscovered" blues artists like Mississippi John Hurt and Lightnin' Hopkins.

In the early 1950s, Elektra put together a jug band in an attempt to compete with Boston-based Jim Kweskin and his Jug Band, who were recording for Vanguard. Besides Sebastian, the band included guitarists Stefan Grossman and Peter Siegel, Dave Grisman on mandolin, Steve Katz (later in Blues Project and Blood, Sweat and Tears), Maria D'Amato (who later married Geoff Muldaur), and pianist Josh Rifkin. Sebastian played a prominent role in folk-rock music.

Another group of young revivalists became determined to promote ragtime music. The difficulty was that ragtime is a complex style, even on the piano, and it presents more difficult technical problems on the guitar. Guitarists Dave Laidman and Eric Schoenberg made finger-busting transcriptions of ragtime piano pieces for guitar and recorded an album of them. Dave Van Ronk was less of a purist, but his guitar arrangements of such tunes as the "Saint Louis Tickle" were more playable for the medium–advanced-level guitarist. Stefan Grossman was another young blues revivalist who was intrigued by ragtime, and he did arrangements of piano rags for guitar.

In subsequent years, Joshua Rifkin made a pioneering album of Scott Joplin piano rags, which he played on the piano at the slow tempos that Joplin advocated.

THE INTERNATIONAL AND CABARET ARTISTS

Cynthia Gooding and Theodore Bikel each recorded a number of albums for Elektra consisting of songs from different parts of the world. Their fans tended to be a somewhat more refined and sophisticated group, compared to the scruffier "beatnik" devotees that constituted the audience for most of the urban revivalists. Several Israeli singers, including multilingual singer Geula Gil and Israeli artists Ron and Nama and the Dudaim Group, also recorded and sometimes performed in New York. Martha Schlamme was a cabaret singer whose material included quite a few folk songs in various languages. Will Holt was a performer and songwriter who also bordered on being a cabaret singer, and who became involved in various theatre shows. His song "Lemon Tree" was a hit for Peter, Paul & Mary, among many others. Ruth Rubin was a scholar as much as a performer, and she published important collections of Yiddish folk song. Her work also influenced the much later revival of klezmer music.

THE INSTRUMENTALISTS

A number of innovative instrumentalists were part of the urban revival. Some of them have already been mentioned in the context of studio work, but their ambitions extended beyond playing on other people's recordings. Billy Faier was an unusual banjo player who utilized the techniques of the old-time classical music banjo players of the 1900s. At his best, he seamlessly integrated these influences with traditional American folk tunes as well as music from other cultures. He made a very influential Riverside recording, *The Art of the Five String Banjos,* following that up with another Riverside solo album, and a banjo trio album with Eric Weissberg and myself. Billy was a very energetic fellow; at times he ran a radio show, and he edited *Caravan* magazine when Lee Shaw bowed out of that role. Billy's music was difficult to master and his influence was more indirect than specific. His career was limited because of his modest vocal talents.

Frank Hamilton was the superb guitarist who played on Faier's album. Frank was also quite a good banjoist, and he has had a lengthy musical career—teaching in Chicago and Los Angeles, doing several years in the Weavers as Erik Darling's replacement, and pioneering the use of guitar in various world music aggregations. He has also done a fair amount of studio work, including the rather raw but spontaneous and intriguing *Nonesuch* album with Pete Seeger.

Sandy Bull grew up partly in New York and took some banjo lessons with Erik Darling. Bull recorded his first Vanguard album in 1963, but even during the late fifties he was gigging, first in New York, then in Boston. He also played on the streets of Paris. Over the years, he absorbed many influences, recording as a banjoist and guitarist, and also playing oud and bass. Of all the instrumentalists on the scene, he probably blended the most world music influences into his work. His career was hindered by drug use and unreliability, and the pioneering nature of his work has not been sufficiently recognized.

Dick Rosmini was a banjoist, photographer, and recording engineer who grew up in Greenwich Village. He was one of the many revivalists who became intrigued by the recordings on the *Anthology of American Music*. Dick was an excellent player who never developed a particularly identifiable style, but he was versatile and he performed on a number of recordings. He later became a recording engineer, active in audio education, and a photographer. Rosmini recorded several solo albums and played on the soundtrack of the biographical film about Leadbelly.

Eric Weissberg appears in various parts of this book, but an extensive profile of his career will appear in the chapter on folk music in the 1970s.

Pete Seeger has been, and remains, an enormously influential figure in the folk music revival. He is rarely analyzed as a musician, but he certainly belongs on any list of instrumentalists. Together with Earl Scruggs, his bluegrass contemporary, Seeger introduced the five-string banjo into the folk music revival. He also wrote the first guide to folk banjo styles, pioneered the use of tablature as a system of notating music for banjo and guitar, and reintroduced the twelve-string guitar to the folk music revival after the death of Leadbelly. Seeger's recognition as an instrumentalist has probably been constrained by his occasional instrumental sloppiness, and by the fact that he has been so intimately involved with other aspects of the revival such as politics, world music, audience participation, and songwriting. Seeger's instrumental inventiveness is best glimpsed on his solo *Goofing Off Suite* album, and his *Nonesuch* collaboration with Frank Hamilton.

The instrumentalists in the folk revival had almost as many goals as there were players. Some simply wanted to re-create traditional music styles. Others were experimenting with adapting traditional tunes to modern musical concepts, changing a rhythm here or a chord there. Some players, like Sandy Bull, wanted to integrate the music cultures of the entire world with American folk styles. The most ambitious of the players were writing original music based loosely on folk themes and instrumental practices, but integrating instrumental styles and techniques that came from the world of classical music and jazz.

Bob Dylan is discussed at length a little later in this book. He first appeared in New York in the bitter winter of early 1961. In 1965, he introduced an electric band at the Newport Folk Festival, ending the revival as it had existed up until that moment and beginning the era of folk-rock.

*   *   *

Recording engineers rarely receive much credit for their role in making records. Bill Schwartau was one of the most creative engineers in New York City. He engineered albums by Peter, Paul & Mary and Charles Mingus, and by day he did jingles. He was technically fearless and never hesitated to try the goofiest things, operating under the oftentimes correct principle "you never know." He taught me a great deal about record production, and I did several projects with him—including a very nice Jean Ritchie album. Bill worked extremely long hours, and over time he developed a serious drinking problem. He stopped working in the studio, broke up with his wife, and was rumored to be living on the Bowery.

One day I had an afternoon session playing on a jingle in the studio where Bill no longer worked. We were about halfway into the session when Bill lurched into the room. There were a dozen studio musicians there, and all of us knew him at least fairly well. No one knew what to say to him. Everyone exchanged perfunctory greetings and suddenly Bill was escorted out of the building. I never saw him again.

*   *   *

Many of the urban revivalists came to New York to pursue professional opportunities. Usually, they were searching for a record deal and a personal manager to guide their careers. They would spend some time living in New York and would then either give up their careers or leave after finding these opportunities.

One of the most interesting of these artists was singer Judy Roderick. A native of Connecticut, Judy started her performing career while attending the University of Colorado in the late fifties and early sixties. She was a small woman with a powerful voice, particularly adept at singing blues but also quite capable of singing folk and country music.

Judy came to New York around 1962 and landed a Columbia Records contract. Her first album was produced by jazz-pop pianist–songwriter Bobby Scott, and for reasons never clear to the people who knew Judy best, he decided to turn her into a young, white Billie Holiday. The first Columbia album came out to a resounding chorus of silence and did little to enhance popular demand for Judy's services. A second album was begun, but tabled when Judy and Scott were unable to agree on the musical direction of the record.

Woman Blue, a 1965 album for Vanguard, was the record that Judy should have recorded two or three years earlier. The *Music Hound Essential Folk Album Guide* describes it as "some very original treatment of original material." Unfortunately for Judy's career, by 1965 the folk boom had ended, and Judy's acoustic album was overshadowed by the folk-rock boom. She returned to Colorado and recorded one folk-rock album for Atlantic with the band 60 Million Buffalo. That album never caught fire either, and later Judy moved to Montana. A diabetic since childhood, Judy died in 1992 in Montana.

In 1993, Vanguard reissued the *Woman Blue* album, and a few years later Tim and Mollie O'Brien recorded the song "Floods of South Dakota," coauthored by Judy Roderick and Bill Ashford. There's an old cliché that timing is everything, and had Judy's Vanguard album come out in 1962, she might well have become one of the better-known folk revivalists. In the music business, talent is definitely not everything.

chapter 6

The Revival Outside the Big Apple, 1950–65

As mentioned, this book is not designed to cover every single city that boasted a coffeehouse, an acoustic-music store, or a folk music radio show. I remember, for example, going to Jacksonville, Florida, on a working vacation in the winter of 1962 and being startled to discover an almost laughable coffeehouse seemingly inspired by a Jack Kerouac novel. It was called the Weird Beard, and its logo was a penciled caricature of a classic beatnik.

Instead, I will be looking at some influential scenes that were going on at about the same time as the events discussed in the previous chapter. The reader also needs to consider that there was a great deal of back-and-forth traffic between the various cities; a performer like Odetta, who started out in San Francisco, achieved popularity in Chicago through her performances at the Gate of Horn and then moved to New York, where she recorded, performed, and lived. She could be considered important in all of these burgeoning folk scenes. I have tried to avoid repeatedly covering the same artists as they moved from town to town.

PHILADELPHIA

Philadelphia is only ninety miles south of New York, but there was a whole group of artists who developed there, many of whom could best be described as semiprofessionals. This is not to demean their talents, but simply a realization that they were not full-time touring professionals. There was a downtown coffeehouse called the Gilded Cage where folksingers gathered in the back room on Sunday afternoons and took turns singing or playing. On weekend nights, Esther Halpern, the owner's wife, entertained. Some of the people who gathered on Sundays starting in the mid-1950s were Harry Tuft, who later founded the Denver Folklore Center; Donny Leace, later a protégé of pop singer Roberta Flack; and me. Many of the others were avocational singers who simply wanted to have fun and play the occasional song.

Another group of performers, notably Joe and Penny Aaronson and Tossi and Lee Aaron, played quite a few gigs in the area, as did George Britton, who became the premier guitar instructor in town.

Philadelphia was a rather conservative city at the time, and the police captain of the area where the Gilded Cage was located was a gentleman named Frank Rizzo. Rizzo was a tough cookie who hated beatniks and wasn't especially fond of anyone or anything that in his mind went against the prevailing cultural mores. On several occasions, he busted teenagers for hanging out at the Cage, presumably for capital offenses like playing chess. One of the habitues of the Cage was the mayor's daughter, and we all lived in hopes that somehow Rizzo would eventually bust the mayor's daughter. That never did actually occur.

By the late fifties, an entrepreneur named Manny Rubin opened the Second Fret, a folk club and coffeehouse in the downtown area. A young African American named Jerry Ricks started out working in the kitchen and later became the manager of the club. During his sojourn at the Fret he learned how to play guitar. Many of the visiting artists such as Doc Watson and Mississippi John Hurt stayed at Jerry and Sheila Ricks's apartment, and the black blues artists in particular were thrilled to find a twenty-something black man who wanted to learn how to play the blues. Doc Watson has credited Jerry with essentially saving his career when he played the Fret during one of his first trips away from home. He has written that Jerry and Sheila's friendship and hospitality enabled him to understand that his work was important and appreciated. Besides being an excellent blues player, Jerry has an encyclopedic knowledge of country music and, later, even did a stint playing lead guitar in an Austrian bluegrass band. You will meet Jerry again in our later discussions of the blues revival.

In later years, the Fret closed and the music scene shifted to a club in suburban Philadelphia called the Main Point. Another music club, Geoffrey Daniels, started in Bethlehem, some sixty miles north of Philadelphia. In suburban Bucks County, an acoustic-music store called the Bucks County Folk Shop opened its doors in 1962, and it continues to this day under the same ownership and management. The Philadelphia Folksong Society dates from 1957, and its large and successful folk festival, now in its forty-first year, started in 1964.

The other significant development in Philadelphia was the strong folklore and folk life program at the University of Pennsylvania. A number of revivalists, including harmonica player Saul Brody, got doctoral degrees in the program. In those days, it was run by McEdward Leach. Later, Kenneth Goldstein abandoned his career as a record producer to take over the program. During the late fifties, a young Philadelphia native and folklore student named Roger Abrahams was living just south of downtown, writing his thesis by collecting toasts, insults, and other bits of folklore from neighborhood African Americans. He compiled these tidbits into his first of many books, *Deep Down in the Jungle*. After a lengthy stint at the University of Texas, he now teaches in the folklore program at the University of Pennsylvania.

Another college scene built up around the interest in folk song at suburban Swarthmore College. The school held some of the earliest college folk festivals and one of the young students there was Ralph Rinzler, discussed earlier in this book.

BOSTON AND CAMBRIDGE

Eric Von Schmidt and Jim Rooney have written an entire book, *Baby Let Me Follow You Down*, about the Boston–Cambridge folk scene. The book details the various personalities, clubs, and musicians on the scene. At the center of the action is the Club 47 in Cambridge, which started out as a reluctant forum for music but turned into a sort of house gig for Joan Baez.

There are more colleges in the metropolitan area around Boston than anywhere else in the United States. Consequently, it is no great surprise that there were a large number of participants in the Boston-area chapter of the folk revival. Von Schmidt himself was a blues singing artist who functioned as a source of songs for many of the younger revivalists. Wearing his other hat, he also went on to design many of their album covers.

Jim Kweskin is a guitarist and singer who started a jug band in 1963. The jug band included a number of musicians who went on to achieve considerable careers in later years. The aforementioned Geoff Muldaur, possessed of a unique blues sensibility with his airy, light vibrato, later made records with his wife, Maria, and studied arranging at the Berklee College of Music. After a long hiatus from the music business following his divorce, he has recently made some very interesting recordings, adding arrangements for horns and miscellaneous instruments. Among these arrangements are charts for Bix Beiderbecke's impressionistic piano pieces. Maria Muldauer defected from New York's Even Dozen Jug Band to join Kweskin's band. Many years later, she scored an enormous hit with the odd song "Midnight at the Oasis." Kweskin's original banjo player was Bob Siggins, who played in the Boston bluegrass band the Charles River Valley Boys. He was replaced by Bill Keith, whose musical adventures have ranged from coinventing the melodic style of banjo playing and practicing it with the Bill Monroe Band, creating technical mechanical devices for the banjo, mastering the pedal steel guitar, and becoming an apostle of modern jazz adapted to the banjo. Fritz Richmond played the jug and washtub bass, and he has gone on to play on numerous recordings and also worked as a recording engineer at Elektra Records' Los Angeles studio. Mel Lyman was the harmonica player in the band, and he later became a sort of spiritual leader for a Boston commune and was almost worshipped by them. In the later part of the band's career, Richard Greene signed on as a fiddler. He has since played on many recordings and has trod the slippery ground between bluegrass and jazz. This was certainly an extraordinarily talented lineup, coming from a single band.

But the Kweskin band was just the tip of the Boston iceberg. Rolf Cahn moved to Boston from Berkeley. Cahn was a flamenco guitarist who gave guitar lessons and performed frequently. Tony Saletan was a performer in the Pete Seeger mold, expert at getting the audience to sing along. Peggy Seeger, Pete's half sister and Mike's sister, was a student at Radcliffe College and she often played at jam sessions at a house known as Old Joe Clarke. Peggy had an enormous repertoire, growing up in a house where her mother was transcribing music for some of the Lomax's song collections. Jim Rooney formed a duo with Bill Keith, managed the Club 47 for several years, and went on to produce records in Nashville.

Sandy Bull attended music school in Boston before returning to New York. Tom Rush was a student at Harvard who became an influential artist and recorded a number of songs written by other songwriters, notably Joni Mitchell. Similarly, Taj Mahal was attending the University of Massachusetts at Amherst. He has credited his days hanging out at the Club 47, and later at the Ash Grove in Los Angeles, as basic building blocks in the development of his music.

In the blues world, Al Wilson, later in Canned Heat, was a music student in Boston. Chris Smithers, one of the most convincing of the white blues artists, was a regular performer and he still performs and records today. A young Paul Geremia was also active on the scene. He went on to become one of the most tasteful of the white blues singers.

Robert L. Jones was a ballad singer who later worked for impresario George Wein on the Newport Folk Festival and many jazz festivals around the world. Bobby Neuwirth, a performer–songwriter and later a road pal of Bob Dylan's, was another Boston artist. Jackie Washington was one of the few African American artists on the scene, and he recorded for Vanguard. Fanatic blues enthusiast Dick Waterman was beginning his career as a blues entrepreneur, booking many of the blues rediscoveries and then managing Bonnie Raitt, another Radcliffe student.

A number of attractive and talented young women performed or attended performances at the Club 47. Debby Green was an excellent guitarist and a talented singer who never pursued a career as a professional musician and who later married singer–songwriter Eric Anderson. Joan Baez often held forth at the Club 47, as I will discuss in the next chapter. Her younger sister, Mimi, also a singer and an excellent guitarist, was also often part of the scene. Joan made an early album, *Folksinger Around Harvard Square,* with veteran folk performer Bill Wood and Ted Alevizos, who sang Greek songs. Jerry Corbett, later to join Jesse Colin Young's band the Youngbloods, was another local musician. Paul Arnold was a local singer–songwriter whose song "One Note Man" had a brief run on the pop music charts.

From a bluegrass standpoint, besides the Charles River Boys, the Lilly Brothers, a traditional West Virginia bluegrass group with banjo ace Don Stover, went into residency in Boston and played regularly at a downtown bar. Peter Childs was a young instrumentalist who developed the skills that enabled him to play with a short-lived bluegrass band called the Knoblich Upper Ten Thousand. Peter Rowan was another young musician who went on to play in Jerry Garcia's side groups, where Garcia played bluegrass as a sort of stimulant or antidote (you choose) to his work with the Grateful Dead.

Besides the Club 47, there were many other clubs in Boston and Cambridge that hired musicians. There was Tulla's Coffee Grinder, the Golden Vanity, Club Passim, and the Café Yana. Dave Wilson edited *Boston Broadside,* a magazine that had articles about folk music and schedules of performances, and was not related to its New York namesake.

Another key figure in Boston was Manny Greenhill. An ex-union organizer, Manny promoted concerts with both local and touring artists and became Joan Baez's manager. A dedicated radical with a reputation for honesty, he also represented Pete Seeger in the New England area. Greenhill and Baez ended their relationship in the mid-1970s and Greenhill moved his booking agency to southern California, where it survives today, run by his son and grandson. When the Jug Band began to split up during the seventies, many of the members of the band left Boston and its important role in the folk revival diminished.

My second and most recent reading of *Baby Let Me Follow You Down* left me wondering what the musical interactions were between the many talented people on the Boston scene. So much of the book is about alcohol, sex, and marijuana. We were all growing up during the folk revival, and maybe that is what the authors remember best. It would have been fascinating to know exactly how Bill Keith and Geoff Muldaur developed their styles and how the other musicians reacted to their music.

THE NEWPORT FOLK FESTIVAL

The Newport Folk Festival was a logical outgrowth of the jazz festival held in the posh seaside resort of Newport, Rhode Island. The first festival was held in 1959 and mixed urban revivalists with pop-folk groups, including the Kingston Trio. The biggest stir at the festival was Joan Baez's guest appearance with Bob Gibson, when he brought her onstage to sing two songs. She tore the audience apart, in effect becoming a star with this single appearance.

Gradually, the festival enlisted some of the important tradition-minded "bridge" artists and scholars, such as Pete Seeger, Peter Yarrow of Peter, Paul & Mary, Theodore Bikel, and conscientious folk scholar–musician Ralph Rinzler. With Seeger's impetus, it was agreed that there would be an increasing number of traditional performers and music workshops. His intent was to make the festival an educational process as well as entertainment.

After a couple of years' hiatus created because of riots at the Newport Jazz Festival, such major blues rediscoveries as Mississippi John Hurt, Skip James, and Son House performed at Newport in front of thousands of people. The board turned away from attempting to draw fans by featuring folk-pop groups, and it also established equity in fees paid to the various performers. The successful revivalists realized that they were, to an extent, being used to create an audience for traditional performers. Most of the revivalists were conscious of the fact that they wouldn't have had careers if not for the music that they had learned from traditional performers. It was a noble attempt to redress the extreme popularity of the pop-folk groups who were making millions of dollars, often through mining the repertoire of traditional performers. The sponsors did their best to create programs that mixed traditional artists with polished performers in order to keep the rather heterogeneous audience happy. The board also used the profits made by the festival to fund traditional music performances at regional festivals and to finance the collection of traditional music. Using these financial resources, Ralph Rinzler played an important role in the encouragement and revival of Cajun music in Louisiana.

It was at the 1965 festival that Bob Dylan introduced a high-volume electric band, a story told in the next chapter.

DENVER

The folk scene in Denver began to crystallize at a club in the downtown area, the Exodus. It booked a number of touring artists, many of whom were on their way from one coast to the other. The owner of the club died in an airplane crash in 1962, and although his wife kept the club going for a while, it didn't last long.

Walt Conley was another pillar of the Denver folk scene. Walt was an African American singer-storyteller who booked the talent at the Satire bar and restaurant, a down-to-earth Mexican restaurant east of the downtown area. Walt also frequently sang there. A performer could almost literally walk in off the street and Walt would give him or her a slot as an opening act at the club. Walt was funny, friendly, and usually even-tempered, and everyone in town knew him. Over the years, he vacillated between singing and pursuing an acting career in Los Angeles. Toward the end of his life, in the early 1990s, he returned to Denver and from time to time performed there.

Meanwhile, folksinger Harry Tuft moved to Denver from Philadelphia. Fresh from conferring with Izzy Young in New York on strategies for opening a folklore center, Harry opened a shop six blocks east of downtown in 1962. He drove a taxi all night and lived in a loft in the store. When someone knocked on the door, he threw himself out of bed and opened the store. A couple of doors down from the shop was a coffeehouse called the Green Spider. The Spider was designed in classic beatnik style, with fat, waxy candles on the tables and very little light. God's eyes decorated the scene. People sat around and jammed. Don Lane, the owner, was your archetypical beatnik proprietor. He crafted handmade jewelry, was a bit of a lady's man, and was a character waiting for a Jack Kerouac novel.

Over the years, the Folklore Center became the key to the folk revival in Denver. There are a large number of distinguished alumni who worked at the store in one capacity or another. Early alumni included banjoist Mike Kropp, later a studio musician and record producer; Kim King, later the lead guitarist in psychedelic rock group Lothar and the Hand People;

banjoist Ray Chatfield, who later worked at the Ode Banjo Company; Mac Ferris, also to become a folk-rock musician; and Paul Hofstadter, today a musician and luthier in northern California. David Ferretta managed the guitar shop for a while and later became a friendly competitor, with his own store a couple of miles away. George Downing was a fine semiprofessional ballad singer and a professional carpenter who helped Harry design his store.

Gradually, Harry's store took over an entire small city block. The Green Spider disappeared and Harry added a concert hall at one end of the street, a store where he sold musical instruments, a record shop, a space for repairing guitars and other stringed instruments, and finally something he called "the funk shop." The funk shop sold beads and fashionably hip used clothing. The concert hall provided a regular venue for local musicians and for everything from rediscovered blues musicians to touring revivalists.

It would be difficult to overestimate the importance of the Folklore Center on the Denver folk revival of the 1960s. The store was a place for musicians to hang out and have constant jam sessions. The teaching studios provided musicians with a way to make a living. Mostly, it was a place where people felt at home, friendships were made, romances were struck up, and people felt a sense of community. A great deal of the "vibe" was Harry's own personality, just as Izzy Young established a certain atmosphere at the Folklore Center in New York. Traveling musicians with Denver-area gigs dropped in and other musicians who were just passing through town got in the habit of checking the action at the store. Another part of the store's personality was that the music wasn't as segmented as it was in New York. The same people who liked blues could be found singing country songs, or even traditional ballads. People played together and learned from one another. They experimented and their music and their personalities matured.

Later alumni of the store included Jerry Ricks, who moved out for a couple of years in the seventies, and Otis Taylor, an important blues singer today who took lessons in the store when he was a teenager. During the 1970s, the entire bluegrass band Hot Rize had some connection to the store as teachers, repair persons, and sales people. Mary Flower, who is currently an active blues guitarist, singer, and songwriter, was often found at the store and her ex-husband Jeff Withers worked there.

Another influence in Denver was an organization called the Denver Friends of Folk Music. It sponsored concerts, regular song circles, and jam sessions. By the mid-1960s, Denver was a hotbed of folk music and people from both coasts knew about it. Following the example of San Francisco's free-form FM radio stations, KFML broadcast a format that was idiosyncratic and unstructured. The disc jockeys played whatever felt good to them. Among the DJs were Harry Tuft himself and mandolin player Jerry Mills. Both of them always featured generous helpings of folk music in their shows. KVOD was the local classical music station, and John Wolfe had a regular folk show. He was also active in the Denver Friends of Folk Music organization.

From the early 1970s into the '90s, a unique women's folk group made a definite imprint on the Denver Scene. The group was called *The Mother Folkers*—as they put it, the most carefully pronounced name in the music business. The group was originally formed to do some performances for International Women's Week, and it became a fixture and virtually a legend in Denver. Mary Flower, Eileen Niehaus, and Mary Stribling were the original sparkplugs, and a number of other musicians, including Bonnie Carol, Ellen Klaver, Suzanne Nelson, Bonnie Phipps, Mollie O'Brien, Julie Davis, and Ellen Thompson, performed at various times. The performances were musically varied and often quite funny. Occasional male guests were allowed if they observed a feminine dress code. Over the years the number of performances expanded to about ten a year, but keeping it together became too much of a burden.

The town of Boulder is about thirty miles northwest of Denver and is the home of the University of Colorado's main campus. Boulder had its own folk music scene. A club called Tulagi's featured such artists as a young Judy Collins, and the Attic was a coffeehouse that featured such performers as Judy Roderick and blues guitarist Ed O'Riley. (Judy Collins is discussed in some depth in the next chapter.)

Chuck Ogsbury was a UC student who started building a line of very reasonably priced banjos under the name Ode Banjos. Soon he had a half-dozen employees, including Kick Stewart, who went on to found his own banjo and guitar supply company in Ohio, and Ray Chatfield, who ended up moving to Galax, Virginia, to get closer to the heart of traditional music. There was a lot of music played around the banjo factory, and there were many parties, jam sessions, and social gatherings with music as their center.

Max Krimmel was making fine-finger style guitars in town and his wife Bonnie Carol was making and playing dulcimers. They lived in an unincorporated town called Wall Street. It was located in neighboring Four Mile Canyon, and since the town was accessed by a tortuous dirt road, the name was something of a joke. There were lots of music parties around Boulder and all of the people listed above were liable to show up, along with a banjo player named Mike Ford, who later wrote one of the early bluegrass banjo methods.

* * *

Just as there had been tension between the Philadelphia police and the Gilded Cage coffeehouse, the city fathers of Denver weren't thrilled with the presence of the Denver Folklore Center. A friend of Harry's who worked in the District Attorney's office called and warned him that the city fathers were planning to set him up for a bust. Since he was risking his job through this warning, he refused to give any details about how he knew about this or just what was going to happen.

Harry summoned his staff and warned that whatever they did in private, if they were seen smoking pot or doing anything else in the store or anywhere near it, they were jeopardizing the future of the business. No one ever commented on Harry's "speech," nor did anything ever happen. Presumably, the town fathers didn't want to see a bunch of longhairs disrupting their image of the town. Never mind that the lower downtown was a skid row area full of drunks and panhandlers. We don't want them beatniks in our cowboy town.

CHICAGO

The initial focal point of the folk revival in Chicago was the Gate of Horn. It was initially owned by Les Brown and Albert Grossman, opening its doors in 1956. Two performers made their reputation at the club, Odetta and Bob Gibson. Odetta came to the club from San Francisco and had a run of four months. Gibson performed as a soloist and also later in a duo with actor–singer Hamilton Camp. He also later recorded a live show at the club. The Gate of Horn developed a strong reputation and many significant touring professionals appeared there.

One of the two house musicians at the club was guitarist Frank Hamilton. When he decided to get married he began to think more seriously about establishing a more secure life for himself. Hamilton began giving guitar lessons at the house of Dawn Greening, who Hamilton has described as a "magnet for the folk music community." She lived in suburban Oak Park and, in addition to letting Frank use her home as a studio, the house was a virtual hotel for traveling folksingers, with constant jam sessions.

In 1957, Hamilton and a Chicago vocalist named Win Stracke established a teaching facility called the Old Town School of Folk Music. Stracke had dreamed of starting a music school that would serve as a bridge to all of the ethnic communities in Chicago, and over time the school has fulfilled that vision. Frank used a teaching method that had been invented by Bess Lomax Hawes at UCLA's Extension Department. Students would study an instrument in large groups—usually guitar, banjo, mandolin, or fiddle. They would have a group lesson on the instrument followed by a break for coffee, snacks, and socializing. After the break, all of the students and teachers would get together and sing and play. The teachers had their hands full, because between trying to keep all of the instruments in tune and supervising players who had different levels of skill, things could get a bit chaotic. The school created its own songbook and the students would jam on songs from it. Dawn Greening, a booster of the school from the beginning, soon came on board on a regular basis. The school's orbit that involved teaching and/or concertizing included banjoist Fleming Brown, George and Gerry Armstrong, vocalist Ginny Clemens, and singer–storyteller Art Thieme.

Old Town was extremely successful and had a major impact on the audience for folk music in Chicago. In addition to the teaching aspect of the school, there were workshops offered by touring professionals and concerts. Roger McGuinn, who later founded the Byrds, was one of the early students of the school, and so was Stu Ramsey, a fine young blues player. Frank Hamilton left in 1962 to continue his performing career but was replaced by Ray Tate, a Chicago guitarist and studio musician, and later Michael Miles, a fine banjoist, replaced Tate. Today, the school is housed in an abandoned public school and also includes an acoustic-music shop. Some twenty years later, Old Town was also the inspiration for the second largest school of its kind, the Music Association of Swallow Hill, which is discussed later in this book.

CHICAGO BLUES

Two other important folk music scenes were going on in Chicago at about the same time. Chicago was the destination point for thousands of African Americans who moved north from Mississippi. One of these people was a man named McKinley Morganfield, better known as Muddy Waters.

Well before the explosion of black emigration from Mississippi, Chicago had been a significant blues town. In the 1920s, Blind Lemon Jefferson was one of the first major folk blues recording artists and Blind Blake was a legendary guitarist who played on dozens of recording sessions for himself and others. Paramount Records was one of the primary blues labels and another label, Gennett, was headquartered in nearby Wisconsin. Tampa Red and "Georgia Tom" were also living in Chicago, and they recorded as a duo, in addition to Tampa Red's extensive solo work. Big Bill Bronzy was another blues artist who recorded and composed hundreds of blues.

By the time the folk revival hit Chicago, the blues had begun to turn electric. Muddy Waters was one of the pioneers of the idiom, playing electric guitar with a slide and using a drummer and an acoustic bass. Little Walter, followed by a string of other musicians, played amplified harmonica, and there was also a piano in the group. The recordings of these artists made the rhythm and blues sales charts and weren't well-known to most of the urban folkies. Big Bill Broonzy was sort of the bridge between the more urban blues and the earlier country blues, and he essentially put aside his electric guitar and took on a less sophisticated musical image as a commercial concession to the folkies. Many of them were unaware of his recordings of the 1940s, which included sax and drums in the lineup. This is oddly similar to what happened with Doc Watson, the superb country guitarist, who was playing electric rockabilly guitar when Ralph Rinzler ran across him in North Carolina and persuaded him that there was a market for the music that Doc had grown up with in the mountains.

The bridge between the blues scene and the revivalists was a bunch of young white college students at the University of Chicago. Harmonica player Paul Butterfield and guitarists Michael Bloomfield and Elvin Bishop were among these students. They took to hanging out in the South Side clubs to see, and eventually jam with, the many fine black blues musicians. Ironically, they were re-creating a scene that had occurred twenty years earlier, when young white jazz musicians like Benny Goodman and Eddie Condon went to the South Side clubs to see Louis Armstrong and King Oliver. It wasn't long before Butterfield and Bloomfield broke down the barriers between folk-blues and electric blues for the folk audience.

In 1953, a group of University of Chicago students founded a folklore society, bringing a number of folk artists to the campus. In 1961, under the leadership of Mike Fleischer, these activities expanded into a major folk festival featuring a large number of artists of all descriptions. This was one of the first significant festivals outside Newport, and other such events later proliferated around the country, notably in Philadelphia and Berkeley.

The college students also did some recordings on their own and one song with Bob Gibson, "Chicago Mob Scene." Some of the people involved were Pete Stone, Pete Stein, Carl Gottesman, and Moe Hirsch.

Another important part of the Chicago folk scene was the activity generated through writer and radio personality Studs Terkel. An incredibly energetic fellow, Studs promoted a series of concerts that he called "I Come for to Sing," and he had a radio show on WFMT. Terkel also produced some records from his radio show, notably the last recordings of Big Bill Broonzy. The Saturday night Midnight Special radio show was run for years by Norm Pellegrini at the same station. It was an important factor in the Chicago scene and featured many live performances as well as recorded music.

Frank Fried was an ex-steelworker who promoted concerts all over the midwest through his Triangle Productions. Robert Cantwell, in his book *When We Were Good: The Folk Revival,* stresses the role of Jewish performers in the folk music revival. In my opinion, he exaggerates. Although there were quite a few Jews represented in the revival, it was the infrastructure of the folk music business that was largely dominated by Jews. The major managers and promoters included Fried, Albert Grossman, and Manny Greenhill. Many of the club owners were also Jewish. The record company owners and executive positions were even more heavily occupied by Jews. The major folk labels were Folkways, Elektra, and Vanguard. All three were owned and founded by Jews. Jews were generally politically liberal, and folk music had developed an association with radical politics. The revival was, initially at least, largely centered in New York; New York has a large Jewish population. Many Jews are likewise involved in entrepreneurial pursuits. It is also true, by the way, that the record business as a whole has historically been dominated by Jewish and Italian executives.

Alan Ribback took over the Gate of Horn when Grossman moved to New York, but there were also a raft of other coffeehouses including the Fickle Pickle, Poor Richard's, and, later Somebody Else's Troubles, Mother Blues, and Holstein's. The latter was run by two singer–songwriter brothers named Fred and Ed Holstein. There was also a suburban version of Old Town called Charlotte's Web in suburban Rockford, Illinois. Singer-songwriter Steve Goodman was also a fixture on the scene, with his epic ode to the Chicago Cubs' fans, and "The City of New Orleans," a much-recorded song that was a hit for Arlo Guthrie.

Chicago was certainly one of the most important towns in the folk revival. When we turn to the blues, we will see that it was *the* most significant place where the blues were alive and well. It continues in that role today. Although there were no folk record companies in Chicago, Mercury Records was a major independent label headquartered in Chicago during the years of the folk boom. Chess Records, of course, was a blues powerhouse.

CALIFORNIA DREAMING

Because California is such a large state, the folk scene was dispersed between the cities of San Francisco and Los Angeles. In San Francisco, there was a commercial folk scene happening in the North Beach section of town, where the Purple Onion and the Hungry i were located. There was even a folk business infrastructure established when the Kingston Trio and their manager Frank Werber bought a building at Columbus and Kearney. They built a recording studio in the building and Werber and his partner, Renee Cardenas, operated a personal management firm there. Barbara Dane operated Sugar Hill, a blues club nearby. Dane was an excellent blues artist herself and she brought in touring blues and jazz artists. The revivalist scene was taking place at clubs such as the Fox and Hounds coffeehouse and the Drinking Gourd, a local bar. Faith Petric was a local performer who began a long role as a sparkplug of traditional music in the Bay area. Malvina Reynolds was a contemporary songwriter whose work was published in *Broadside,* and whose song "Little Boxes" became a widely performed and recorded folk standard.

Berkeley had its own scene, and a whole other group of musicians were developing there—much as the Colorado scene had a Boulder and a Denver contingent.

Berkeley spawned a bunch of talented artists whose lives eventually moved outside of the music scene. Al Young was a smooth-voiced young African American performer who had a large and varied repertoire of folk songs; he went on to become a famous novelist, poet, and music critic. He often sang at a local bar called the Blind Lemon. Steve Talbot had a reputation for being a fine blues and ragtime guitarist, but he made a living working on the railroad. Pete Berg was an excellent musician and a creative jazz-influenced guitarist who seemed to be attending the University of California on a ten-year program, changing his major repeatedly until he got a degree in anthropology and became a bamboo farmer in the Phillipines.

The center of the action in Berkeley was Lundberg's, a music store run by Jon and Deidre Lundberg. Musicians from all over the country sent their old acoustic guitars for Jon to repair or rework, and as with the Denver Folklore Center, a number of musicians worked for Jon. Marc Silber worked as a repair person before moving to New York to partner with Izzy Young. Mark is still at it today. Other Lundberg alumni are singer–songwriter–guitarist Janet Brown and Tony Marcus, a wonderful fiddle player and multi-instrumentalist. Mary Ann Pollar, possibly the only black woman folk entrepreneur, was an important local promoter. Barry Olivier produced a folk music festival in Berkeley beginning in 1963. San Francisco was much more self-consciously hip than Los Angeles, and Alex Hassilev of the Limeliters, speaking at a recent panel on the history of California folk music, commented that commercial success was considered "suspect." The San Francisco area was one of the most important incubators of folk-rock, and bands like Joy of Cooking, the Grateful Dead, and the Jefferson Airplane all contained at least some members who had deep roots on the folk scene.

*   *   *

My band played several times at the Hungry i. To give the reader a feeling of what life was like in Berkeley in 1963, I rented a one-bedroom apartment for fifty dollars a month. It had a large kitchen where I kept a sofabed for visitors, and since the apartment was on the second floor, the flat roof could be used as a sort of solarium most of the year in the mild Northern California climate. You really couldn't lock the door; if you hit it with your shoulder, the door would open. It never even occurred to me that someone would try to break in and steal some of my instruments. There really wasn't anything else that I owned, so that would have been the only target for theft. One floor below me, Pete Berg was living with a fine blues singer named Toni Brown, who cofounded an important folk-rock group a few years later, called Joy of Cooking.

When we fired the management team of Werber and Cardenas that were representing us, we all moved back to the East Coast. I couldn't bear to give up an apartment that rented for fifty dollars, so I kept paying rent for a couple of years, until I admitted that I wasn't ever going back.

*   *   *

Los Angeles had two major clubs in the Hollywood area that specialized in folk music. The Ash Grove began as a home for both commercial and traditional acts, but it moved more and more in the direction of traditional music. Many of the blues rediscoveries played there, and so did everything from ballad singers to flamenco guitarists. The other club, the Troubadour, featured more commercial pop-folk acts. Both clubs had regular hootenannies or open-mic nights, and a large group of future recording artists would often attend. Some of the local musicians were Ry Cooder, Linda Ronstadt, David Lindley, and David Crosby. All of them later enjoyed important music careers in various bands and musical formats. The Dillards were the preeminent bluegrass group, and they had moved out from their native Missouri. Actor–singer Theodore Bikel owned the Unicorn on Sunset Strip with manager–entrepreneur Herb Cohen.

Another music scene was happening in suburban Orange County. There was another set of clubs out there, including the Paradox Club and the Mecca. Some of the participants included Penny Nichols, Mary McCaslin, John McEuen, Jeff Hanna, Steve Noonan, and Jackson Browne. McEuen and Hanna went on to start the Nitty Gritty Dirt Band. Future Monkee Mike Nesmith was another habitué. Every one of these performers had a place in the folk revival and/or the singer–songwriter movement of the 1970s. Other clubs included the Garret and the Ice House in Pasadena, and Ledbetter's in Hermosa Beach.

McCabe's, in Santa Monica, was the music store where people hung out. It was the center of the action and today it has evolved into a major source for lessons and a weekend concert space where folk-oriented performers play. Westwood Music, near UCLA, was another music store where quite a few musicians hung out or taught lessons.

When Frank Hamilton left Chicago, he resumed his teaching career at Westwood.

I have already mentioned that Bess Lomax Hawes established a curriculum for group guitar lessons while teaching for the extension department at UCLA. Four different radio shows that feaured folk music were another influence. Les Claypool, Ed Cray, Skip Wechsner, Jeff Miller, and John Davis all had folk radio shows during this period. Howard and Roz Larman have a show that has had a thirty-year run and is currently on internet radio. After Theo Bikel moved to New York, he had a radio show called at *At Home with Theo Bikel.* It was taped in New York but also broadcast in Los Angeles.

By the 1960s, Los Angeles had started to become an extremely important recording center, and by the end of the decade it had surpassed New York in importance. New York has remained the center for recording commercials, but Los Angeles was always the movie capital of the United States, and it rapidly became the source of most television work as well. Doug Dillard played banjo on many of the recording sessions, and David Cohen was playing guitar on pop, rock, folk, and country records. David Lindley and Ry Cooder were sought-after multi-instrumentalists who were used as colorists—people who could add exotic instrumental sounds to a record or film. It wasn't really until the 1970s that folk music assumed importance in Hollywood, but since that time Ry Cooder has done a number of film scores where he utilized various traditional and urban revivalist musicians.

There were a bunch of touring California singers who did pretty well during the revival, but who never became famous. They included Stan Wilson, Don Crawford, and Bob Grossman. Coloradans used to call these acts "West Coast folksingers." They all seemed to sing lengthy versions of John Henry and they pounded on the guitar with broad strums. In short they weren't the subtlest of performers. They all seemed to sing an odd dramatic ballad called "The South Coast," about a card game where the protagonist, a Mexican of noble birth, loses his wife in a card game. The song came from a poem by Lillian Boss Ross. Folklorist Sam Eskin wrote the melody and Rich Dehr and Frank Miller, members of the folk-pop band the Easy Riders, adapted it for performance purposes.

THE REST

In most major cities there were influential people that seemed to play a central role in the folk revival. In Portland, and later Seattle, John Ullman was a concert promoter and a manager; in Salt Lake City, Jim Sorrels and his then-wife Rosalie were at the center of the action; in Phoenix, Dolan Ellis, later to be a member of the original New Christy Minstrels, seemed to be the key performer. Paul Endicott booked and managed acts out of his Detroit office. Some of the coffeehouses and clubs that dated from the 1960s, such as the Café Lena in Saratoga Springs, New York, and the Ark, in Ann Arbor, Michigan, still exist today. Koerner, Ray, and Glover were performing original and traditional blues, Bob Dylan was hanging out, and critics Jon Pankake and Paul Nelson were delivering their critical edicts about folk music on the Minneapolis–Saint Paul front. There were scenes in places like Gainesville, Florida, Austin, and Dallas, and Austin later became a sort of singer–songwriter haven and an important outpost for blues and country-rock music.

For the folk scene to really emerge in a city, there needed to be an infrastructure to support it. That infrastructure included a variety of elements. Below is a list of these factors.

- **Music stores:** Not just any music stores, but ones that featured old and new acoustic instruments, and offered lessons on the instruments and repair services;

- **Entrepreneurs:** Business people who promoted concerts, booked, and/or managed talent;
- **Clubs or venues:** Bars or coffeehouses that featured live acoustic music;
- **Teachers:** Instrumentalists who could impart their skills to aspiring talent and to devoted amateurs, who would become an audience for the music;
- **Radio stations:** DJs and music directors who had folk shows and also featured interviews with local and touring artists (we've mentioned a few of them already; some others with long-running shows are Gene Shay in Philadelphia and Dick Cerri, Mary Cliff, and John Dildine in Washington, D.C.);
- **Record companies and recording studios:** For anyone seeking to develop a serious career, making records is a necessity. When a city didn't have adequate studios, performers had to go elsewhere. Most cities during the sixties revival didn't have record companies. This situation, as the reader will see later, is entirely different today;
- **Studio work:** For accomplished musicians and vocalists, work was available playing or singing for commercials, records, and films;
- **Folklore societies:** In cities like Portland, Seattle, and San Francisco, there are folklore societies that sponsor concerts and song circles and, in general provide a support network for people interested in folk music. They usually publish periodicals with schedules of folk performances and other articles of interest to folk fans;
- **Colleges:** Many of the folk groups met in college, or were actively involved in folk song clubs at colleges. Colleges were also a source of gigs, with the many parties, social functions, and concerts. Oberlin College in Ohio, for example, was the nurturing environment for Joe Hickerson (for years the archivist at the Library of Congress folk song division); Bill Svanoe, later in the Rooftop Singers; folk promoter-performer of hobo songs Fred Starner; folklorist and performer Neil Rosenberg; some ten years after the revival period, Richard Carlin, who has edited dozens of books on folk and other kinds of music and has written some of his own; and Brad Leftwich, an excellent fiddle and banjo player, recording artist, author of instructional materials, and whose family were traditional folk musicians. Oberlin even spawned the Folksmiths, who recorded an album for Folkways;
- **University folklore departments:** Despite the fact that during the 1950s and '60s many folklorists looked down their noses at the folk revival, many people who graduated from these programs themselves

played a role in the revival. I am thinking of such people as Roger Abrahams, Ellen Stekert, Neil Rosenberg, and Gene Bluestein, to cite a few;

- **The intangibles:** Sometimes it was the presence of a single individual or some sort of place to hang out and develop one's craft that created an atmosphere that seemed to inspire people to take a deeper interest in the music;
- **Folk dancing:** The folk revival also included and was fed by an interest in square dancing or in regional dance styles like contra dancing in New England.

It wasn't necessary for all of these elements to exist for a city to develop some sort of cachet in the folk revival. Obviously, it was the larger cities that had more of the ingredients, yet there was a strong interest in the revival at many of the colleges, such as Oberlin, that were not located in close proximity to a large city. Perhaps it was this very isolation that brought people closer together and helped to develop a sense of community.

FOLKLORISTS AND THE FOLK REVIVAL

In the early chapters of this book I paid considerable attention to the role of such folklorists and music collectors as John and Alan Lomax and Howard Odum and Guy Johnson, as well as the numerous collectors of regional folk song and folklore. I have also referred to the fact that a number of folklorists despised the use of music for political purposes and bridled at the notion that these rewritten topical songs had anything at all to do with a proper scholarly definition of folk music. It therefore shouldn't come as a surprise that folklorists had a somewhat less than strong appreciation for the work of the urban revivalists, let alone the folk-pop performers.

It was left to a band of informal folklorists, folk aficionados who hadn't studied folklore in college, to locate some of the surviving musicians who had recorded the sort of blues and country music songs found on the *Anthology*. Mike Seeger, John Cohen, and Ralph Rinzler traveled in the southern mountains and found such artists as Dock Boggs and Clarence Ashley. The "discovery" of Doc Watson is an even stranger story. Rinzler found Doc while on a field trip to east Tennessee to record Clarence Ashley. Doc was playing electric rockabilly guitar in a hillbilly band, and Rinzler only became interested in him when Doc revealed that he also played some banjo, and it turned out to be traditional banjo. Rinzler persuaded

Watson that he could have a career playing the music that he had learned as a child in Deep Gap, North Carolina. Think of the irony of the situation. A city-bred, college-educated musician and folk song collector convinces the "primitive" folk musician that he ought to abandon commercial folk and perform the mountain music that he had learned in his youth. In any case, Doc went on to pursue a career as a musician and singer, and developed a tremendous reputation as a guitarist. Yet it is his heartfelt and straightforward singing that really has marked his musical achievements. As good as Doc's guitar playing is (and it is very, very good), anyone who sees him just as an instrumentalist doesn't understand the integrity or achievement of his performances. It turned out that Doc also loves blues, and he was influenced by a rediscovered Mississippi John Hurt to add fingerpicking blues-based music to his repertoire. (One can only imagine folklorists agonizing over Watson adding archaic black music styles to his already suspect repertoire.)

Alan Lomax was in England from 1950 to 1958. During his absence from the U.S., there seemed to be little interest in the collection of traditional African American music. Oddly, when Lomax returned, he wasn't the one who located the lost great American blues artists of the 1920s and 1930s. It was a group of musicians and blues freaks—including guitarists John Fahey, Henry Vestine, and Bill Barth and blues fanatics Ed Denson, Tom Haskins, Dick Spottswood, Nick Perls, Phil Spiro, and Dick Waterman—who tirelessly scrutinized old phone books, pestered other blues musicians with questions, and drove many miles in successful searches for Mississippi John Hurt, Skip James, Bukka White, and Son House. Brilliant blues guitarist Lonnie Johnson was found shining shoes at the Benjamin Franklin Hotel in Philadelphia in 1960 and he then resumed his musical career.

Where were the folklorists? First of all, remember that they were ballad specialists. They didn't like blues in the first place and they disliked anyone who had made records for commercial record companies. But there is more to it than this. There was an implied superiority of ballads over later African American musical forms that seemed to govern the aesthetic tastes of the folklorists. There were exceptions, of course, such as D. K. Wilgus, who taught at the University of Western Kentucky and, later, at UCLA. I have to see this picture not just as a form of snobbery, but of racism. The implication, quite simply, was that white music was better than black music. The implied, if not quite stated, thought was that black music wasn't real folk music anyway.

There were a couple of discoveries, as opposed to rediscoveries, of blues artists. Alan Lomax did find Fred McDowell in Mississippi in 1959, and McDowell went on to record a number of albums as well as influence such urban blues revivalists as Bonnie Raitt. And Harry Oster, a folklorist who taught at LSU, found a wonderful blues artist named Robert Pete Williams at the Angola prison in Louisiana in 1958.

Other artists who had never had substantial music careers until the folk revival were John Jackson, a songster from the Washington, D.C., area and Mance Lipscomb, a songster from Navasota, Texas. Songsters are defined as African American artists who perform a broad repertoire that includes blues but is not limited to that genre. Lipscomb was discovered by playwright and unofficial folklorist Mack McCormick (by "unofficial" I mean that he did not teach at a university). McCormick brought Lipscomb to the attention of Chris Strachwitz, and he was the first artist on Strachwitz's Arhoolie label in 1960. Strachwitz also recorded Jackson, beginning in 1965.

The blues rediscoveries had a varying effect on the newly discovered artists. Mississippi John Hurt had never been a full-time musician and his creativity seemed to thrive when he finally had the opportunity to play without having to pursue other sources of income. Many of the young fans who found these artists were not equipped to handle their musical careers. They had no background in music-business procedures and in some instances the musicians might have been better left alone. Dick Waterman was about the only one of the fans who learned enough about the business to handle booking or managing his artists. He has recently written a book, *Between Midnight and Day: The Last Unpublished Blues Archive,* that combines his sensitive photographs with stories of the rediscovered blues men and the travails of handling their careers.

In the history of the blues, another genre was the recordings of the women who were basically pop-blues artists. These included Ma Rainey, Bessie Smith, and another dozen artists whose backgrounds were in vaudeville and tours in black theaters. Several of these artists were retired or semiretired and had settled in New York. They began to reappear during the folk revival. Victoria Spivey, a songwriter and one of the most entrepreneurial of the group, started her own record company, Spivey Records, in 1963. In addition to her own recordings she recorded a number of her friends, including Lucille Hegamin, Alberta Hunter, and Hannah Sylvester. Hunter had retired from music and worked for years as a practical nurse. She became a virtual institution at the Cookery, a Greenwich Village restaurant. Other divas of the 1920s who resurfaced included Sippie Wallace and Ida Cox.

The reemergence of the female blues divas influenced a number of younger white women in their careers. Bonnie Raitt, in particular, toured with Sippie Wallace and recorded with her.

In 1958, Jimmy Driftwood, a high school principal from the Ozark mountains in Arkansas, recorded a bunch of his original folk-based songs for RCA. One of them, "The Battle of New Orleans," used an old fiddle tune, "The Eighth of January," as the melody for its verses. The song became an enormous hit in a country-pop version by Johnny Horton. Some of Driftwood's other songs, especially "The Tennessee Stud" and a sort of metaphorical freedom song, "He Had a Long Chain On," became staples in the performances of urban revivalists. Later, Driftwood helped to establish the Ozark Heritage Festival in Mountain View, Arkansas. Although not much attention has been paid to Driftwood's contributions to the folk revival, he was probably the first folk-oriented singer–songwriter, and one of the few people with deep traditional roots, who participated in the folk revival.

A later scholarly generation of folk song and blues collectors were often ethnomusicologists rather than folklorists. Consequently, they did not share the prejudices of the old ballad scholars. Such collectors as Kip Lornell, David Evans, Bruce Bastin, and Jeff Todd Titon collected and published dozens of blues, and Evans even started a record label at the University of Memphis, where he teaches. But none of this happened during the early-to-mid-1960s, the heart of the folk revival. During the high point of the folk revival, the two people doing the most collecting and analysis of blues were an American musician–poet–critic named Sam Charters and Paul Oliver, a British architect and fanatic blues fan, neither of whom were folklorists.

chapter 7

Music, the Civil Rights Movement, and the Folk "Superstars"

When World War I ended in 1918, African American soldiers came home and resumed life in a world of poll taxes, lynchings, and segregation. The Ku Klux Klan was revived in the South in 1915, two years before the U.S. entered the war, and during the 1920s became a powerful force not only in the South but also in the midwest and Rocky Mountain states. Consequently, although there were some instances of southern blacks attempting to assert their rights, the racial situation in the South quickly returned to the status quo. There were floggings, burnings, and, according to historian John Hope Franklin, more than seventy lynchings of blacks in 1919. There were also twenty-five race riots all over the United States, including a serious outbreak in Chicago.

In World War I, many black soldiers were assigned as laborers, although some did fight on the battlefield. World War II was a different story, with hundreds of thousands of black soldiers drafted. As in the previous war, African Americans fought in segregated units, with white officers commanding them. American participation in the second World War lasted much longer, and many more blacks were drafted. Black soldiers were an important part of the invading, and later occupying, army. As such they were surprised to find that many of the racial barriers found in America were not as strictly observed in Europe. This even applied to the bête noire of American life, social contact between black men and white women. When the war ended in 1945, once again the soldiers returned home. Many of the southern black soldiers were determined to change social conditions in the South. They had risked their lives for their country and now they wanted a level playing field in education, politics, and other aspects of daily living.

Franklin Roosevelt had generally stayed away from attempting to create profound changes on the racial front. Under pressure from black leaders, though, he did create the FEPC (Federal Employment Practices Committee). This was an attempt to increase the number of black employees in the federal government and in the defense industry.

Roosevelt died in 1945, and was succeeded by Harry S Truman. Truman was considered a moderate democrat, and as a former senator from the border state of Missouri, he was not expected to agitate for the expansion of civil rights. Like Lyndon Johnson in later years, he exceeded these expectations. In 1948, he issued an executive order that mandated fair employment by the federal government. This led to a revolt by southern democrats, who formed their own political party, the Dixiecrats.

In 1950, the North Koreans invaded South Korea and the United States entered the conflict. Initially, the American forces experimented with integrating some units of the army, and by 1951 all American forces were integrated. Other advances came with Truman's appointments of African Americans to various federal court positions and cabinet appointments.

DESEGREGATION IN THE SCHOOLS AND THE CIVIL RIGHTS MOVEMENT

For many years, public schools in the United States were segregated. The U.S. Supreme Court had created the notion of "separate but equal" facilities for white and black students in an 1896 decision. Starting in 1946, African Americans started to sue for admission to white universities and in 1950, the U.S. Supreme Court started to demolish the separate but equal philosophy that it had endorsed over fifty years earlier. In 1954, segregation in the public schools was outlawed.

The end of segregation was followed by successful efforts to integrate restaurants, hotels, and transportation systems. To summarize some of what was taking place:

- In Montgomery, Alabama, Rosa Parks refused to move to the back of the bus. This led to a boycott of the bus company, and to the emergence of Martin Luther King as the most important leader of the civil rights movement;
- There sit-ins at lunch counters, and dozens of blacks, mostly college students, were arrested;
- Freedom riders came South to test segregation in transportation. In many instances, the integrated groups of riders were beaten up and mobbed;

- John F. Kennedy was elected president in 1960, and he was success-fully pressured to protect civil rights workers and to promote integra-tion. Despite the intervention of the FBI, civil rights workers were beaten and murdered;
- Black political organizations became more militant. The NAACP, traditionally the forum for black leadership, was replaced in the fore-front of the struggle for civil rights by the SNCC (Student Non-vio-lent Coordinating Committee) and CORE (Committee for Racial Equality). Younger blacks found the NAACP too passive and conser-vative;
- Many African Americans went to jail during this period of political agitation, and so did some of their white supporters;
- The civil rights movement was a singing movement. Music sustained and supported the cause, and people sang in the jails and on the picket lines;
- A number of folksingers, mostly the younger urban revivalists, came down South and sang their support for the cause of civil rights.

MUSIC AND THE CIVIL RIGHTS MOVEMENT

Earlier, I examined how the political singers of the 1930s into the 1950s attempted to initiate social change through the use of folk music. In virtu-ally every case, with the outstanding exception of the music of the coal miners and textile workers, the change was initiated by largely urban, edu-cated artists who had little or no personal connection with the working class. This is why so much of this music had relatively little effect. For a Pete Seeger or a Millard Lampell to sing at a union rally and expect to change the ideology of the workers was naive and, in some respects, rather arrogant. What made these middle-class performing artists think that they knew enough about local issues and working conditions to feel that they could offer guidance or solutions to the problems that the average long-shoreman was experiencing? In hindsight Seeger, for one, has tended to be amused at his own style of dress, for example. The average worker only wore work clothes at work, and the visiting folksingers, dressed in their flannel shirts and blue jeans, were in effect *playing* at being workers. More-over, the visiting folkies were singing songs that represented their own tastes, but not necessarily the musical preferences of, for example, auto workers in Detroit.

The music of the Kentucky miners, by contrast, was music that the miners had grown up singing. It wasn't something imposed by New York radical intellectuals, but was part of the culture. It is interesting that when some of the singing miners or their relatives, such as Aunt Molly Jackson, her brother Jim Garland, or her half-sister Sara Ogan, came up to New York, after an initial flurry of interest, the New York radical movement for the most part had little interest in them or their music. Even the Almanacs, let alone the Weavers, were professional musicians, and more to the point, they were entertainers. They knew how to work a crowd, they were good, or at least competent, players, and their singing was not nasal or difficult for city folks to understand.

The textile workers' music was more localized, and sung on radio, records, or in southern communities. It did not have the direct affiliation with the New York radical singers, and with the exception of one or two songs the music was not performed by topical singers.

This brings us to the music of the civil rights movement. There is a long and rich tradition of African American music in the South, ranging from the music of the church to secular work songs, hollers, blues, and protest songs. These musical forms were used on a daily basis at work, dances, parties, and in rough juke joints. Furthermore, it was a living tradition, easily familiar to the people in the community. It isn't really surprising then that when the sit-ins resulted in jail time, the prisoners sang. What they sang were the songs that they had grown up with, but since black music is often highly improvisational, they changed the words to reflect the times. Religious tunes were often used, but the words reflected political sentiments, not just religious ones. SNCC even formed a group called the Freedom Singers, and Bernice Johnson Reagan, one of the members of the group, still performs with her group Sweet Honey in the Rock forty years later.

Because many of the people in the movement were young, they not only rewrote gospel songs, but they also rewrote some of the gospel-oriented pop songs of the day. The Percy Mayfield song that Ray Charles had popularized, "Hit the Road Jack," was transformed into "Get Your Rights Jack." A number of Curtis Mayfeld's songs were also used in the movement, with his permission. According to singer-activist Jimmy Collier, Mayfield's trio, the Impressions, were known as "movement fellows." Beginning in the early 1960s, Mayfield began writing a series of songs that spoke to issues like black pride and hope. Many of these songs used metaphors for the civil rights struggles. They became crossover hits, popular on both white and black radio stations. To the black listener, phrases like "people get ready" or "keep on pushing" had a specific and current meaning that was probably overlooked by white teenagers, not to mention white-owned radio stations. The latter rarely welcomed music that was politically controversial. And, of course, since the songs were current hits, everyone knew the melodies. The older New York political activist singers had pretty much avoided any popular music in their parodies, with the exception of a handful of Broadway-style songs that were composed during the Wallace presidential campaign.

Another key source for the use of music in the movement was the Highlander Folk School in Monteagle, Tennessee. Founded by two white political radicals—poet Don West and Myles Horton—the school held workshops for union organizers and civil rights workers from its inception in the late 1940s. Horton's wife, Zilphia, was a musician and a song leader and she encouraged and nurtured the music of the "students" who participated in the school. After her death, Guy Carawan, a young revivalist from California, essentially gave up his performing career to work at the school and to participate in the civil rights movement. Guy and his wife, Candy, helped civil rights workers put new words to some of the old gospel-flavored songs and he landed in various southern jails for his trouble. Highlander still exists today, outside of Knoxville, and the Carawans are still there.

WHITE REVIVALISTS AND THE CIVIL RIGHTS MOVEMENT

Many of the young white urban revivalists traveled down South to support the civil rights movement, especially during the Mississippi summer campaign of 1964. That movement was designed to assist African Americans to register to vote and to help them through encouragement, support, and even tutoring for the absurd tests that blacks needed to pass in order to register to vote in Mississippi.

With the exception of the Carawans, who have essentially dedicated their lives to the civil rights movement, most of the visiting singers spent very limited amounts of time in the South. The usual commitment was a week or two. It is important to distinguish between someone like Bob Dylan, for example, singing at a few rallies and urban (black) revivalist Len Chandler, who stayed in the South for months and spent time in numerous southern jails. Performers like Pete Seeger, Theodore Bikel, Phil Ochs, Judy Collins, and Joan Baez gave their support, but took comparatively few risks and spent very little time as activists compared to the people in the trenches. (In fairness, Baez continued her political work in protesting against the Vietnam War, and did log considerable prison time for those efforts.)

It must have been odd for African Americans to see and listen to the urban white folksingers performing music that was closer to the listeners' traditions than to anything that the singers themselves had grown up with. There was also, inevitably, some resistance to the notion of white singers participating in the movement. For example, in the famous 1963 March on Washington, Dick Gregory, for one, objected to having Joan Baez and Peter, Paul & Mary featured as singers. He felt that it was fine for them to be there, but that they shouldn't be usurping prime stage time with Martin Luther King. On the other hand, long-time activist Harry Belafonte felt that it was useful and important to have white singers publicly involved in the event.

In 1965, Malcolm X was assassinated, and in 1968 Martin Luther King was killed as well. These events radicalized the African American community; the Black Panther Party and other groups began to renounce King's nonviolent tactics. By that time the civil rights movement had fragmented and whites were no longer welcome. After King's death, the country became increasingly racially polarized and there were race riots in a number of cities. The folk boom itself had diminished, and the major issue in radical politics was the war in Vietnam.

Another interesting musical sidelight that surfaced during the late 1960s into the early 1970s was that black popular music itself became increasingly political. While Curtis Mayfield's lyrics had been somewhat subtle or metaphorical, and his music a sort of soft-gospel sound, the black-owned record companies such as Gamble and Huff's Philadelphia International and even Motown began to issue records with strong messages, and even the rather politically conservative James Brown jumped on the bandwagon with "Say It Loud, I'm Black and I'm Proud." Gamble and Huff-produced recordings by groups like the Chi-Lites and the O'Jays even referred to issues like slavery—hardly the usual purview of popular music. Motown's catch phrase was "the sound of young America" and owner Berry Gordy had resisted taking any political positions with the company's recordings. Some of his artists, like Marvin Gaye and Stevie Wonder, pushed for and got creative control of their recordings and Motown producer Norman Whitfield also wrote and produced songs about social issues. Many of these songs—especially those of Gamble and Huff, and Whitfield's recordings of the Temptations—used much heavier, angry

instrumental textures in addition to their explicit lyrics. None of the recordings by the white topical singers approached this level of intensity.

The music of the civil rights movement is so intertwined with the music
itself that the two cannot be separated from each other. The music was
not, as so much of the Almanac Singers' music was, an add-on to a social
issue. The music and the issues were part of the same fabric. It was probably the most effective use of music as a political tool in American history.
Many of the gospel songs were constructed with lyrics where someone
threw out a line and the group answered back. This allowed for a free and
spirited improvisational quality, and the lyrics could be adjusted to the situation. The lyrics about the Albany (Georgia) jail could easily adjusted to
fit the conditions in, say, Birmingham. Singers like Jimmy Collier, Matt
Jones, Julius Lester, Mabel Hillary, and Fannie Lou Hamer didn't become
famous performers, but their songs helped to fuel the movement. The song
"We Shall Overcome" became a sort of rallying cry for the movement. It
was adapted from an old spiritual by Zilphia Horton at Highlander, and
re-arranged by Pete Seeger, Guy Carawan, and Frank Hamilton. It became known in the movement through Guy Carawan's workshops at
Highlander starting in 1960. It became traditional to sing "We Shall
Overcome" at the close of rallies, usually with participants crossing their
arms and swaying. The authors donated all of their royalties to the cause
of civil rights.

*   *   *

In 1963, my band was involved in a thirty-day Hootenanny '63 bus tour
along with Glenn Yarbrough, the Geezinslaw Brothers from Texas, Jo
Mapes, and the Halifax Three, a Canadian folk-pop group. A few days
before we were scheduled to appear in Jackson, Mississippi, at the city auditorium, we received a call from SNCC. They asked us not to do the
show in solidarity with the civil rights movement. At the time, the city of
Jackson had a town ordinance requiring that the audience be segregated.
The city fathers knew that the law would not survive a court test, so they
would simply arrest any black person that came within 100 yards of the
auditorium on a loitering charge. The charges would later be dismissed,
but no black person could get into the auditorium if there were whites in
the audience.

The members of the tour held a group meeting. We voted not to play,
as did Glenn and Jo. The Geezinslaws wanted to play, as did the Halifax
Three (all of whom were Canadians), except for Zal Yanovsky, their gui-

tarist, who voted against playing. (Yanovsky's father was the editor of Communist newspaper the *Daily Worker* in Toronto.)

SNCC then asked if we would do a concert at Tougaloo College, a largely black but integrated college that was one of the centers for civil rights agitation in Mississippi. The three acts agreed, and the Journeymen rented a car to get there. John Phillips pulled up to the Greyhound bus station and asked me to check a brown paper bag in a locker. As I walked into the station, I realized that in the bag were several ounces of marijuana. This incident was rather ironic, since John was a "frequent user" and I never had much of an interest in drugs. As I walked into the bus station, I imagined myself getting busted and spending a number of my young-adult years in a Mississippi prison. Fortunately for me, no one seemed to notice.

We then drove to Tougaloo, which was located in the middle of rural nowhere. We ended up doing a full concert for the students. Looking around us, we noticed that some of the students were adorned with heavy bandages. Clearly, they had been beaten up by southern cops or thugs. When we got to the end of the show, we all sang "We Shall Overcome," locking arms in the style I described above.

When we left, the students warned us to drive slowly and to absolutely come to a full stop at any railroad crossing or stop sign. They informed us that we would probably be followed by cops and if we came even close to violating any laws, we would have the book thrown at us.

We drove away without incident. The next day, the story was carried on the newspaper wire services all over the South. We got to our next concert destination in Louisiana and the first people off the bus were the Geezinslaw Brothers. They were met with baseball bats and told that if Jackson wasn't good enough for us to perform in, then they didn't want any part of us either. Our greeters also tossed the usual epithets at us, like "nigger lovers." We drove away, the tour continued, and a few more weeks into the tour John Kennedy was assassinated.

Years later, my friend Scott McKenzie sent me a story posted on the internet. It seems that at the point when we performed, morale was very low in Tougaloo, and our willingness to honor the boycott and to perform for them was an important event for the students. It seems embarrassing in retrospect that doing the only humane thing was a significant contribution in the eyes of people who were risking their lives on a daily basis for their ideals. Granted, there were some risks in our doing what we did, but they certainly seemed insignificant in the overall scope of courage and risk-taking that was so much a part of the civil rights movement.

THE SUPERSTARS OF FOLK

I recently read a book coauthored by David Crosby called *Stand Up and Be Counted: Making Music, Making History*. The opening chapter describes music in the civil rights movement, but oddly, the music that Crosby is writing about is not the music *of* the movement, but the music sung by people like Peter, Paul & Mary and Joan Baez. The only part of the movement itself that he refers to in any detail is Martin Luther King's famous "I Have a Dream" speech. The bulk of the book is devoted to benefit performances given to support an end to the war in Vietnam. Apparently, the author doesn't comprehend the differences between, say, the Journeymen singing for one night at Tougaloo College, undertaking a mild level of risk, and putting one's life on the line on a consistent basis, as the students at Tougaloo were doing. The remainder of this chapter is devoted to the notion of superstars and how a movement designed to preserve and promote traditional music became infected by the disease that Joni Mitchell has referred to as the "starmaker machinery" behind the popular song.

ODETTA AND PETE SEEGER

Odetta is a magical performer who has always been accepted in the community of urban folk revivalists and fans. Anyone who has ever seen her or gotten to know her has been affected by her warmth, personality, and friendliness. Originally a classically trained singer in Los Angeles, through friends and fellow thespians in a production of *Finian's Rainbow* she became entranced with folk music and took up the guitar.

An engagement at the Tin Angel in San Francisco led to a recording for Fantasy Records with her then-singing-partner Larry Mohr, but it was engagements at the Gate of Horn in Chicago that began to establish her reputation. Odetta then became a client of manager-club-owner-impressario-music biz hustler Albert Grossman. She is one of those performers whose performing magic has never quite been captured on records, and she never had the good fortune of finding the one hit song that would have opened up more lucrative areas of performance and acceptance. Grossman seemed to lose interest in her when he started acquiring more immediately lucrative clients such as Bob Dylan and Peter, Paul & Mary. She was later managed by her husband, Danny Gordon.

Odetta has never made claims of authenticity, and possibly she lacks the competitive spirit and aloofness that seems to distinguish superstars. I

A young Pete Seeger, performing for a 1944 CIO function in Washington, D.C. *Joseph A. Horne, photographer. The Library of Congress*

In the words of Bob Dylan, nobody sings the blues like Blind Willie McTell. *Library of Congress*

Alan Lomax – better known as a folklorist – performing at the Mountain Music Festival in Asheville, North Carolina. *Library of Congress*

Leadbelly, lifting a car out of the snow at the Wilton, Connecticut, home of English professor Mary Elizabeth Barnicle in 1939. *Library of Congress*

The cover of Woody Guthrie's *Dust Bowl Ballads,* his 1940 RCA Victor album.

A 1930s photo of a banjo player and his wife. *Library of Congress*

Jesse Fuller, "The Lone Cat," one-man band and composer of "San Francisco Bay Blues." *Courtesy Folklore Productions*

At the right-hand table, Eric Weissberg, Dick Weissman, Jane Saltzman, Wendy Scribner, and "Papa" John Phillips (as he was later known), listening to Brother John Sellers at Gerde's Folk City in 1961. *Courtesy* New York Times

A one-man band at the Mountain Music Festival, Asheville, North Carolina. *Library of Congress*

Bob Dylan performing at the Isle of Wight, September 1, 1969. *United Press International Photo*

The Band when they were still known as Ronnie Hawkins (LEFT) and the Hawks. *Photographer unknown*

Publicity photo of Odetta Felious. *Photographer unknown*

Bruce Langhorne, unsung and distinguished guitarist who played on recordings by Bob Dylan; Peter, Paul & Mary; and many others. Langhorne was the composer of the film score for the underground classic *The Hired Hand. Photo by Caleb Deschanel*

Multi-instrumentalist Mike Seeger and banjo player Mike Kropp at the Denver Folk Center. *Photo by Duke McDermott*

Harry Tuft, founder and owner of the Denver Folklore Center talking to Manny Greenhill and Mitch Greenhill, who are also at the booth at the North American Folk Alliance. *Photo by the author*

Utah Phillips and Ani DiFranco, Righteous Babe Recording Artists and comrades in arms. Photo by Steve Stone, *courtesy Righteous Babe Records*

still remember walking through Greenwich Village in the late 1950s and hearing people whisper to one another that they had seen Odetta walking down the street or drinking coffee in a Village restaurant.

Pete Seeger is the antisuperstar. Of all the folk artists, he has been one of the most influential. He has inspired hundreds of musicians to become professional folksingers, and to look deeply into the music. As an original member of the Weavers he sold millions of records. As the cowriter of "If I Had a Hammer," "The Bells of Rhymney," and the author of "Turn, Turn, Turn" and "Where Have All the Flowers Gone," this reluctant idol has been the author of major hit songs. Along with bluegrass banjoist Earl Scruggs, Pete has introduced thousands of people and dozens of musicians to the five-string banjo, and his book, the first to describe folk banjo styles, has been used by everyone from the Kingston Trio to many urban revivalists. After the death of Leadbelly, Seeger introduced the twelve-string guitar into American popular music. Millions of people all over the world have sung along with Seeger in concert. As a political folksinger, he refused to cooperate with congressional investigations of his personal politics, thereby effectively handcuffing his own music career. His children's records and dozens of other albums have sold thousands of copies, and he was one of the first folksingers to embrace the notion of environmental preservation. He has probably performed more benefits than any other artist, and he may be the only artist who has ever told his manager to *reduce* his fees because he felt he was being overpaid. Seeger has also written a half-dozen books, including collections of his own songs and songs of the civil rights movement.

On a certain level, for a person with his incredibly diverse list of musical accomplishments, Seeger has never really become a superstar. Because he is a private person, he doesn't make the gossip columns,. He hasn't fathered children except the three that he shares with his sole wife, Toshi. David Dunaway's biography of Seeger points out that on the few occasions when he has been accosted by "groupies," he has immediately diverted them with fatherly, rather than lascivious, behavior. He rarely drinks; he isn't interested in drugs. In short, he would make a terrible candidate for the VH1 series *Behind the Music* because there simply isn't any scandal or suicidal behavior governing his life. He reportedly is not fond of Dunaway's biography, and he probably won't be pleased at getting this much attention in this book. Now in his late eighties, he has never wanted to be regarded as a superstar.

Seeger is a complicated person, and this can best be seen by looking at his dealings with the ABC *Hootenanny* TV show of 1963–64. This was a series of folk performers taped at colleges. Seeger was not chosen to appear because of the blacklist, but the producers of the show shamefully claimed that he wasn't good enough, or contemporary enough, to suit the image of the show. Various performers decided to boycott the program, but Seeger himself urged the New Lost City Ramblers to appear because he felt that bringing tradition-based music to television was important. He also subbed for the Tarriers at a New York nightclub engagement so that they could appear on the show. He did this because the Tarriers were a racially integrated group and he felt, once again, that their appearance on television was more important than his personal cause.

After I discuss some of the performers who are more comfortable with the superstar label, I will turn to the notion of stardom and its relationship, if any, to folk music.

JOAN BAEZ, BOB DYLAN, ET AL.

Joan Baez is the daughter of an astrophysicist. She briefly attended Boston University, but became entranced with the Boston coffeehouse scene. Baez's autobiography, *And a Voice to Sing With,* offers many details about the singer's fundamental sense of loneliness and her involvement with so-cial and political causes. Of all of the urban revivalists, Baez has contrib-uted the most money and the most time to political causes, particularly the antiwar movement.

Eric Van Schmidt and Jim Rooney's *Baby Let Me Follow You Down* reveals a whole other side of Joan's character. From the day she started to play the guitar, she felt competitive with anyone else that was performing. The authors describe her learning singer-guitarist-friend Debby Green's entire repertoire and then performing it when she was the opening act for Ms. Green. This left Debby with nothing to do at the concert. This was then rationalized by Joan asserting that Debby was not ambitious, and would never really apply herself to career goals anyway. Van Schmidt and Rooney also describe Joan sitting in the back of Cambridge's Club 47 and singing harmony parts from the rear of the club in such a way that they overpowered the performer, even though the performer was singing with a microphone, and Joan wasn't.

Joan became a superstar from a two-song performance at the Newport Folk Festival when Bob Gibson invited her to perform with him. This led to a recording contract with Vanguard Records, although during a brief business flirtation with Albert Grossman, he attempted to push her to record with Columbia Records. Baez felt more rapport with Vanguard, and was also impressed that they had fought the blacklist by signing the Weavers. She also decided to sign with Boston manager Manny Greenhill, an ex-union organizer who certainly was not the business shark that Grossman was generally acknowledged to be.

Baez's repertoire was initially a combination of English and American folk songs. Her first record was minimally produced—simply her performance with some guitar accompaniment by Weaver Fred Hellerman—and it became a gold record (a gold record has sales of over 500,000 copies). This was an astounding feat for a small label like Vanguard and certainly went way beyond their expectations. Baez had a strong soprano voice and, because she was half-Mexican, a sultry appearance, which she embellished with her long hair, simple outfits, and the avoidance of makeup. One of the distinguishing characteristics of superstars is that their styles are imitated not only by other performers but by fans modeling themselves after the star. All over the United States, young women wore their hair straight and used minimal makeup, or abandoned it entirely.

In Baez's case, it wasn't only her physical appearance that resonated with young women. Baez was a follower of Gandhi's nonviolent approach to social change and she demonstrated against the war in Vietnam, spent some time in jail, refused to pay federal income taxes, and founded a school for nonviolence in her new home in Carmel.

Just as Bob Gibson had in effect sponsored Joan Baez, she in turn introduced Bob Dylan to *her* audience. Because Dylan was never a great natural singer, he badly needed the endorsement of more conventional singers who had captured the folk audience. This task was assumed on a business level by Peter, Paul & Mary, who made hit recordings of Dylan's songs "Blowing in the Wind" and "Don't Think Twice, It's Alright." Dylan's own early records hadn't sold well, and it was these recordings that initially gained him national attention.

*   *   *

I was in the audience at the 1964 Newport Folk Festival. Newport is a naval base, and a number of tickets had been given away to sailors. I was sitting next to two of them when Dylan sang "Blowing in the Wind." One sailor commented that this was about the worst singing he had ever heard. His friend looked over at him and said in a worshipful tone that this was the guy who had written that song, the one that Peter, Paul & Mary recorded. The first sailor immediately quieted down and gave Dylan his full attention for the rest of his performance. It was then that I understood just how important PP&M's endorsement was to Dylan.

*　　*　　*

Baez's sponsorship was more of a personal endorsement, bringing him on concert tours and recording a number of his songs. She was also clearly enamored of him, and their affair was the subject of much speculation and gossip. If this is the sort of thing that interests you, I suggest that you read David Hadju's lengthy gossip-column treatise, *Positively 4th Street: The Life and Times of Joan Baez, Bob Dylan, Mimi Baez Fariña and Richard Fariña.* In this book, Hadju describes the complex web of personal relationships that developed between Baez and Dylan, Joan's sister, Mimi, and young author-musician Richard Fariña. He goes so far as to say that Fariña recommended to Dylan that he "go after" Baez because it would assist his career. Which he did. According to Baez's autobiography, she in turn accepted a role as a sort of second banana in the Dylan bandwagon. She followed him to England, assuming that she would be asked to sing as a guest artist with him, in the same way that she had paved the road for him. Seemingly Baez had found someone more ambitious and calculating more cold-hearted than she was. She was transformed from a guest artist to a mere member of Dylan's entourage. She was largely ignored and occasionally humiliated, and so she left the tour.

This brings us to the seemingly inexhaustible story of Bob Dylan. Dylan was actually Bob Zimmerman, the son of a Jewish furniture-and-appliance dealer in the northern Minnesota town of Hibbing. After a year at the University of Minnesota, Dylan came to New York, assuming a new identity and claiming to be an orphan. He ended up with a Columbia Records recording contract through meeting John Hammond Sr. at a recording session for Carolyn Hester. Hester had enlisted Dylan to play harmonica on her Columbia album. At about the same time, *New York Times* folk music critic Robert Shelton had written a rave review of a Dylan performance at Gerde's Folk City. It is very likely that Hammond saw this review, and Hester and her then-husband Fariña both praised Dylan to Hammond.

There have been dozens of books written about Dylan, including his own best-selling autobiography, *Chronicles, Volume 1.* Fans and critics have exhumed his songs, his personal garbage cans (literally), his connections with religion and politics, his ex-girlfriends, his childhood, and his importance as a songwriter and literary figure. I will have more to say about him in the ensuing chapters about folk-rock and singer–songwriters, but for now it is worth looking at his connection to stardom.

FOLK MUSIC AND THE CONCEPT OF SUPERSTARS

In reading the various tomes about Dylan and Baez, a few commonalities emerge that set them apart from Odetta and Seeger. If Seeger is self-effacing and somewhat reclusive, and Odetta is warm and accessible, what stands out about both Baez and Dylan is their fanatical ambition and their narcissism. Being an artist in twentieth- and twenty-first century America is obviously not the easiest choice of career, and there are clearly many more people who aspire to fame and fortune than there is fame and fortune. What are some of the qualities that separate the "winners" from the "also-rans," and what does any of this have to do with folk music?

It seems to me that the single-minded quest for success is a game that involves using people to get what one needs to achieve, then abandoning these people once they have served their purpose. Gibson may have helped Baez, but there is no particular public acknowledgment on her part of what he did, nor did she, to my knowledge, ever try to give him any career assistance. She never asked *him* to appear with her, and she didn't record his songs. His own autobiography seems to indicate that he had no expectations of her doing so, and these expectations were accurate. Nor is there any evidence that Baez did anything in particular to recognize the role of the people that had helped to introduce her to the Boston folk community. In later years, when Baez wanted in on a more contemporary singer–songwriter scene, she broke her handshake deal with Manny Greenhill. She does, however, remember him fondly in her autobiography.

Dylan's behavior represents a somewhat more extreme case, possibly because he had more competition to deal with than Baez did. In his Minnesota college days, it is said that Dylan stole some rare records from Paul Nelson and Jon Pankake, only returning them after a peculiar facedown with Pankake. Interestingly, among these records were British releases by Jack Elliott. Jack was the first and foremost Woody Guthrie imitator, and these records certainly influenced Dylan's early folk persona and repertoire. Before going to New York, Dylan stayed with Denver folksinger Walt Conley and repaid his hospitality by stealing a number of albums from Conley's record collection.

In his early days in New York, Dylan relied on several people for free lodging and he had Mike Porco sign papers as his "guardian" (remember, he was an "orphan") in order to join the Musician's Union. He made good use of Izzy Young, who promoted Dylan in an early concert, talked him up to all his friends, and helped to create a buzz for Bob on the folk music grapevine. Dave Van Ronk was an early confidant, and he relied on Dave and his ex-wife, Teri, for hospitality, food, and political enlightenment. Teri was managing Dylan very early in the New York days and when Dylan switched to Albert Grossman he didn't bother to tell her about it.

Dylan started out as a protest singer, modeling himself after Woody Guthrie. In that vein, he wrote a bunch of talking blues, songs where the artist talks over a set group of chords rather than singing a melody. Dylan was lionized by the left, sang at all sorts of political functions, and his early songs appeared in *Broadside*. Although he is more generous in the autobiography, biographers reveal that, at the time, Dylan was contemptuous of Phil Ochs, his competitor in the political-song sweepstakes, as well as Tom Paxton, who was writing both political and lyrical songs. Dylan was friendly with the New Left leaders of SDS (Students for a Democratic Society), went to some of their meetings, and even expressed interest in working with them. By 1965, Dylan had become an antiprotest singer; he proclaimed that he had only been involved in protest music because he was able to break into the music business that way. A few years later he divested himself of Albert Grossman. A cynical observer might say that Dylan no longer needed the shark since his own teeth were now sharp enough to handle any exigency.

FOLK MUSIC AND SUPERSTARDOM

Don West was the cofounder of the Highlander Folk School and the father of folk performer Hedy West. In two articles in the magazine *Appalachian South,* he discussed the notion of what he called "folk stars." West argued that the whole notion of folk stars "violated the nature and spirit of folk song." In his articles, he described the relationship between the folk songs of the southern mountains and the living conditions of such people as cotton mill workers, and the sacrifices of coal miners and textile workers in their attempts to form unions.

West points out that the people who wrote and sang these songs wrote them out of inspiration and hope, with no sense of competing against other writers and no expectations or interest in gaining financial rewards from their musical creations. He went on to roast the pop-folk stars with the sentence "'Success' is measured in terms of affluence, and trampling on others, if necessary, to get it. The 'folk song' show world comes to resemble a jungle with sometimes bitter, unprincipled, throat-cutting competition." It is certainly a far cry from the Almanac Singers, a group so casual that the personnel shifted from day to day. And what was it that the artists wanted? Money, power, acclaim? The point that West seems to be raising is that the world of the pop star had taken over a musical form that was intended to be a platform for a sort of communal sharing, rather than having a platform for the artist set himself above his audience. But is it reasonable to expect that an artist in, say, 1960, let alone 2005, would be content to play music in a community for a small group of like-minded people? Certainly it was Pete Seeger more than anyone who dragged the music into the pop world, by stressing that if you want to use music to create social change, you are going to need to have a mass audience. Another problematic aspect of this sort of analysis is that, clearly, folk music in anything resembling a traditional folkloristic view is music played in communities where there is little or no separation between performers and listeners. Certainly, by 1920, mountain musicians and blues singers were starting to record and to perform on the streets or in small venues. These performances then became monetized, so to speak, through such outlets as the *Grand Ole Opry* radio show and royalties or fees paid to performers by record companies and music publishers. Before the widespread use of the automobile and the building of highways, touring was not a practical option outside of the occasional thespian or opera star taking culture to the hinterlands. Once it became possible for a musically talented, nonclassically trained artist to develop a musical career, some performers in the folk vein became full-time professional musicians. It was inevitable that some of these performers would become more popular than others, either because their music "spoke" to more people, or their performances were particularly interesting or dynamic. In a sense, West is whipping a dead horse. Should an artist deliberately choose to perform for smaller audiences because there is more interaction? The musical infrastructure of concert promoters, personal managers, and record companies—professionals whose income is determined by large concert grosses and record sales—cannot be supported by intimate performing situations. If the artist feels that he or she has a valuable message to impart, whether it be political, emotional, or aesthetic, then isn't it natural for that artist to want to develop a larger audience? This inevitably puts the artist in competition with other musicians who have the same goals. How many artists deliberately limit the size of their audience or, for that matter, their fees, in order to stimulate the notion of audience interaction? Even Pete Seeger has to support managers, booking agents, and promoters.

How do our folk superstars measure up against this analysis? Certainly both Baez and Dylan did, and do, have the competitive drive to succeed in the world of the music business. Possibly, West was naive to believe that the folk music he loved and grew up with could possibly exist in the technological world of the late twentieth and early twenty-first century. Part of what has happened to Baez and Dylan is that they have felt the need to change, bringing themselves into alignment with the changes in the music business itself. Under the spell of Dylan, Baez became a song-writer, even writing her most famous song, "Diamonds and Rust," about Dylan. She also left Vanguard and recorded for A&M, certainly a "commercial" record company. Because she is a woman, Baez has had to sustain a career when she can no longer rely on her physical charms and when her image is seemingly more historical than interesting to young people. We all know that this is not fair or reasonable, but in our culture older women are at a disadvantage compared to younger, "sexier" women. Living a relatively quiet life as she ages, generally living alone, Baez's superstardom over the years has turned her into a major musical figure in historical terms, rather than as a contemporary performer. If there is one certain thing in Baez's life, it is that she knows that Bob Dylan will remember her, but he will never do anything for her.

Dylan has employed a different set of tactics, ones that have enabled him to remain in the public eye, even if his records are not best-sellers and his newer songs don't seem to get recorded by other artists. For years, he attempted to be a trendsetter rather than a follower. He would change musical styles, recording country albums in Nashville, going back to New York to record more rock-influenced albums. He has written books and attempted ill-fated movies; there are documentary films about him, and he became something of a recluse, first in Woodstock and later in Los Angeles. He became variously a born-again Christian and then flirted with Orthodox Judaism. Dylan also radically changed his recording modus operandi. Originally noted for such impatience in the recording studio that he would only record one or two takes of a song, he more recently has employed renowned (and opinionated) record producers Jerry Wexler and Daniel Lanois. Lanois's odd fascination with electronics, technology, and roots music on the face of it doesn't seem to jibe well with Dylan's roots aesthetic. Perhaps what was behind this choice was a perceived need to go with something a little more contemporary than the loose style of recording that he had utilized for so many years. Maybe it was simply the desire to try something new and different. Or maybe he simply wanted to sell more records. Every artist has to face the fact that after making twelve or fifteen or twenty albums; unless a new audience is cultivated, album sales aren't going to continue at the same high level. How many albums does an avid fan want to buy? Four, six, eight, ten? Older artists are not apt to appeal to new generations of record buyers. Certainly in the world of popular music, who wants to see a grandfather on stage?

Dylan toured comparatively little during his early career, and now he seems to constantly be on the road. It's one thing for a "road rat" like B. B. King to continue his lifelong pattern of intensive touring. It's quite another for someone deep into middle age to suddenly take on the role of the traveling man.

On a personal level, he has gone through a serious motorcycle accident, several divorces and marriages, and like Ray Charles and B. B. King, he has fathered a number of children, some with his various wives, and, like Ray Charles, some with his backup singers.

Yet, beyond all of this, Dylan does indeed seem to love and care about folk music. In his autobiography, he describes seeing Mike Seeger at a party at Alan Lomax's house and realizing that he would never rival Mike's skills as a musician or even as an interpreter of folk music. As he tells it, it was then that he decided that he had to focus on writing songs. Periodically, Dylan has become involved in causes, particularly agitating for the freeing of jailed boxer Rubin "Hurricane" Carter. In writing a song like "Blind Willie McTell," he has acknowledged his own debt to the blues, and to that fine blues artist. It appears that the aging Dylan has come to terms with the notion that he may be a superstar and a pop singer, but an important segment of his personal roots came out of the folk music revival and the rediscovered traditional artists that formed a significant part of it.

*   *   *

My friend guitarist-singer–songwriter Artie Traum took care of one of two houses that Bob Dylan owned in Woodstock some thirty-five years ago. The house had thirty-seven rooms! As Dylan has discussed in his autobiography, people would come by to visit uninvited and calls would come in from all corners of the world. Artie was instructed not to give out Dylan's phone number to any caller. The first caller was Joan Baez and Artie followed instructions, calling Dylan at the other house to relay the call. At one point, Al Grossman, Dylan's manager, asked Artie to pay the winter heating bill, which of course was far more than a mortgage payment on an

"ordinary" house. The moral of that story is that some people are artists
and others are businessmen!

At one point during Artie's housesitting chores, I visited him. He took
me on a brief tour of the house. In one room were sacks and sacks of mail.
We randomly read a half-dozen of the letters. The one that I remember
came from a female fan in North Dakota. She had been to a Dylan concert
and reminded him that they had met. She plaintively added that if he
didn't remember her, then maybe one of the members of Dylan's group,
the Band, would remember her. There was something touching, though
pathetic, about the letter. It certainly had little relationship to Don West's
notion of folk music. Dylan had become one of the mythical figures in
pop-rock, whether he wanted to be or not. His autobiography makes it
clear that there are many days when he might prefer to go to a movie or a
restaurant like an ordinary human being.

JUDY COLLINS

Like Odetta, Judy Collins is a classically trained, literate musician. Her
father was a performer and radio personality in Denver, but she studied
classical piano with pianist and conductor Antonia Brico. As a teenager,
she became interested in folk music and the guitar. Judy has written three
autobiographical works where she discusses her musical and personal experiences at length. Early in her career, she was influenced by a mystical
character named Lingo the Drifter. Today, Lingo is remembered as a
little-known but legendary character who lived on the top of Lookout
Mountain, occasionally performed in Denver, and pursued a fanatical interest in the functioning and potentiality of the human brain.

Judy started to perform in Boulder, and then in Denver. Because she
was married and had a child, she was conflicted about her musical career.
Her husband was a psychology student, and got a graduate assistantship at
the University of Connecticut. Judy got some opportunities to perform, at
the Gate of Horn in Chicago and also in New York. The first of many
Elektra albums was released in 1961.

Possibly because of her classical music background, Collins has moved
in more musical directions than most of the urban revivalists. Her early
records concentrated on her folk repertoire, but she soon became noted for
performing the work of other songwriters such as Bob Gibson, Billy Edd
Wheeler, John Phillips, and Tom Paxton. She had several gold albums,
but her career reached a new level with her 1967 recording of the song

"Both Sides Now," written by a (then) little-known Canadian writer named Joni Mitchell. After that, she began to record with classically oriented arrangements and to try her hand at sophisticated cabaret songs by Kurt Weill, Stephen Sondheim, and others. Her recording of the Sondheim song "Send in the Clowns" became a hit single. She also began to write songs herself, wrote a novel, and produced an award-winning film about her piano teacher that detailed Brico's career struggles as a woman who wanted to conduct major orchestras. Collins continues to record and she sometimes performs with symphony orchestras. Because of her musical training, this is a logical step for her. She still tours and has a radio show of her own in New York City, where she has lived for over forty years.

SUPERSTARS, FEMINISM, AND AUTHENTICITY

Of the people discussed in this chapter and those to be discussed in the folk-rock and singer–songwriter sections, few of the better-known women singers have had much direct association with the feminist movement. Judy Collins has probably been the one most associated with the women's movement, through her network of associations in New York and her film about Brico. The other artists, like Odetta and Joan Baez, have been feminists more by example than by direct involvement in the movement. Later, I will discuss how the 1970s spawned a women's music movement, but possibly because of its strong lesbian connections, none of these artists were directly involved in it.

None of the superstars had any direct links to traditional folk music. Seeger, Odetta, and Collins all had classical training. Dylan grew up in a middle-class Jewish family in Minnesota and invented a persona that, depending on which interview you read, had him being reared an orphan, a disaffected kid who ran away from home on numerous occasions, or a wandering boy who had ridden the freight trains, hitched rides on the highway, traveled to New Mexico, and so forth. Baez began her career in the rarified college environment of Boston and Cambridge and her father, as noted, was an astrophysicist—not exactly a folk occupation.

Why weren't all of these artists subjected to the same scathing criticisms that greeted the Kingston Trio or the Limeliters? The folk fans, particularly those who did have concerns about authenticity, wanted their heroes and heroines to be authentic. Baez looked like a "folk chick," Dylan dressed like a hobo and talked like a Woody Guthrie clone, Seeger constantly referred to traditional people whose work had influenced him, Collins projected a certain dignity and class, and so did Odetta, who is also African American. None of them told jokes written by New York or Hollywood writers, they did not run onstage, and they all projected an aura of sincerity. Dylan, Seeger, Odetta, Baez, and Collins were all political supporters of the civil rights movement on one level or another of involvement. All of them, except Dylan, were also openly opposed to the war in Vietnam. In an interview with *Sing Out!*, when interviewer Happy Traum tried to get a statement from Dylan opposing the war, Dylan responded by asking whether Happy had considered the possibility that he supported it.

It seems to me that what people sensed was an "authenticity of spirit." Maybe Dylan was faking it, but he has made it clear that he really does love traditional music. Of the others, only Collins has to some extent backed away from the folk music label. The problem is that one person's authenticity is another person's insincerity. Nevertheless, the superstars, many of whom made as much money as the pop-folk singers, managed to maintain an aura of authenticity that eluded all of the pop-folk groups, except perhaps for the Weavers and Peter, Paul & Mary. It simply wasn't cricket to refer to Dylan as a fake. That sort of critique was reserved for the Brothers Four and the Kingston Trio, neither of whom ever pretended to be anything other than what they were.

chapter 8

Folk-Rock, Country-Rock, and the Singer–Songwriters

Most of the books about the folk revival date the end of the urban revival and the beginning of folk-rock from Bob Dylan's Newport Folk Festival performance in 1965. It might be more accurate to view the emergence of the Beatles as marking the inevitable end of the folk boom, or as Utah Phillips calls it "the folk scare."

The Beatles first arrived in the United States in February 1964. Musicians and fans quickly picked up on the group's magnetism and sense of humor, but no one had any notion of how important the Beatles would become to the history of popular music. More significantly, no commentator or critic had any idea of how far the Beatles would take the recording process, and the whole nature of popular songwriting.

DYLAN AND ELECTRICITY

If Bob Dylan hadn't decided to use electric instruments and drums at Newport, surely someone else would have done so sooner or later. When folk music leaped to general popularity, the initial energy that drove the introduction of rock 'n' roll had greatly diminished. Elvis' creativity had descended into a mediocre film career, and his early contemporaries were either dead (Buddy Holly) or, in the cases of Jerry Lee Lewis and Chuck Berry, removed from the scene for alleged moral infractions. A group of white singers that included Bobby Rydell, Frankie Avalon, Fabian, and Annette Funicello were dominating the pop charts. These entertainers were not songwriters, but rather they were traditional sex symbols who were possessed of something less than sterling vocal talent or dynamism.

There was another musical movement bubbling under the pop charts, but the performers were black artists and they were mostly relegated to the rhythm and blues charts. Folk music provided a temporary haven for more adventurous lyrical sentiments, which were overtly or vaguely liberal and greatly appealed to college students.

By 1965, the urban revivalists and pop-folk artists had plumbed most of the archives of folk music. There wasn't really anywhere to go, in terms of continuing the evolution of folk music. The other problem was that pop music has generally involved dance styles, and folk music wasn't suitable for dancing.

The Chicago blues artists and their young white protégés had already gone electric, so there was some precedent for harnessing electricity to the folk movement. Dylan elected to use some of these Chicago musicians, notably harmonica player Paul Butterfield and electric guitarist Michael Bloomfield, as his backup band at Newport.

The story of Dylan's electric band has assumed mythical proportions, and it has been told in countless books not only about the folk revival but about the history of rock 'n' roll. To recapitulate the event briefly: Dylan appeared with a combo rock band—electric bass, drums, harmonica, and electric guitar—and totally confused not only the audience but also the august folk fathers. In a sense, the stage had already been set for conflict at an earlier event in the festival when Alan Lomax made a rather patronizing introduction of the Butterfield Band, making fun of their need for extensive electrical equipment and ended by saying that the audience would now see whether they could play. Al Grossman, who was managing the band and Dylan as well, took violent exception to Lomax's comments, and he and Lomax proceeded to have a wrestling match when Lomax left the stage.

At Dylan's performance, Pete Seeger was appalled at the sound levels and tried to find a way to unplug the band. Seeger himself has stated that it wasn't the use of electricity that bothered him, but the high level of distortion that made lyrics unintelligible. In any case, the audience reaction was mixed; some liked the new sound and others hated it. There were some boos. Dylan left the stage and returned to sing "It's All over Now Baby Blue" with a hastily borrowed acoustic guitar.

I need to point out that the Byrds had already pioneered electric folk-rock at the time of Dylan's Newport debacle. Dylan himself had even experimented with some electric instruments backing him on a song called "Mixed Up Confusion," which was not released on an album at the time. The point is that to the average folk fan Dylan was a protest singer in the Woody Guthrie tradition. Just to see him dressed like a rocker, playing electric guitar in a loud band was a shock to the folk establishment. He had changed the rules without asking anyone's permission, not the elder statesmen of the folk world, his fans, or his peers.

The urban folk revival would never be the same. At first, artists and critics chose sides. The naysayers thought Dylan was selling out to the commercial pop establishment, and others saw a new horizon looming, with folk music evolving into new and exciting forms. People's opinions largely revolved around their approach to the notion of innovation, a subject that this book has already explored. The innovators pointed out that microphones and tape recorders were not part of folk culture, and the traditionalists felt that the use of electrical instruments and drums was an unnecessary concession to commerciality. A flood of British groups appeared that were successful in the American market, including Peter and Gordon, Chad and Jeremy, and the Searchers. They too contributed to the folk-rock mania. Along the way, some other factors emerged.

THE NEW APPROACH TO SONGWRITING

The Beatles and Bob Dylan shared a similar approach to songwriting. The popular music of America during the 1930s, 1940s, and into the 1950s consisted of novelty or sentimental love songs. They were generally written by professional songwriters and not by the artists who recorded them. Both Dylan and the Beatles wrote most of the songs that they recorded, and when they did record other people's songs, they tended to be either other folk songs or folk-pop songs, in Dylan's case. The Beatles' recordings of other people's songs were drawn from rock 'n' rhythm and blues songs.

Both Dylan and, a bit later, the Beatles wrote songs that were based on their life experiences, on historical or social events, or on fantasies. In short, they wrote about any subject at all. Dylan, with his run-on sentences and odd rhyme schemes, created a universe of songwriting discourse that was parallel to what the beat generation writers like Jack Kerouac or Alan Ginsberg were doing with their novels and poems. It all seemed to happen so quickly—within five years songwriters like Paul Simon, Stephen Stills, Neil Young, Laura Nyro, Joni Mitchell, James Taylor, and so many others followed Dylan's example and moved songwriting in new and ever more creative directions.

Besides the notion of writing one's own songs as a means of aesthetic fulfillment, there were also financial pressures involved. When a hit song emerged from an album, there were serious monetary advantages for the writer, in terms of royalties from record sales and income that derives from radio and television performances. Not only did the artists want to write their own songs, but the artists' business teams encouaged the artists to write their own songs. Many of the artists' managers, like Dylan's manager Al Grossman, reaped a rich financial reward from their participation in the publishing royalties (remember that that the songwriter and publisher split royalties, usually on a 50–50 basis).

PEACE, LOVE, DRUGS, FLOWERS, AND MUSIC

Within two years of Dylan's Newport performance, it seemed as though virtually the majority of the urban revivalist folk song movement had been transformed into folk-rock. Among the important early folk-rock groups were the Byrds, the Buffalo Springfield, and the Lovin' Spoonful. All of these bands were filled with urban revivalists. Roger McGuinn of the Byrds had studied banjo and guitar at the Old Town School of Folk Music in Chicago, and he had accompanied the Limeliters and played with Bobby Darin. David Crosby of the Byrds had been a member of Les Baxter's Balladeers, one of the many New Christy Minstrel clones. Richie Furay and Stephen Stills of the Buffalo Springfield had been in yet another Christy Minstrels imitation group, the Café Au-Go-Go Singers. Neil Young had been a Canadian coffeehouse folkie in Toronto. John Sebastian, leader of the Spoonful, had been in the Even Dozen Jug Band and had played harmonica and guitar on a number of folk-oriented recordings. Guitarist Zal Yanovsky had been the guitarist for Canadian pop-folk act the Halifax Three. By virtue of plugging in their guitars and adding bass and drums, a pop-folk band could become a folk-rock band. In many cases, the bands were "learning as they were earning" in the sense that they didn't know much about the functions of rhythm sections. The Byrds and the Jefferson Airplane acknowledged hiring drummers that "looked like drummers," whatever that meant. Some of the folk-rockers such as John Sebastian, Jorma Kaukonen, and Jerry Garcia did have a strong blues background, but it was mostly oriented toward acoustic blues.

In Los Angeles in 1965, a band formed called the Rising Sons. It featured Taj Mahal, Ry Cooder, and Jessie Lee Kincaid, and they quickly were able to get a Columbia Records contract. Only one single was released and the band quickly splintered. It was one of the first interracial bands and this, plus musical conflicts, probably didn't help matters commercially. In 1993, after both Taj and Ry had become musical institutions, the album was finally released. It only took twenty-eight years.

As the folk-rock bands practiced and played together, they began to develop an ear for rock as well as rhythm and blues rhythms and some of the rhythm players, such as the Airplane's bassist Jack Cassady and the Grateful Dead's Phil Lesh, became strong bass players. Roger McGuinn developed an original sound on the electric twelve-string guitar and, in fact, the Byrds' hit records all featured his twelve-string and lead vocals. Even the Byrds' first major hit, Dylan's "Mr. Tambourine Man," featured McGuinn's guitar, although all of the other musicians on the recording were hired studio guns. And it was McGuinn's guitar that set the mood for the song, and it is the sound that the listener remembers. Another set of musicians who were half-way between studio musicians and folk or jazz players emerged in New York and played on many of the folk-rock and singer–songwriter records. This included Sebastian on harmonica and guitar, and on acoustic and electric guitarist, Bruce Langhorne. Bill Lee, father of film director Spike, played acoustic bass on many sessions, and electric bass parts were often handled by Harvey Brooks or by studio player Russ Savakus. The drum chair was frequently filled by New York session players, including Herb Lovelle and Bobby Gregg. In Los Angeles a group of young players who called themselves the "wrecking crew" were the musicians who played on sessions of acts such as the Mamas and Papas and Barry McGuire. They included drummer Hal Blaine, bassists Joe Osborn and Carol Kaye, pianoman Larry Knechtel, and guitarists Glen Campbell and Mike Deisy, and jazzman Barney Kessel.

But it was not just a matter of adding electricity and a rhythm section. Folk-rock became intertwined with an ideological component. If the early folksingers had been connected to radical political ideas and then to the civil rights movement, the folk-rock artists were loosely intertwined with the so-called New Left movement. The New Left rejected the traditional Marxist-Leninist ideology; it had more of a free-wheeling approach to radical politics. The most important group was SDS, Students for a Democratic Society. Earlier in the book, I described their brief connection with Bob Dylan. The SDS members were all college students or recent graduates and, unlike the communists, they were willing to entertain some criticisms of communist ideology. Although they were supporters of the civil rights movement, by the mid-to-late 1960s that movement was focusing more on black power and black leadership and less on racial integration. The SDS turned to the war in Vietnam as their primary issue. Very few of the musicians were specifically political. They essentially followed Bob Dylan's example, looking at the personal, rather than political, aspects of life. The folk-rock musicians could be counted on to play benefits or to appear at occasional antiwar rallies, but for the most part they lacked the sort of direct movement connection that the Almanac Singers and People's Songs artists had maintained. By the late '60s, a left-wing faction of SDS called the Weathermen took a more violent approach to social change. They took their name from a Dylan lyric that proclaimed that you didn't need a weatherman to know which way the wind was blowing. Dylan had no apparent connection to them, and they were involved in bank robberies, shoot-outs, and even kidnappings. This ideology really didn't appeal to the peace, love, and flowers notions of the musicians.

There were other issues that were not political, but became associated with radical politics. By the end of the folk boom, marijuana had become a popular drug among folksingers. By the time folk-rock reared its head, marijuana was superseded by LSD. Marijuana had been seen as a recreational drug, but LSD was viewed as a source of personal enlightenment.

The widespread use of birth control pills created another aspect of a changed social environment. Sex became as available as marijuana and it was another aspect of a youth culture rebelling against their parent's values, or at least what they assumed to have been those values.

Much of the drug movement was connected to the explosion of folk-rock in San Francisco. There was a proliferation of bands in the Bay area and, as with the groups mentioned in the previous section, many of the musicians had come out of the urban folk revival. Jerry Garcia of the Grateful Dead had played bluegrass banjo. Jorma Kaukonen of the Jefferson Airplane was a folk and blues guitar teacher in San Jose. Paul Kantner of the Airplane had run a folk club in San Jose. Barry Melton and "Country Joe" McDonald of Country Joe and the Fish had been folk performers who toured the northeast for SDS. Janis Joplin had been a country and folk singer in Austin, and some of the members of her band, Big Brother and the Holding Company, also had backgrounds in folk music and blues. Every once in a while, the folk-rockers would reveal their folk background. Sometimes it was through their lyrics, as in Neil Young's "Nowadays Clancy Can't Even Sing," or perhaps a folk instrumental touch might be added, such as Charley Chin's frailing banjo in Stephen Stills's song "Bluebird."

The San Francisco folk-rock scene was transformed from folk-rock into psychedelic rock, which really only meant that many of the bands were under the influence of acid and their performances featured long jam sections, often without too much specific musical form. Interestingly, this format has survived today through the influence of the Grateful Dead and various bands that have much younger personnel. The San Francisco scene was largely fueled by the beginnings of FM radio. In short order KMPX, the "hip" FM radio station, was achieving a major audience share of the airwaves. The jockeys programmed their own sets and frequently played songs of much greater length than had ever been heard before on commercial radio. They also featured live music by the various bands and there were benefits for free medical clinics and other community causes for which the disc jockeys and musicians donated their services. In short, folk-rock in San Francisco existed in a way that created a sense of community that was a kind of modern parallel to the ideal of folk communities.

At the same time, folk-rock music achieved enormous popularity. The Byrds had hit records with songs by Bob Dylan and Pete Seeger. The Buffalo Springfield had their one big pop hit with a rare political song, "For What It's Worth," a song about riots on Sunset Strip. This song, by the way, seems to be part of virtually every film soundtrack that is set in the late 1960s and early '70s. Country Joe and the Fish and the Grateful Dead didn't have massive hit singles but they were extremely popular, and the Fish's "cheer," "Give me an F," etc., became a sort of institution at large outdoor rock festivals.

Other bands that emerged during the folk-rock period of the late 1960s included the enormously popular Mamas and the Papas; the Youngbloods, with their anthemic hit "Get Together"; Earth Opera, never a hit group, but a band that included mandolin player David Grisman and Peter Rowan, later an important figure in country-rock; and Linda Ronstadt and the Stone Poneys, with their one hit, "Distant Drum," which became the launch pad for Ronstadt's long and continually evolving musical career. The Mamas and the Papas' tune "Creeque Alley" actually provides a brief, if somewhat satirical, history of the evolution of pop-folk music to folk-rock. This was certainly fitting enough, given that John Phillips, who cowrote the song with his wife, Michelle, had been deeply involved in the pop-folk arena during his days with the Journeymen. In a bow to the folk influence, Phillips's twelve-string guitar began the song on a seventh chord, a device strongly associated with Leadbelly's music. Peter, Paul & Mary delivered their own lightly sarcastic commentary on the folk-rock scene with their hit record *I Dig Rock and Roll Music*. It is fair to say that folk-rock also influenced some of the pop-rockers. Dion, for example, after many pop-rock hits, had his biggest hit with the song "Abraham, Martin and John," where he transformed his neo-doo-wop style into folk-rock.

THE END OF FOLK ROCK

In a certain sense, folk rock never ended entirely as a musical style. Some singer–songwriters continue to explore it to this day. But all of the groups mentioned in the paragraphs above either broke up or had so many personnel shifts that their original identity evaporated (Jefferson Airplane had so many changes that it changed the very name of the group several times). In many cases, group members elected to pursue solo careers; in other cases there were personal problems, usually ego conflicts, between various group members. In some cases the members' drug habits became so intense that they were unable to continue rigorous performing and recording schedules; others' habits were so intense that they died, or simply left the music scene.

The progressive FM radio station formats became clichés in their own right and the stations became boring and predictable. Rhythm and blues music was transformed into soul music and began to make serious inroads into the pop-record market. By the time the war in Vietnam ended in 1973, followed by Nixon's resignation in 1974, none of the original folk-rock groups existed. Buffalo Springfield had mutated into Crosby, Stills, Nash, and (sometimes) Young, but they were reduced to periodic reunion tours, in typical rock 'n' roll fashion. The party was over.

Part of folk-rock had been the venues such as the Fillmore West and East in San Francisco and New York, with their powerful sound systems and spectacular light shows. Nightclubs began to move into disco music, heavy dance-oriented music that didn't necessarily require the use of live musicians. The stars of the records became the producers, rather than the artists, and rock 'n' roll, as it always does, moved on. Bob Dylan pioneered the country-rock sound, the Byrds, among others, jumped on board, and once again, as Dylan put it, the times were changing.

*   *   *

Around 1967, the Mamas and the Papas did a very successful concert at Forest Hills Tennis Stadium in New York. My old friend John Phillips invited me to a post-concert party at the posh St. Regis Hotel. The party was like something out of a movie about the last days of Rome. Outside the hotel railing, a road manager for the band who was a skilled mountain climber was scaling the hotel walls. Considering that he was clearly reasonably stoned, I found this rather frightening. Inside, John led me to a table with a well-stocked bar and every drug known to man, and many unknown to me. He smiled, described himself as the perfect host, and offered me whatever I wanted to drink, smoke, and so forth.

I had never seen anything like it, and didn't stay very long. Folk-rock had mutated into Hollywood Dionysian excess, and most of the many guests seemed to fit right in. Not many years later, John was busted for exchanging pills obtained with a fake prescription pad from a New York drug store for prescription-quality heroin. When folk rock became associated with all of the vices of the Hollywood rock lifestyle, all bets were off. One of the brightest people I have ever known had become a heroin addict and taken his life to the brink of destruction. As Neil Young put it, "once you're gone, you never will come back." John made a deal with the legal authorities and went into a therapy program, and later appeared in schools and on television testifying to the dangers of drugs.

COUNTRY ROCK

If Dylan and the Byrds led the transition from urban folk music to folk-rock, they were also among the principal players in marrying country music to rock. Lest the reader become seasick at this point, it is important to remember that musical genres are not as easily subsumed into labels as the average record store display might suggest. The Folkways reissues on the *Anthology of American Folk Music* have long broken down the barriers between blues, country, cowboy, and cajun music. What I am referring to as country music here is music played by white string bands, based on Anglo-American folk music, and modified through what I can only call the Nashville organizational meat grinder. The characteristic instruments of traditional, hardcore country include the fiddle, the banjo, and the pedal steel guitar. The vocal style is generally high-pitched and somewhat nasal.

By the late 1960s, Nashville had become the center of country music, and apart from the occasional obligatory bow to traditional country or western styles, the "countrypolitan" sound had set in. This included violin played en masse (rather than rough-edged solos), backup singers, and a smooth vocal delivery. The backup singers always seemed to be either the Jordanaires or the Anita Kerr Singers. At the same time as the folk rockers were beginning to view albums as time-consuming concept projects measured in months instead of days, country music sessions were still finishing songs at a rate of about a song an hour. An album of ten songs could be comfortably completed in three days or less, if the singer's voice held out. There was a core group of a couple of dozen people that played on all of the records, including such musicians as guitarists Chet Atkins, Jerry Bradley, and Owen Bradley; Harold "Pig" Robbins or Floyd Cramer on piano; Henry Strzelecki or Roy Husky on bass; and Pete Drake and Lloyd Green on pedal steel.

During the mid-1960s, the folk-rockers turned to country music. It was a move away from the Los Angeles and New York studio musicians and the cost and intensity of making records in New York. Dylan, Ian and Sylvia, and many of the other folk musicians knew as much or more about country-folk music as they did about folk-rock.

Meanwhile back in Nashville, a group of younger studio musicians began to tire of playing the same old country licks five days a week. Among the group were drummer Kenny Buttrey, bassist Norbert Putnam, guitarists Wayne Moss and Mac Gayden, steel guitarist Weldon Myrick, banjo and rhythm guitarist Bobby Thompson, and harmonica ace and multi-instrumentalist Charley McCoy. By the end of the '60s, these musicians had played on albums by Dylan, Joan Baez, Ian and Sylvia, and Buffy Sainte-Marie—the cream of the urban folk revivalists.

But it wasn't only about the folk stars. A group of young musicians emerged who were rooted in country music itself. Among the most important of these musicians were guitarist Clarence White, Florida singer–songwriter Gram Parsons, a Missouri bluegrass group that had migrated to California called the Dillards, and a group of young West Coast musicians who organized the Nitty Gritty Dirt Band. Chris Hillman, a member of the Byrds, also had a solid background as a bluegrass mandolin player.

Gram Parsons came from a family that owned numerous orange groves in Florida and he transitioned through a pop-folk group called the Shilos, to a brief fling at Harvard College, to the International Submarine Band. Along the way, he turned away from folk in the direction of country music and he joined the Byrds in 1968, staying just long enough to push the band in a country direction with their album *Sweetheart of the Rodeo.*

Various disputes between band members, including the question of a South African tour and Parsons's fascination with his new friends the Rolling Stones, led to his leaving the band after less than a year. The album developed more stature long after its release than it achieved during the period when it was originally released.

Parsons went on to form the more heavily country Flying Burrito Brothers, but was eventually kicked out of his own band because of his ever-growing drug and alcohol dependency. He then hooked up with a young singer named Emmy Lou Harris, who has spread the influence of his music far beyond any success that Gram himself achieved.

According to Parsons's biographer, Ben Fong-Torres, none of Gram's albums ever sold more than 40,000 copies, while Harris became a significant country artist with several gold records. Parsons flamed out in rock-star style, dying from drug abuse. His road manager, Phil Kaufman, fulfilled a request from Parsons and stole his casket from an airport loading dock, cremating him in the desert at Joshua Tree, California, where Gram had been living. Although many of the rock stars who died young, such as Jimi Hendrix, Janis Joplin, and Jim Morrison, became, if anything, more famous after their deaths, Gram Parsons's fame has extended primarily to other musicians. There are almost two-dozen songs that have been written about him. Among the songwriters who have celebrated Gram's life are Emmy Lou Harris, Richie Furay, Bernie Leadon, and John Phillips.

THE WEST COAST

Out in Los Angeles, the Dillards had achieved some success as a bluegrass group, even appearing on the *Andy Griffith* TV show. They also moved in a country-rock direction, amplifying their instruments as early as 1964 and recording some country-rock, but their label, Elektra, was not certain exactly how to promote it.

Clarence White, a wonderful and innovative flat-picking guitarist who had played with his brother Roland in the Kentucky Colonels, replaced Gram Parsons in the Byrds and went on to master the electric guitar, using a mechanical device to help him simulate the sound of a pedal-steel guitar. Later, White's career moved into West Coast studio work, but he died young in 1973 when he was killed by a drunk driver while loading instruments after finishing a gig in a club.

Other Angeleno musicians such as Chris Hillman, Chris Etheridge, and Herb Pedersen have had various stints in bands and on record and film projects.

AUSTIN

By 1970, many country musicians became unhappy with the Nashville musical establishment. Many of these musicians had backgrounds playing folk, country, and rock music, and quite a few of them were songwriters. A few of these musicians were well-known, such as Willie Nelson and Michael (Martin) Murphy. J. W. Stevenson was a one-hit wonder with his song "My Maria." Willis Alan Ramsey to this day has only released a single album, but his song "Muskrat Love" became a substantial hit in a version by, of all people, the Captain and Tennille. Bobby Bridger was a singer–songwriter–playwright obsessed with western history, and he was somehow able to persuade RCA Records to issue some of his mythic music based on western themes. Some of these artists will reappear in the following section on singer–songwriters.

Kinky Friedman had a band called the Texas Jewboys, and he managed to outrage and irritate a sizeable number of people before settling into a subsidiary label of ABC and falling into the mist when the label itself dissipated. Later, Willie Nelson had a hit with Steven Fromholz's song "I'd Have to Be Crazy" and, much later, Lyle Lovett recorded Steve's brilliant "Texas Trilogy." Townes Van Zandt's song "Pancho and Lefty" became a country-folk standard, but although Van Zandt made a number of interesting albums, his career never caught fire. Jerry Jeff Walker became an Austin institution, and his song "Mr. Bojangles" struck paydirt in a version by the Nitty Gritty Dirt Band. Rusty Weir's "Up Against the Wall Redneck Mother" is a true Austin classic. Murphy had his share of hits, then moved to Colorado and later New Mexico, changing his musical focus from country-rock to cowboy music.

*   *   *

I was a record producer for ABC's Command Probe Records in 1968 and 1969. I have a close friend in Denver named Harry Tuft who sent me a tape of Frummox. I ended up producing their album and Eric Weissberg played fiddle, pedal steel, electric bass, and guitar on the album.

The artists had written a song called "There You Go" that I thought could possibly be a hit. I called in piano player-arranger Bob James, and he did a really nice string arrangement that had Eric playing fiddle against a full string section. The record came out in 1969, and FM radio loved it. A station in Austin called it "the most innovative record of the last five years" in a passionate telegram that they sent to the company. A few weeks later, they took it off the air. A minister had called in objecting to the fact that the song used the word "damn." At the time, half of the record business had graduated from pot to cocaine and Billy Joe Royal had a big country hit, called "Cherry Hill Park," about a girl losing her virginity in the back of a car. But he didn't use any curse words.

The label started to fall apart due to an internal power struggle within the ABC mother company. There was one more chapter to the story. *Rolling Stone* belatedly gave the album a great review. The record label couldn't make its mind up whether they ought to drop the act, and they greatly irritated "the Boys" before finally deciding to drop them from the label. It was probably the single most disappointing episode in my long and checkered career in the music industry. Damn!

Years later, Austin became a more intense music business scene, with an annual schmooze-fest called South by Southwest. That's a story I get to later.

THE BAND

This brings us to the subject of The Band. I don't know exactly how to categorize this group of folk–rock–country–blues refugees. The Band consisted of four young Canadians, joined by a funky Arkansas-born drummer. They were the backup band for legendary American rocker Ronnie Hawkins, who had emigrated to Canada. They later became Bob Dylan's backup band, and after his motorcycle accident in 1966, they took up residence in a house near Woodstock. With Dylan, they proceeded to record twenty-four songs, some written by Dylan, some coauthored between Dylan and members of The Band, and some written by Band members themselves.

The songs run the gamut from bluesy rock to country-rock, and the instrumentation includes keyboards, drums, mandolin, electric bass, electric and acoustic guitars, harmonica, accordion, and tenor sax. Recorded in 1967, the songs were used as publisher's demos, but the recordings were fairly well-circulated as bootleg records. Finally, in 1975, they were commercially released.

Greil Marcus has proclaimed these recordings as the Holy Grail of Americana, a sort of modern realization of the old *Anthology of American Folk Music* records. Close listening reveals them to be more like jam sessions of varied inspiration. All of the vocalists seem to have adopted Dylan's vocal phrasing, which, given that his is a reasonably unique sound, is a bit peculiar. In short, the songs are enjoyable but in an odd way; they sound more dated than the songs on Smith's anthology, which are all some thirty or forty years older than anything on the *Basement Tapes*.

Later, the band experienced some success with their own recordings, and Robbie Robertson's song "The Night They Drove Old Dixie Down" became a major country-rock hit in Joan Baez's version. It is an odd sidelight that Robertson's mother is a Mohawk, but only a little more recently has he devoted attention to that side of his heritage. In a sense, the band matched Dylan's fabricated identity (except for Levon Helm). They were a bunch of Canadian rockers transforming themselves into an American roots band. Robertson has claimed that no one would have accepted songs based on Native Indian issues, but the fact is that Peter La Farge and Buffy Sainte-Marie were writing, performing, and recording precisely these kinds of songs before The Band met Bob Dylan.

THE SINGER–SONGWRITERS

Before the 1960s, artists were generally singers who did not write their own songs. There were exceptions, of course, like Peggy Lee, who cowrote some of her songs with her then-husband, guitarist Dave Barbour. Another aspect of the music business was that there were "cover records," songs that got recorded by more than one performer and would fight one another for a position on the popular music charts. In the early days of rock 'n' roll, many of these cover records were white interpretations of rhythm and blues songs with the words and rhythms changed to be more understandable and attractive to white audiences. Sometimes these changes involved rewrites that removed or changed bawdy lyrics to make the songs more playable on the radio.

There were a number of professional songwriters, most of them in New York City, who wrote songs on a daily basis. This division of labor between songwriters and performers continued through the early rock 'n' roll years, although a few of the rock artists, especially Chuck Berry and Buddy Holly, wrote and performed their own songs. By the early 1960s, a group of younger songwriters were working in New York, including Carole King, Gerry Goffin, Jeff Barry, Ellie Greenwich, Neil Sedaka, Howard Greenfield, Neil Diamond, Jerry Leiber, and Mike Stoller. Of this group, only Sedaka and Diamond were performing artists, although later Carole King became a record star and a reluctant performing artist.

For the most part, the urban folk revivalists, at least during the early part of the revival in the 1950s, were not songwriters. Although the political songwriters such as Woody Guthrie and the Almanacs did write songs, by the 1950s most of their careers were declining or ended. The repertoire of the revivalists came from the Harry Smith *Anthology* record, from records by earlier singers like Burl Ives or Richard Dyer Bennett, or from songbooks.

The first person that I can think of as being a singer–songwriter was John Stewart, who started out with a group called the Cumberland Three before being recruited to replace Dave Guard in the Kingston Trio. John is a competent banjoist-guitarist and an adequate singer, but has not really received adequate recognition for his songwriting skills, although he has achieved commercial success with his song "Daydream Believer." John also had a hit as both an artist and writer with his 1977 song "Gold." Although most of John's material is not political as such, during the 1960s he was quite involved with both John and Robert Kennedy's political campaigns and wrote songs that were idealistic and hopeful, rather than the sort of agit-prop songs that the Almanacs had done.

Of all the singer–songwriters of his era, Stewart was about the least swayed or influenced by Dylan's work. John's songs tend to be written along the lines of pop and folk songs, and they are more carefully constructed than those of many of his peers. Besides his idealistic and straight pop songs, he has written many songs that explore various historical and emotional aspects of life and the American historical experience as a whole. His *California Bloodlines* album is generally regarded as one of the best of these works.

Song Structure

In order to understand the influence of Dylan and the Beatles on songwriters, it is necessary to look at the structure of popular music. Pop songs generally contain two or three sections. Folk songs are more apt to have one or two sections. A one-section song uses verses and no choruses and the same melody is used throughout. Many of the songs on the *Anthology of American Folk Music* have only verses, such as "Pretty Polly" or "John Henry."

Two-section songs have verses and choruses. The verses and choruses often use different melodies, although this is not always true. Sometimes the two sections have similar but not identical melodies, like Woody Guthrie's "This Land Is Your Land." Sometimes the verses and choruses use entirely different melodies. Choruses almost always repeat the same melody and lyrics throughout a song, and it is the choruses of songs that most people remember.

Three-section songs have a third melody and lyric called a "bridge." Bridges are used in lengthy songs as a form of musical relief, a sort of left turn on a very straight road. In the pop songs of the 1930s and 1940s, the bridge was often an introductory passage used at the beginning of a song and occasionally repeated once in the song. It was not unusual for these bridges to be dropped in performing situations, and often many musicians knew a song called "Stardust" and were not even aware that thee was another section in the song.

Influence of Dylan and the Beatles

To summarize the innovations of Dylan and the Beatles:

- Subject matter beyond love and novelty songs—places, people, current events, etc.;
- Greatly expanded use of symbolism to encompass historical and current events;
- (Dylan) Greatly expanded rhyme schemes, enjambments, and run-on sentences;
- (Beatles) Using the studio as a playground for adding new musical aspects—backward tapes, electronic additions, odd sounds, natural sounds, etc.;
- Expansion of the notion of story songs—songs that were like short stories or quick movies.

Dylan's influence on the urban folk revivalists was profound and has continued to this day. It is clear that the New York folk and folk-pop songwriters all saw themselves as rivals to Dylan. In Dylan's early protest songs, his "rivals" were Phil Ochs and Tom Paxton. Paul Simon was probably Dylan's strongest competition. Just as ambitious as Dylan, Simon spent some time playing British folk clubs. Like Dylan, Simon is something less than a great singer, but he had dulcet-toned Art Gunfunkel as a foil to reach out to the pop market, and in fact Simon and Garfunkel sold more records than Dylan. Simon was quite a capable guitarist and his songs leaned toward poetic and personal subjects rather than political ones. Simon was also similar to Dylan in the sense that he had literary ambitions beyond the songwriting genre; he attempted movies (*One Trick Pony*) and, years later, a play that briefly appeared on Broadway (*The Capeman*). From time to time, Simon has revealed a more playful side of his songwriting talents, and some of his biggest hits have been with songs like "Feelin Groovy (the 59th Street Bridge Song)" and "50 Ways to Leave Your Lover." Simon's career was certainly assisted by the popularity of his song "Mrs. Robinson," used in the very successful film *The Graduate*.

The influence of the Beatles is harder to specifically delineate than Dylan's effect on the urban folk revival. The Beatles were so versatile and their music moved in so many directions that their influence is perhaps more evident in the way that artists began to approach the recording process than in groups directly imitating them.

The New York Scene

There were a number of talented singer–songwriters on the New York scene in the early-to-mid-1960s. Fred Neil held court at the Café Wha, and he had something of a Johnny Cash–register vocal delivery, accompanying himself on the twelve-string guitar. Fred's biggest successes came through other people's recordings of his material, particularly Harry Nilsson's 1969 recording of Fred's song "Everybody's Talkin'," the theme from the movie *Midnight Cowboy*.

Neil had a bluesy, ingratiating voice and several of his other songs— "The Bag I'm In," "Blues on the Ceiling," "The Dolphin," and "Other Side of This Life"—were covered by other artists on record and in performance. Neil recorded for Elektra and for Capitol, but his career never took off because of his drug problems and his reluctance to tour. He spent the last thirty years of his life in Florida, primarily concerned with the protection and preservation of dolphins.

Like Neil, Tim Hardin had a soulful bluesy voice, as well as a serious drug problem. His life was embittered by Bobby Darin's hit recording of the Hardin song "If I Were a Carpenter." Later, the same song was recorded by the Four Tops as well as Johnny Cash and June Carter. Darin's recording closely followed Tim's demo of the song, and although he did receive songwriting royalties, he felt that this had eliminated his own big chance at success.

As was the case with Fred Neil, several of Hardin's songs were covered by other artists. "Reason to Believe" was recorded by rocker Rod Stewart, The Nice recorded "Hang on to a Dream," and "The Lady Came from Baltimore" and "Don't Make Promises" were also covered by other artists. "The Lady Came from Baltimore" was the slightly edited version of his courtship and marriage to soap opera star Susan Morss.

Hardin's heroin and drinking problems led to his death at age thirty-nine. Tim was an extremely soulful singer, but his melodies tended to sound a bit similar to one another, and some of his records are poorly arranged and recorded.

Other New York singer–songwriters included Tom Rapp, leader of the group Pearls Before Swine, and American Indian writer and singer Patrick Sky, who performed traditional songs as well as his own work. David Cohen, who sometimes recorded under the name David Blue, was a singer–songwriter who was strongly influenced by Bob Dylan. He recorded a half-dozen albums in New York and California and also had some success pursuing an acting career in Los Angeles.

Eric Andersen followed the Dylan influence in his own literary-poetic style. His songs tend to reflect his individual, romantic image and have not been covered by many other artists. Eric has continued to perform and write, and he eventually overcame a peculiar situation where Columbia Records somehow lost an entire album of his material only to discover it twenty years later! To aggravate matters, this event occurred immediately after an earlier Andersen Columbia album had actually made the pop charts.

Tom Paxton has written number of topical, sometimes humorous songs, but he also has a romantic, almost sentimental side, revealed in his songs "The Last Thing on My Mind," "I Can't Help but Wonder Where I'm Bound," and "Rambling Boy." He also had success with his children's song "The Marvelous Toy" and his "My Dog's Bigger than Your Dog" became a successful, and (as commercials go) tasteful commercial for dog food. Tom even wrote a few hit songs, including "Bottle of Wine," a rock hit by Jimmy Gilmer and the Fireballs, and "Wasn't That a Time," a million-selling song in a recording by the Irish Rovers.

Phil Ochs spent a large part of his life and energy trying to compete with Dylan's artistry and popularity. The various Dylan biographies claim that Dylan was not kind to Ochs, treating him like a sort of hack pretender to the protest songwriting throne. Ochs was a staunch defender of Dylan's right to artistic freedom when many of his fellow radicals criticized Dylan for deserting left-wing politics and writing more personal and abstract songs. Ochs himself seemed to believe that he was eventually going to best Dylan in some mythical musical competition that mostly went on in his own mind. Later, Ochs apparently started to reference Elvis as his musical hero and he started to adopt Elvis's dress code. By 1975, Ochs had become frustrated by his lack of success and the fact that the radical movement in the United States seemed to be going nowhere. He became a virtually homeless alcoholic, and committed suicide.

*   *   *

Around 1985, I was one of about fifteen musicians that drove from Denver to the Colorado State Fair in Pueblo. We were the pick-up band accompanying Anita Bryant, who was known as a sort of conservative-religious beauty queen. She was also doing orange-juice commercials at the time. The other musicians were a rhythm section and horn players, and I apparently represented the "folk" element of the show. Before the show, Bryant's then-husband-manager, who she later divorced and accused of embezzling money from her, asked if we wanted to pray before the show (we demurred). One of the features of the show was a patriotic medley, which featured Phil Ochs's song "The Power and the Glory" seguing into "God Bless America." I desperately wanted to ask Bryant if she knew who Phil Ochs was. It did confirm, for me, that this particular song was so vague that an ultraconservative artist could perform it quite comfortably.

Another singer–songwriter of some importance was a Canadian poet and novelist, the enigmatic Leonard Cohen. Cohen's song "Suzanne" became a standard among other performers, and his own records, which featured his modest vocal talents, had some success. Judy Collins was one of the other artists who contributed to his mystique through her recordings of his songs.

Joni Mitchell may well be the most artistically significant of all of the singer–songwriters. Mitchell began her career as a coffeehouse singer in Canada and emigrated to the States when she married Chuck Mitchell. Her first record, produced by David Crosby, was released in 1968. During that same year, Judy Collins had a hugely successful record with Joni's song "Clouds (Both Sides Now)." Mitchell went on to craft an enormously influential group of songs during the 1970s, which will be discussed during the next chapter.

In addition to the artists singing their own songs, certain artists, especially Judy Collins and Tom Rush, were noted for introducing the work of new songwriters. Rush himself wrote some, but somewhat sparingly, and he recorded songs by Joni Mitchell and Jackson Browne and James Taylor. Until she found her own voice as a songwriter during the 1970s, Judy Collins recorded songs by Billy Edd Wheeler, Leonard Cohen, Richard Fariña, and Eric Andersen, among others. Two more artists who are a little impossible to categorize are Tom Waits and Rickie Lee Jones. Waits is renowned for his unmistakable vocal growl and slice-of-life songwriting, whereas his protégé, Jones, is more of a jazz-flavored, offbeat singer-songwriter.

Gains and Losses Through the World of Singer–Songwriters

It became de rigeur for artists to record their own songs. The positive part of this process was that the artist generally had a strong emotional involvement in the music. The flip side was that some of the singer–songwriters were far better writers than they were singers. In effect, they were compelled to record their own material because it became so difficult to get artists to record other people's songs. At other times, as I have pointed out, they wanted to record to stroke their own egos, or to earn money both as performers and songwriters. This situation remains unchanged today. Yet when you think about it, some of the best recordings have been made by artists singing songs that other people have written. For example, I personally would rather hear Aretha Franklin sing "Bridge over Troubled Water" than Simon and Garfunkel.

There are also many artists who are great singers but mediocre songwriters. In my opinion, the notion that one must record only one's own songs has hurt the development of songwriting as an art form and has resulted in the recording of a considerable body of mediocre music.

If you are wondering what any of this has to do with the folk music revival, in the next few chapters you will see just how important a part songwriting plays in the revival, from the late 1960s to the present day.

*   *   *

One of the strangest songwriting odysseys that I know about is the tale of the song "Hey Joe." I lived in New York briefly in 1955–1956, and when I graduated from college in 1956, I moved there permanently from Vermont. The folk music community was relatively small at the time, and I met a young songwriter and occasional performer named Niela Miller. I particulary recall two songs that she sang at that time, "Daddy's Gone to Jail," a song about her ex-husband's arrest for civil rights agitation, and another tune called "Hey Babe, What You Goin' to Do in Town?" The second song used an unusual chord progression, moving in fifths from F to C to G to D to A. I remember going to parties with my friend Happy Traum and hearing Niela sing this song on two or three occasions.

Somewhere during this time, Niela started going out with a bluesy guitarist and singer named Billy Roberts. About ten years elapsed, and suddenly I heard a song called "Hey Joe" on the radio that seemed oddly familiar to me. I soon remembered Niela's song and hoped that she was making a bunch of money from the successful recordings of the song by Jimi Hendrix and a West Coast band called the Leaves.

It turned out that Billy had learned the song from her, changed "Hey Babe" to "Hey Joe," and copyrighted the song in his name. At the present time, there are over eight-hundred documented recordings of the song and it appears in over fifty songbooks. Along the way, singer–songwriter Tim

Rose, who thought he was rearranging a folk song in the public domain, and writer–singer Dino Valente also made attempts to copyright the song. In fact, sometimes the song is credited to Valenti, and a posting on the internet reveals that he received some performance royalties for the song from BMI. Roberts's publisher apparently litigated the song and now controls the copyright. Meanwhile, Miller pursued her career as a psychiatric social worker and never received any money from the song.

In 1968, I was working as a record producer at ABC and ran into Neila Miller, then Neila Miller-Horn, on the street. When I found out that she was not being credited for the song, I had her come up to the ABC offices and talk to a lawyer in an adjoining office from mine. Unfortunately, under the old copyright act, which expired in 1976, when a song was copyrighted there were no grounds for reasonable error, and the lawyer informed Neila that she would not have a legal claim on the song. On an internet posting Neila says, "Please let Billy know that whenever he wants to make amends, I would welcome it." I doubt that this will happen in this particular universe! I'm not sure what the moral of this story is, but there must be something in there about being more suspicious of your lovers than your enemies.

chapter 9

The Seventies: Singer–Songwriters and Women's Music: The Revival Transformed

In 1973, the United States withdrew its troops from Vietnam, and in 1974 Richard Nixon resigned as President of the United States. Folk-rock had become obsolete in the same way that other sub-genres of rock have eventually become passé as new styles and energies replaced them. Rhythm and blues, succeeded by soul music, had increasingly impacted the American popular music scene, and it in turn was superseded by disco.

None of this had anything much to do with the folk revival. The point that I am trying to make is that the mainstream of popular music seemed to be moving farther and farther away from any sort of folk sensibility. On the business front, Elektra Records became increasingly devoted to rock 'n' roll, and the importance of an artist like Judy Collins receded in the eyes of the label as the sales of rock bands, particularly the Doors, climbed into the millions. Of the folk record labels, only Folkways remained essentially unchanged, with Moe Asch, as always, unmoved by sales or pop music trends.

Dylan set the example for many artists and the genre of singer–songwriters became the closest thing on the music scene that related to the urban folk revival. Some of the singer–songwriters leapfrogged back and forth between folk-based music and rock 'n' roll. Possibly the most extreme example was (and is) Canadian-born Neil Young. Young began his career in the early 1960s as a Canadian coffeehouse singer, then had a brief foray into the world of high-voltage rock when he hooked up with R&B crazy-man Rick James in a band called the Mynah Birds. They recorded for Motown, but Rick had some problems with the U.S. Navy when he went AWOL rather than join a ship bound for Vietnam. Motown decided not to release the record, which has never resurfaced.

Neil then moved to Los Angeles and formed the Buffalo Springfield with Stephen Stills and Richie Furay. During their brief existence, from

1966 to 1968, they had one major hit single for Atco and released three albums that were more important for their influence on other musicians than for their sales. The band's repertoire was mostly divided between Stills and Young's songs, and some of the songs, such as Neil's "Nowadays Clancy Can't Even Sing" or Stills's protesty "For What It's Worth," were indicative of their revivalist roots. Both Stills and Young played acoustic and electric guitar, with Stills in particular exhibiting his folk and country chops as well as his rock influences.

In 1969, Young's first solo album was released, an interesting and odd piece of work with elaborate orchestrations by Jack Nitzsche. Young's voice was deliberately halfway mixed out of the record because at the time Neil didn't like his own singing. One of the songs, an acoustic guitar opus called "The Last Trip to Tulsa," is a very peculiar, lengthy Dylan-esque tune that includes the lines "I used to be a folksinger, keeping managers alive." The rest of the album varies from folk-rock to almost pop ballads.

Neil Young is one of the most enigmatic artists in the world of popular music. Over the years, his albums have varied from garage-band rock with his band Crazy Horse to punk-rock, country-folk–oriented albums like *Harvest,* and his intermittent on-and-off relationship with the slick Crosby, Stills, and Nash. Neil's political stances have ranged from outrage at the killing of students at Kent State College to support for Ronald Reagan. The Kent State affair resulted in Crosby, Stills, Nash, and Young's overnight recording of Neil's song "Ohio," with its repeated chant of "four dead in Ohio."

Like Bob Dylan and Paul Simon, Young is captivated by films and has made several attempts at the genre. As is the case with his peers, these attempts haven't been especially fruitful. His most recent foray into the genre was the creation of a DVD called *Greendale.*

Paul Simon split from Art Garfunkel in 1971 and quickly achieved success with his songs "Mother and Child Reunion" and "Me and Julio Down by the Schoolyard." The folk aspect of Simon's work is most evident in his guitar playing. When his '70s successes diminished, Simon hit on the notion of adding more world music elements to his sound and his 1986 album *Graceland* became his biggest solo success. *Graceland* was a bit of a controversial album because at the time the South African antiapartheid forces were discouraging pop artists from coming to South Africa. Although Simon treated the African musicians well in terms of payments and royalties for the recording, there was still some resentment against him on the political left. In a sense, Simon initiated the world music boom-let (it isn't quite big enough to call it a boom). Some dedicated fans of world music have pointed out that it is artists like Simon and David Byrne who recruit world musicians to play on their records, but it is difficult to imagine African musicians asking pop musicians to play on *their* albums. Garfunkel went on to act in films and perform and record as a solo artist. His closest connection to the folk revival was in hiring Eric Weissberg to play in his backup band for about ten years. Essentially, Garfunkel is a smooth-voiced pop singer. Neither Simon nor Garfunkel have been able to escape the reality that the two of them are more popular playing together than either of them are as soloists.

Like Neil Young, Bob Dylan (as noted) has lived his musical life in a regular state of reinventing himself. From the folk-rock tunes of the mid-1960s, Dylan moved in a country-rock direction, even recording in Nashville. In a creative slump by the end of the '60s, Dylan recorded *Self Portrait,* a strange double album that includes everything from old folk songs to covers of songs by some of his contemporaries. Dylan also mostly adopted a crooner's voice in place of his usual rasp.

Throughout his career, critics have written off Dylan's ability to revive his talent, and he has answered with periodic bursts of brilliance in such albums as *New Morning* in 1970 and the 1975 work *Blood on the Tracks.* In 1979, Dylan became, apparently temporarily, a born-again Christian, and his *Slow Train Coming* album testified to that transition.

Pop and Otherwise

Crosby, Stills, and Nash and Jackson Browne were among the singer–songwriters who were extremely popular during the 1970s. Stills's *Suite for Judy Blues Eyes,* a series of songs that documented his relationship with Judy Collins, included a large dose of acoustic guitar, as did a good deal of CS&N's work. Browne's song "Take It Easy" was the first big hit for country-rock band the Eagles, a band that had one foot in rock and the other in country music, and possibly, one sock in folk music.

Other male singer–songwriters of the '70s danced back and forth variously between folk music, country music, and rock 'n' roll. Steve Goodman wrote the hit song "City of New Orleans," which was a huge hit for Arlo Guthrie, and other Goodman songs dealt with such Americana ephemera as baseball's Chicago Cubs' futile quest for success as well as his attempt at the ultimate country song, "You Never Call Me by My Name."

James Taylor has established a long-term career as a singer–songwriter, beginning with his 1970 hit "Fire and Rain." As is the case with Paul Simon, much of Taylor's connection to folk music is in his acoustic guitar playing and his relatively straightforward delivery. He has even played the Telluride Bluegrass Festival. It is reasonable to place Taylor in a variety of categories—soft-rock, pop-folk, etc.

Another artist who is a bit of a category-buster is Canadian singer–songwriter Gordon Lightfoot. Lightfoot rose to great popularity with his songs "Early Morning Rain," "That's What You Get For Loving Me," and "Ribbon of Darkness." Lightfoot had two big '70s hits, his 1974 bluesy "Sundown" and his 1976 "Wreck of the Edmund Fitzgerald." The latter was a rare A-form song. Written in the style of a traditional folk ballad, the repetition of its many verses was masked by a clever production, with additional instruments coming in during the performance giving the illusion of the melody itself changing.

The biggest neo-folk artist of the 1970s was John Denver. Denver replaced Chad Mitchell in the Chad Mitchell Trio in 1964. During the 1960s, he was best known for his hit song, "Leaving in a Jet Plane," recorded by Peter, Paul & Mary. In 1969, he began his solo career and in 1971, he hit paydirt with the song "Take Me Home Country Roads," coauthored with Bill Danoff and Taffy Nivert. Denver moved to Colorado and wrote a series of songs about the Rocky Mountains, especially "Rocky Mountain High," which caused a veritable population explosion in the area. Denver's sociopolitical interests were not directed so much toward politics as to environmental change. He set up a foundation to that end.

Denver's music was really pop music with (mostly) acoustic guitars and the occasional fiddle, banjo, or pedal-steel guitar. He had a dozen hit songs through the 1970s, including the country tune "Thank God I'm a Country Boy," written by John Sommer, a member of his band. Denver's popularity became so widespread that he even won awards from country music associations, to the discomfit of the more conservative members. By the end of the '70s, Denver had drifted into a career as an actor and TV personality and his music had diminished in popularity.

Harry Chapin was another singer–songwriter who experienced a meteoric rise to fame during the 1970s. Son of a well-known New York drummer, Chapin briefly sang with his brothers Tom and Steve during the mid-1960s. Tom has gone on to establish his own successful but less dramatic career as a singer–songwriter and performer of music for children, with an award-winning TV show, *Make a Wish.* Harry specialized in story-songs, pop songs that followed a folk format in the sense that they resembled short films about real or imaginary characters. His lengthy 1972 opus, "Taxi," was a hit song and he followed it up with "WOLD," a sad portrait of a disc jockey in decline, and "Cats in the Cradle," a portrait of a non-communicative family who never found time for one another.

Chapin's academic background was in film, and he wrote a play called *The Night that Made America Famous,* which won two Tony Award nominations. Chapin was a very energetic person; he became deeply involved in the battle against world hunger, doing many benefits for that cause.

Because Chapin used a cello in his backup band and his arrangements tended a bit toward art-rock, he did not receive much recognition from the folk movement. The structure and subject matter of his songs makes an argument in favor of such recognition. His songs differed from those of most of the singer–songwriters in the sense that Chapin's primary subject was not himself. His career was cut short by a 1981 automobile accident.

The Eighties and Nineties and Other Singer–Songwriters

During the 1980s and '90s, a number of other singer–songwriters emerged. Some of them were already mid-career. Although Loudon Wainwright III began his songwriting career during the 1970s, he began perform during the late-'60s in Greenwich Village. After huge media hype, notably from a trade paper columnist named Ira Meyer, Loudon signed a fat contract with Atlantic Records. After two Atlantic albums, Columbia signed him, and he had his only hit with the rather uncharacteristic and childlike "Dead Skunk." His songs were recorded by others, most notably Kate (his wife at the time) and Anna McGarrigle. Since then, Wainwright has toured as a solo act and has also had some success as an actor. His son, Rufus Wainwright, is a contemporary pop artist. Loudon's songs tend to be humorous and sophisticated. They often concern his personal and family relationships.

There are a number of male singer–songwriters whose careers began during the 1980s. Jack Hardy was an important figure in the singer-songwriter movement because he started a magazine-album called *Fast Folk,* which included recordings of Hardy's songs and also the songs of numerous other New York singer–songwriters.

Other singer–songwriters who emerged in this period were Cliff Eberhardt, Bill Morrissey, Greg Brown, John Gorka, and David Wilcox. Each of them has toured widely and recorded a number of albums, but for some reason these collective careers have not approached the success of their female peers. Brown has toured widely and, in addition to his own compositions, has set some of William Blake's poems to music. Wilcox is known

for his use of guitar tunings and his sensitive songs about personal relationships. Gorka has written a number of songs that touch on social-political
subjects, and Eberhardt was one of the *Fast Folk* community of writers and
has toured as a side musician as well as doing solo work and touring with
a band. Morrisey is a published novelist as well as a singer–songwriter.
Husband-and-wife team Robin and Linda Williams have also benefited
from numerous appearances on Garrison Keilor's radio program, *The Prairie Home Companion,* which has provided a consistent and valuable asset
for folk music performers.

Tom Waits has had a long and by and large successful career with his
quirky slice of life songs and smoky, gruff voice, and a parallel, somewhat
more jazz-oriented path has been taken by Rickie Lee Jones. Kenny Log-
gins and Kenny Rankin are singer-songwriters who owe something to the
folk music world but have moved in more of a pop music direction. John
Prine's career as an artist and a songwriter is centered in Nashville, where
he operates Oh Boy, his own record company. Many of his songs, like
"Angel From Montgomery," have been recorded by a number of artists.

*   *   *

One of the true wild cards of the 1970s was the hit recording of "Dueling
Banjos," the theme from the movie *Deliverance.* James Dickey wrote the
novel that the movie was based upon, and in the course of a short college
teaching engagement in Portland, Oregon, Dickey became friendly with
banjoist Ron Brentano and guitarist Mike Russo. Dickey particularly enjoyed their version of "Dueling Banjos," a song originally performed on
tenor- and five-string banjos by Arthur Smith and Don Reno. Dickey as-
sured them that he would use them in the film, but Warner Brothers preferred to stick with more experienced studio players. Banjoist Bill Keith
got the original call for the gig, but he was about to go on tour in Europe
and he turned the gig over to Eric Weissberg, as noted, a renowned New
York studio musician. Weissberg flew down to Atlanta with guitarist Steve
Mandel and they recorded numerous versions of the song at different
tempos.

The next thing that Eric knew the song was on the radio, with no artist
credited. Eric had to enlist a New York attorney in order to receive the
proper credit and royalties. When the song became an instant hit, Eric
called Warner Brothers to discuss making a follow-up album. To his an-
noyance, they had gone ahead and released an album that Eric had done
with banjoist–screenwriter–director Marshall Brickman some years before.
On the original album, Eric had composed a very nice piece called "No

Title Yet Blues." To avoid paying any songwriting royalties, the record company took that tune off the new album, replacing it with "Dueling Banjos." To aggravate matters, Warner Brothers insisted on crediting the song to Eric, although he informed the company about the history of the tune. The record sold two million copies and Eric toured with a band for several years, going out on weekends and racing home to do studio work from Monday through Thursday.

Eric is one of the most versatile studio musicians anywhere and has played fiddle, mandolin, pedal-steel guitar, banjo, acoustic and electric guitar, harmonica, and acoustic bass on hundreds of recordings, film scores, and commercials. He is also one of the best trained of the musicians in the folk revival, having studied piano, violin, and bass, even taking flute lessons during the height of his career as a studio musician. He has played on recordings by Dylan, Peter, Paul & Mary, Chicago, and Barbra Streisand to name a few, besides performing in the Tarriers. Recently, Eric performed Lee Hays's parts singing bass and also playing acoustic bass in a film that included a reunion of the Weavers.

For reasons that are entirely unclear to me, Eric is one of those people whose contributions to the revival have never been adequately discussed or recognized. He is an incredibly versatile musician, but not a hot-licks player intent on always showing off his technical skills. Nor is he idenified with a particular stylistic innovation, as, for example Bill Keith is identified with the so-called melodic style of banjo playing. Possibly, it was because Eric committed the cardinal sin of having a hit record. I recently asked Eric if he had received negative feedback from Nashville musicians because here was a New York Jewish Yankee with the biggest bluegrass hit record of all time. He told me that Russell George, a mutual friend of ours and a New York studio mainstay bass player, had done a session in Nashville where one of the country multisession stars complained about this New York guy exploiting "their" music. One of the other session players shut him up, pointing out that Eric was probably a friend of the New York guys.

The *Deliverance* record initiated a tremendous boom in the sales of banjos, records featuring the banjo, bluegrass music in general, and instructional materials for the instrument. I was one of the beneficiaries, because a banjo method that I had written months before the release of the record came out just after *Deliverance* hit. To this day, I am convinced that many people bought my instruction book thinking that it was written by Eric Weissberg. We sold about 50,000 copies in a couple of years. Basically it paid my way through music school. Thanks Eric!

Female Singer–Songwriters and the Women's Music Movement

Traditionally in American popular music, women have been relegated to the role of "chick singer" in bands. Swing bands almost invariably had a female vocalist, as much for the image as for musical reasons. Even though a number of these performers such as Jo Stafford, Billie Holiday, or Rosemary Clooney were excellent musicians, the general public and even many of the male musicians viewed them as a sort of necessary evil.

Women played a more obviously significant role in the folk revival. Susan Reed and Jean Ritchie were soloists during the early part of the revival, and Ronnie Gilbert was an important part of the Weavers' sound. Ritchie started out as a traditional singer, singing the songs of her family, but went on to write a number of interesting songs about the economic hardships that have come to her native Kentucky, especially the areas like Harlan County where strip mining, with its low wages, has decimated the United Miner Workers Union.

Gilbert was an important role model for many of the urban female singers because of her powerful voice and her major onstage role in the Weavers. Holly Near, for example, has cited Gilbert as an important influence on her own career.

During the 1960s, Joan Baez and Judy Collins quickly established themselves as major figures in the revival. Both Baez and Collins played guitar, and Collins had an extensive musical background as a piano player. Although both of them used additional musicians on their records, they were clearly the dominant musical influences on these albums (although later on in her career, Collins utilized music arrangers and larger orchestras).

JONI MITCHELL

When Joni Mitchell appeared on the scene in the mid-1960s, she brought a whole another musical sensibility to the music. Mitchell wrote her own songs, and the songs almost immediately established her as one of the most significant songwriters on the scene. After Judy Collins turned Joni's song "Both Sides Now" into a major hit record, Mitchell recorded her first album in 1968. Unlike Baez or Collins, Joni had a major label contract, recording for a subsidiary of Warner Brothers.

Mitchell's *Blue* album, which was released in 1971, may be the outstanding singer–songwriter album ever. In a sense, it crystallized the gap that had developed in the revival between the performance of traditional music and the singer–songwriter's emphasis on the personal. In a searching interview with Bill Flanagan in his excellent book *Written in My Soul,*

Mitchell mentioned that when she recorded this album she had no de-
fenses, and that she was so emotionally vulnerable that she and her engineer–coproducer Henry Lewy locked everyone else out of the studio. One
of the songs on the album, "Little Green," describes a mother giving up
her child for adoption. Some thirty years later, Mitchell revealed that the
song was literally about herself, and that she was able to find her child and
meet her.

There are many interesting things about Mitchell's career. She was one
of the first woman artists who assumed an active role in producing her own
records. In addition to her superior talents as a lyricist, Joni was also a
creative musician. She pioneered the use of numerous alternate guitar tunings, many of which influenced and encouraged other musicians to follow
suit. After the *Blue* album, Mitchell started to work with various studio
musicians in Hollywood and it is arguable whether their work added another dimension to her music, or whether their musical contributions
brought her more toward the mainstream of popular music. Studio musicians, after all, are basically skilled hired hands and many of them resist
emotional involvement with their work because the various commercial
and artistic demands of artists and producers tend to induce a high degree
of cynicism. In any case, Mitchell was finally able to achieve a hit record
of her own, "Help Me," in 1974.

In 1979, Mitchell made a violent left turn and worked on a collaborative
album with jazz bassist and composer Charles Mingus. This noble experiment succeeded in losing Mitchell her mainstream audience, a loss that
she has never quite recovered. In various interviews that she has given,
Mitchell has expressed some bitterness about the current state of the music
business and, especially, the narrow policies governing the music played
on radio stations. Something that she has *not* discussed is the fact that
women in the entertainment industry are generally treated like old hags
once they get much beyond the age of forty-five. To put it another way, it
seems necessary for women to be young and sexually attractive, while senior citizens like Mick Jagger and David Crosby can rock on into their
golden years. In the folk music movement, women like Judy Collins and
Joan Baez can maintain a reasonable-size audience as they age. Unfortunately, Joni Mitchell has placed herself, or been thrust into, the role of a
rock star.

Aside from her musical influence on such other writer–singers as Shawn
Colvin and Mary Chapin Carpenter, Mitchell's lyrics also asserted her
right to choose and abandon lovers, while at the same time expressing her
personal vulnerability. Some of the songs describe her affairs with such

musical luminaries as Graham Nash and James Taylor. Mitchell was asserting the rock star's prerogative of treating men in the same way that
male rock stars treated women. Although Baez and Collins reveal in their
autobiographies that their own romantic lives were somewhat parallel to
Mitchell's, their recorded works were not, for the most part, as explicit
about these choices. Mitchell's lyrics covered many other bases as well, including suburbanization, conformity, and environmental issues.

OTHER SINGER–SONGWRITERS

Several of the female singer–songwriters who emerged in the 1970s, and
even earlier, have had long-lasting musical careers. Janis Ian, like Eric
Weissberg, Happy Traum, and Béla Fleck, attended the High School of
Music and Art in New York City. As a fifteen-year-old in 1966, Janis Ian
had a hit record with "Society's Child," her song about an interracial romance. The record was originally too controversial for the disc jockeys and
it received a peculiar and important boost from Leonard Bernstein, who
spoke about it on a television show.

Ian's career included unsuccessful major label recordings, until she
wrote and recorded the hit song "At Seventeen" in 1975. Ian currently
lives in Nashville and is more active as a songwriter than as a performer.
She has survived a disastrous business relationship that led to problems
with the IRS, and she came out as a lesbian in the early 1990s.

Carly Simon is another New York singer–songwriter whose musical career started in the '60s when she had a folk duo with her sister, Lucy. Although Carly continued to make occasional children's records in a
somewhat folkish vein with her sister, she is best known for her folk-pop
hit singles, "That's the Way I've Always Heard It Should Be" (1971) and
"You're So Vain" (1972). Simon does not enjoy live performing and her
career has been somewhat impacted by that problem, as well as her years
of raising a family with her (then) husband, James Taylor. More recently,
she has moved even farther away from anything resembling folk music by
recording an album of pop standards.

THE WOMEN'S MUSIC MOVEMENT

The modern women's movement in the United States dates from around
1963, when Betty Freidan's book *The Feminine Mystique* was published.

This book revolutionized the attitudes and behaviors of women, more specifically middle-class white women. Women began to question their family roles and demand the ability to pursue career goals in addition to raising families. Some of the impetus of the movement may have been the changing situation of women in the middle-class household. Washing machines and dishwashers reduced the necessity for women to be perpetual homemakers, and women all over the country formed groups for "consciousness raising." At these gatherings, women began to express years of frustration at being stuck in menial tasks while the men were the family breadwinners. In 1970, radical women's manifestos were published, such as Kate Millett's *Sexual Politics,* Shulasmith Firestone's *The Dialectic of Sex,* and Robin Morgan's *Sisterhood Is Powerful. Ms.* began publication in 1972, and such organizations as the Women's International League for Peace and Freedom and WITCH (Women's International Conspiracy from Hell) moved the impetus of the women's movement to more radical postures.

A significant impetus of the women's movement centered on a woman's right to assert her sexual identity, and in some cases this meant coming out as a lesbian or a bisexual. It was only a matter of time before these notions were translated into music. A group of women formed a co-op that founded Olivia Records. They included singer–songwriters Meg Christian, Cris Williamson, and coordinator Judy Dlugacz. The first recording issued was Christian's *I Know You Know,* released in 1974. Cris Williamson's *The Changer and the Changed* was released a year later, and over the years it has sold well over 300,000 copies. The musical content of Williamson's album fits into the folk-rock genre, and she sometimes adds string instruments to the arrangements as well.

Olivia's ideology was not only limited to recording songs by and about women. They wanted women to assume all aspects of the recording process, from engineering to artwork, background singing, session playing, and even the distribution of the records. The records were sold by the artists at their performances and also at the women's bookstores that had grown up all over the country as the result of the women's movement. The music itself included songs that celebrated women's love and women's issues, sometimes in a very direct way. During the '70s, Olivia also recorded other women's artists, such as Tret Fure and African American artist Linda Tillery. Today, Olivia has abandoned the record business and exists as a travel agency that sponsors cruises for lesbians.

Another major figure in the women's music movement was Holly Near. She established her own label, Redwood Records, which recorded her own music as well as other artists, male and female, who expressed radical social-political sentiments. As she expressed it in her autobiography, *Fire in the Rain . . . Singer in the Storm,* Olivia recorded women's music and supported world peace, while Redwood recorded political music and supported women's music. Near's role in the women's music was a complex one because she was openly bisexual, and she often used men as her piano accompanists. Some of the lesbian artists were opposed to Near appearing at women's music events because they didn't want anything to do with women who maintained relationships with men.

Women's music festivals began to appear all over the country. At one of these festivals, Near found herself in a bitter dispute with her friend Malvina Reynolds when the festival would not allow Reynolds's husband, a confirmed political radical, into the event. Reynolds had been one of the first women singer–songwriters, and her songs "Turn Around," recorded by Harry Belafonte in the '50s, "Little Boxes," recorded by Pete Seeger in the '60s, and "What Have They Done to the Rain" had inspired many women, including Near herself. There were also other women artists who issued records on their own labels, including Alix Dobkin, with her album *Lavender Jane Loves Women,* and composer Kay Gardner.

The festivals and concerts by the various women's artists were social-political statements in themselves. There were booths with literature and petitions supporting various women's causes, and in general these performances constituted a sort of feminine safety net not only for lesbians but for women in general. Festivals were held in Sacramento, San Diego, Missouri, Illinois, Michigan, and Boston. The Michigan venue was so successful and organized that its organizers purchased a 650-acre site for their annual festival, which continues to this day. As Portland women's music activist Mary Rose wrote in an email to me, "we didn't have to subsume our interests to husbands."

Obviously, women's music festivals featured women's music. In Ellen Schwartz's book *Born a Woman,* Canadian singer–songwriter Sylvia Tyson reports that she was invited to perform at a women's festival, but she refused when she was told that she could not bring any of the members of her male backup band and she would not be able to perform any songs about men. In retrospect, this may seem a rather limited view, but consider for a moment that none of the folk festivals in the United States featured women's music artists. The Canadian folk festivals began including women's music artists in 1961 at Mariposa, and the Winnipeg, Vancouver, and Edmonton festivals soon followed suit.

By the same token, none of the books published about the folk revival consider women's music as part of the revival, even though it is quite possible to argue that women's music was the most active segment of the folk revival during the 1970s. By the end of the decade, the impetus for women's music became greatly diminished. To some extent, the issues in the women's movement had become part of the consciousness and lifestyle of many young women, many of whom did not consider themselves feminists. Women who aspired to a career in the music business quickly caught on that espousing feminism was not a positive gesture to record company executives, and coming out as a lesbian was an even less positive gesture.

The women's music movement is waiting for a scholar or a participant–observer to write its history in detail. Until then, Holly Near's autobiography and *Girls Rock!*, a recent book by Mina Carson, Tina Lewis, and Susan M. Shaw that is more focused on women in rock music, provide useful information.

Other Female Singer–Songwriters

There were other female singer–songwriters during the 1970s. Melanie achieved some success as a singer–songwriter during the early '70s with her "Nickel Song" and the somewhat goofy, childlike "Brand New Key." Kate Wolf was a highly respected folk artist during the 1970s and 1980s, and despite her premature death in 1986, she has retained something of a following. There are two songbooks of her work, much of which she wrote herself, as well as a tribute album recorded by other artists.

During the 1980s, there was something of an explosion of female singer–songwriters. Suzanne Vega was a dance student at the High School of Music and Art in New York, and had sung with Pete Seeger at Carnegie Hall at the ripe age of twelve. Vega's first album was released in 1985, but it was her second one that established her career. It included the hit "Luka," a song that she wrote about child abuse. "Tom's Diner," another song Vega wrote, was a hit twice: first in her 1987 version and three years later in a dance mix by the British group DNA. Vega plays acoustic guitar, but her more recent records have included electric instruments and more elaborate production.

Michelle Shocked became an unlikely star through a bootleg recording of her singing around a campfire at the Kerrville Music Festival in 1986. Shocked had been living in Europe, and ironically it was a British record producer who recorded the tapes, releasing them without her permission and without compensating her. The album became a hit in England, resulting in a seven-year court battle before Shocked finally gained control of the tapes. The incident created a giant buzz in the music industry and resulted in Michelle receiving a healthy contract from Polygram Records. Shocked comes out of a modern version of the Almanac Singers' topical-political notions, and she was never entirely comfortable with a major label deal. Eventually, she got out of the Polygram deal, and she has subsequently recorded for several other labels. Some of her recordings, notably the 1992 *Arkansas Traveler,* are heavily based on traditional American folk music, but others highlight her interest in New Orleans jazz and rhythm and blues.

Tracy Chapman made her recording debut in 1988. Two of her songs, "Fast Car" and "Talking 'bout a Revolution," became enormously popular hit records. The album that contained these two songs sold over ten million copies. It was in a folk-rock vein, with little instrumentation beyond Chapman's guitar and a rhythm section. Chapman is black, and her husky voice, as well as the fact that she plays acoustic guitar, has created many critical comparisons to an excellent British singer–songwriter named Joan Armatrading. The latter has never achieved the kind of success that Chapman enjoyed.

Chapman's socially aware songs and her acoustic guitar playing make her a logical choice for folk clubs and venues, but her huge record sales thrust her more into arena-rock venues, where she was not entirely comfortable. Chapman has many fans but she has neither received much recognition for her role in the relatively recent reincarnation of the folk revival, nor has she *ever* received airplay in the "urban contemporary" stations that dominate the market for African American poplar music.

Peggy Seeger was an important influence on the folk revival in the mid- and late-1950s. She grew up in a household where her mother was transcribing and arranging song for some of the Lomaxes' books, as well as her own collections of children's songs. Peggy was also Pete Seeger's half sister, and the result of these circumstances was that she developed an enormous repertoire, and she taught a number of songs to various revivalists. After she moved to England and married Ewan MacColl, Seeger began to write songs, notably "The Ballad of Springhill" in 1958 and her 1971 feminist anthem "I'm Gonna Be an Engineer." Many of her songs, like the two mentioned, are about social and political issues. After MacColl's death in 1989, she continued to perform, write, and record. She moved to Asheville, North Carolina, in 1994 and continues to tour and record.

Country–Folk

By the 1980s, the word "folk" was not a favorable one to use in negotiating a record contract. Several artists filtered into the world of major label record deals by coming in the door marked "country." Nanci Griffith and Mary Chapin Carpenter are two women whose records were classified as "country," but whose folk influences were clearly evident.

Griffith's first recording was released on a homegrown Austin label called B. F. Deal. She then moved to an '80s folk label, Philo/Rounder, and in 1987 shifted to MCA. MCA never quite figured out how to market her, and her continual frustration with the label moved her from their Nashville country operation to recording for the pop-rock division in Los Angeles.

Many of Griffith's songs, like Harry Chapin's, are like short stories. Her biggest songwriting success came come Kathy Mattea's recording of "Love at the Five and Dime," which was based on a short story that Griffith had written in college. Although she is widely respected in the revivalist movement, particularly as a songwriter, her biggest American record success came from her 1993 Elektra album *Other Voices, Other Rooms,* where she recorded seventeen songs by other songwriters. For some years, Griffith's recording career has been more successful in England and Ireland than in the States.

Mary Chapin Carpenter has pursued a clever and extremely successful strategy on her Epic albums. An artist who peaked in the 1990s, recording for a major label and being classified as a country singer, Carpenter has sprinkled a few country-rock hits, like "Down at the Twist and Shout," "Passionate Kisses," and "I Feel Lucky," amidst albums that contain sensitive and literate offerings like "John Doe No. 26," a song based on the death of an anonymous homeless man. Most of her albums have been produced not in Nashville, but in a studio in Virginia by her guitarist John Jennings, and they include elements of folk music, country, and rock.

Carpenter writes songs that vary from social-political concerns to literate and intelligent songs about romance. She has acknowledged the influence of Joni Mitchell, not exactly a member of the Nashville songwriting mafia. I have always wondered what the fans who like her dancey upbeat tunes make of the more introspective, sensitive, and complex songs that comprise most of her recorded material.

Kathy Mattea is not a songwriter, but is a country star whose work has moved more and more toward folk, bluegrass, and Celtic influences. Besides recording Nanci Griffith's "Love at the Five and Dime," she has recorded several songs by songwriter–fiddler–singer–guitarist Tim O'Brien.

Women in Music

During the 1990s, there was a proliferation of female artists in the rock field. Some of them, like Natalie Merchant, Shawn Colvin, and Sarah

McLachlan, showed strong folk influences. Others such as Melissa Etheridge, Alanis Morrissette, Sheryl Crow, Tori Amos, Jewel, Fiona Apple, and the seemingly ageless Cher and Madonna were much more pop-derived. McLachlan is also important in women's music because she started a three-year series of performances by women artists called Lilith Fair. Missy Elliott and Lauryn Hill have established extremely successful careers as producers, writers, and artists.

The thread that tied these artists, or at least most of them, together was their songwriting. Although there had obviously been female artists who wrote songs before the '90s, like Grace Slick of Jefferson Airplane or Karla Bonoff's successes of the late 1970s, it was not a common occurrence.

Although Holly Near and Cris Williamson continue to perform today, there is no important women's music label as such. As Williamson and others have pointed out, perhaps there isn't a need for these labels today. Melissa Etheridge, k. d. lang, Janis Ian, and the Indigo Girls have all outed themselves as lesbians. An increasing number of women have also established reputations as instrumentalists as well as vocalists. Among them are guitarist Patty Larkin, the Indigo Girls, bluegrass music superstar Allison Krause, bluegrass banjoist Allison Brown, and guitarist–banjoist–songwriter Lynn Morris. Although the music business is still clearly dominated by white males, there are women at the top, such as Sylvia Rhone, the black woman who headed Elektra Records and is now an executive at Universal Records.

There is little question in my mind that the women's music movement opened the doors that many of the above artists have walked through.

chapter 10

Roots and Branches

Just as the singer–songwriter movement evolved out of the urban folk revival, a number of other genres connected to the revival became increasingly important. This chapter will consider some of these musical branches of the urban revival.

THE BLUES AND THE BLUES REVIVAL

Dozens of books have been written about the blues. They include autobiographies and biographies of blues artists, survey histories of the genre, books that explore regional styles, and even essays on folk poetry and the blues. What I would like to do here is to briefly discuss the history of the blues, highlight its relationship to the urban folk revival, and take a look at contemporary blues.

History and Beginnings

The blues are generally believed to have emerged sometime between the Civil War and the turn of the twentieth century. Most scholars have settled on the period between 1880 and 1895 as the era where the blues was born. Unfortunately, the folk song collectors were not active until after the 1900s.

The first serious blues collecting was done by Howard W. Odum, working in Georgia and Mississippi from 1905 to 1908. Odum was not a folklorist but a sociologist, and he and his academic partner published two collections of southern black work songs and blues in 1925 and 1926.

The first blues recordings were not folk blues, but rather a sort of cabaret–pop–blues, generally sung by female vaudeville performers. Mamie Smith was the first of these artists to make a record, and her record company was pleasantly surprised by its sales. Other labels jumped on the bandwagon and by 1925 such artists as Ma Rainey, Bessie Smith, Clara

Smith, Victoria Spivey, Sippie Wallace, and quite a few others were recording. Many of these artists were relatively sophisticated urban products and the instrumental music accompanying their vocals often consisted of jazz musicians, sometimes including horn players. Folk blues didn't get recorded until 1924, when Daddy Stovepipe made his first recordings. He was followed by the first commercially successful blues artist—Papa Charlie Jackson. Almost all of these recordings featured guitar, played either by the artist or by fine studio players like Blind Blake or Lonnie Johnson.

Scholars make a distinction between blues artists and songsters. The latter are musicians who perform a varied repertoire that includes blues, rather than one that is solely blues-based. Jackson definitely falls into the songster category, and his records show influences of ragtime, vaudeville, and blues.

The first blues superstar was Blind Lemon Jefferson, a Texas artist who did most of his recording in Chicago. Blind Lemon's records date from 1926. Because he was so successful, Lemon made a large number of records and he was in effect forced to come up with more and more original songs in order to keep recording. Although all of the books about the blues acknowledge Lemon's importance, few of his songs are performed by contemporary blues singers or blues revivalist singers, and his versatile guitar technique is rarely copied or even acknowledged today.

Piedmont, Delta, and Texas

Blues scholars generally divide the blues into the Piedmont and Delta styles, while some insist that Texas blues deserves its own category. The Piedmont blues developed in the Carolinas, Georgia, and Virginia. The singing style is almost recitative, with a sort of friendly conversational tone. The chord progressions and the guitar technique show ragtime influences. Delta blues features a tortured and intense style, both in the vocals and the guitar accompaniments. A knife or a slide made of metal or glass is often used in the Delta style, creating a tortured emotional effect similar to crying. (Some of the Chicago slide players, like Tampa Red, used the slide more as a melodic device, similar to the sound of a Hawaiian guitar.)

By the 1930s, many African Americans migrated to northern cities in search of higher paying jobs and a better life. The Mississippians tended to go to Chicago, the Piedmont people came to New York, and a number of Texans moved to California. By 1940, several developments had taken place that influenced the direction of the blues.

Rhythm and blues became the prevalent style of popular black music. It utilized rhythm sections that included bass, drums, and piano. Sometimes a horn or two, especially the saxophone, was added. Electrical instruments were introduced in the late 1930s. Guitarists began to use electric guitars, and the harmonica was also often amplified. The Chicago South Side blues clubs were loud and the patrons wanted to dance. The older folk-blues styles were considered old fashioned by younger African Americans, and it became difficult for acoustic musicians to compete with electric bands.

When Muddy Waters moved to Chicago, he took up electric guitar, often playing with a slide. He brought the blues into the rhythm and blues world. Soon artists such as Muddy, harmonica ace Little Walter, John Lee Hooker, and Lightnin' Hopkins were able to enjoy hit rhythm and blues records, singing folk-blues but playing electric guitar, usually with a rhythm section.

In New York, another strand of the blues was unraveling. Josh White moved to the city in the mid-1930s, followed soon after by Leadbelly and then Brownie McGhee and Sonny Terry. Josh specialized in blues, but his repertoire spilled over to include contemporary protest songs, and even some ballads and pop songs. Leadbelly was a songster from Louisiana who spent time in Texas and Louisiana jails and prisons, essentially being rescued by John and Alan Lomax. McGhee and Terry were contemporaries of Piedmont blues artist Blind Boy Fuller. They hooked up in New York and established a long though somewhat contentious partnership that lasted through hundreds of performances throughout the world. All of these artists made records and many of the records sold to white audiences, something that Robert Johnson, for instance, had never been able to accomplish. The three blues artists were all recruited and lionized by the New York radical movement. Josh made some records with the Almanac Singers and Leadbelly was friendly with Pete Seeger and Woody Guthrie, among others. Both Josh and Leadbelly wrote songs that advocated racial justice and protested against the treatment of black Americans. Brownie and Sonny were also friendly with the Almanacs and their descendants, although less involved in political music. Big Bill Broonzy fulfilled a somewhat similar role in the Chicago blues scene.

The final piece in the New York blues puzzle came when Gary Davis moved to New York from South Carolina in the early 1940s. Davis was a minister who accompanied his music with his superb blues guitar playing. His music has been described as "holy blues."

Prior to the *Anthology of American Music* reissues, there was a relatively insignificant interest in blues on the part of white Americans. The *Anthology* included recordings by Blind Lemon Jefferson, Mississippi John Hurt, Ragtime Henry Thomas, jug bands, and even white blues artists. All of the young New York folk revivalists, such as John Sebastian and Dave Van Ronk, were heavily influenced by the *Anthology* recordings. A number of them ended up taking guitar lessons from the transplanted blues artists. Among the people who I personally knew who studied with the blues men was Happy Traum, who studied with Brownie McGhee. Stefan Grossman, Barry Kornfeld, Andy Cohen, Ernie Hawkins, and Jorm Kaukonen all studied with Reverend Gary Davis. In Dave Van Ronk's colorful memoir, *The Mayor of MacDougal Street*, Dave acknowledges Davis's influence, although they never had a literal student–teacher relationship.

The Rediscoveries

By the early 1960s, a sort of underground blues record collecting world had emerged. Many of the collectors were fanatical blues fans and they began to wonder whether any of the blues artists of the 1920s and 1930s were still alive. Diligent detective work on the part of these informal scholars turned up Mississippi John Hurt, Skip James, Bukka White, Buddy Moss, and Son House by 1965. Almost all of them played at the Newport Folk Festivals, and most of them got the chance to record and perform. Ironically, this time their audience was the folk revival audience, a white middle-class group. There was very little interest on the part of the African American population. They were listening first to rhythm and blues, and by the mid-1960s, soul music. Blues were something their parents or grandparents were invested in.

When older blues artists were rediscovered, the effects of their reemergence weren't always positive. Some of the blues fans involved in the rediscoveries appointed themselves as managers and booking agents, with mixed results. Dick Waterman was one of the ringleaders of these blues fanatics, and his recently published collection of photographs and reminiscences, *Between Midnight and Day: The Last Unpublished Blues Archive*, details some of these stories. One of the strangest odysseys was that of John Hurt. He had never been a full-time musician during his 1920s career, but as a result of his reemergence, he had more time to practice and create, and he also was in reasonably good health. Some of the other musicians in this group—for example, Son House and Skip James—were not in good health, and although their newfound exposure may have been emotionally rewarding to them, their musical skills were not on a par with their earlier work. Whereas some of the folklorists of the 1920s had regarded blues as a risqué pop music form, the younger generation of collectors treated the music with respect and interest.

The White Revival

In New York the revival was largely based on Gary Davis and his students. Sam Charters's book *The Country Blues* was published in 1959. Charters shortly assembled a record for RBF, a subsidiary of Folkways, that contained the work of many of the artists he had been writing about. Paul Oliver, a British architect who was a somewhat more meticulous blues scholar, wrote a series of books beginning in 1960, and he also edited a series of books about specific blues styles and blues singers ten years later. Some of these biographies discussed comparatively little-known blues figures such as Delta artists Tommy Johnson and Charley Patton. The interest that the folk boom created in traditional blues guitar styles resulted in a seemingly neverending series of blues books by New York revivalist Stefan Grossman.

In Chicago, the revival involved the fascination with the blues that a number of University of Chicago students developed. Guitarists Michael Bloomfield, Elvin Bishop, and harmonica player Paul Butterfield all hung out in the tough South Side clubs. They were all mentored by Muddy Waters, who by the 1980s had started to hire white musicians to play in his band. Record producer–music scholar Jim Rooney pointed out in his book *Bossmen* that Muddy and bluegrass pioneer Bill Monroe played a seminal role in transmitting their musical styles, because so many young musicians played in their bands, and were mentored by them.

Can White Folks Sing the Blues?

By 1970, when *Living Blues* magazine was born, there were a couple of dozen white urban blues singers plying their trade. In New York, there were Dave Van Ronk and John Hammond Jr.; New England had Geoff Muldaur, Eric Von Schmidt, Chris Smithers, and Paul Geremia; and on the West Coast Ry Cooder was making his reputation as a marvelous slide guitarist. There were also white women blues artists on the scene, especially East Coasters Rory Block, Bonnie Raitt, Lisa Kindred, and Judy Roderick and West Coasters Alice Stuart and Barbara Dane. One of the best of these artists was Tracy Nelson, who never seemed to be able to make up her mind whether she was a country singer or a blues artist. Sometimes versatility can be a curse in the image-driven music business.

There was an inevitable backlash against the white blues artists. For years, *Living Blues* simply would not provide any press for the white artists, proclaiming that blues were an art form invented by African Americans and it was their work that was important. This put the magazine in a difficult position, because until the 1990s, there simply weren't any young black blues artists to speak of. Taj Mahal was the great exception, although he never really limited himself to blues in the way that John Hammond, for example, did. Jerry Ricks was virtually the only other young black artist playing blues, and although Jerry was a major influence in Philadelphia, by 1970 he had moved to Europe, where he spent most of the next twenty years. Larry Johnson, a young New York protégé of Gary Davis, was an excellent Piedmont-influenced blues artist, but he never became widely known.

Another bizarre aspect of the blues revival were the young British rock artists such as the Rolling Stones, Eric Clapton, and the Animals, who became rock superstars in the United States. All of these performers were absolute blues freaks. They recorded songs by traditional blues artists—in the case of the Stones even toured with blues artists—and recorded at the same Chess Studios in Chicago where Muddy Waters, Howling Wolf, and Little Walter had made their records. Clapton, in particular, was always generous in crediting the sources of his inspiration, both in terms of never pretending to compose songs that he had learned from blues artists and in interviews.

It is difficult to ignore that many of the young American revivalists were good enough players, but with a few exceptions, their ability to sing the blues was less than outstanding. Although Jagger and Eric Burdon were not in a class with, say, Muddy Waters, they were able to sing the blues convincingly, and with some power. And unlike some of the white Americans, Jagger, Burdon, and the young Stevie Winwood did not attempt to imitate a particular singer. Blues bands developed, such as Canned Heat, Janis Joplin's various bands, and the J. Geils Band, that had hits songs and sold millions of albums.

Guitarist–singer Robert Cray scored a big pop hit in 1986 with his song "Strong Persuader." His work preceded the emergence of a whole string of younger black blues musicians. Among them were Eric Bibb, Guy Davis, Ben Harper, Corey Harris, Alvin Youngblood Hart, Keb' Mo', and Otis Taylor. Sensing that maybe his time had come, Jerry Ricks returned from his self-imposed European exile.

Like folk music, blues suddenly became a big business. A chain of nightclubs called the House of Blues featured blues and, along the way, sold T-shirts, ridiculously overpriced blues guitars, and started its own record label. Major festivals grew up all around the country, everywhere from Chicago to Denver, New Orleans, and Portland, Oregon.

Record labels that specialized in blues reissues and new recordings proliferated all over the place. Among them were Yazoo, Origin, and Arhoolie. Other labels, like Folkways and Rounder, issued many blues recordings alongside their other offerings.

The Legend of Robert Johnson

Most music fans realize that in popular music, dying young actually seems to be a fact of life that brings great monetary rewards to an estate. Rock stars Jimi Hendrix, Jim Morrison of the Doors, and blues-rock diva Janis Joplin have sold millions of records since their premature deaths. Robert Johnson, more than any other blues artist, also seems to fit the bill.

Johnson recorded a couple of dozen songs during the mid-1930s and, as best we can tell, was murdered shortly after by a jealous husband. Columbia Records reissued two albums of his work in 1961 and 1970. The impetus for these reissues seems to have come from John Hammond Sr., since during his short lifetime Robert's best-selling record had only sold about 5,000 copies. In 1991, after years of work and agitation within the blues community and Columbia Records, that company released everything Johnson had ever recorded in a boxed set of two CDs. The booklet contained notes and tributes by Eric Clapton and Keith Richards and some extremely rare photos of Johnson. To everyone's amazement, the set sold over a million copies and Columbia then proceeded to reissue quite a few other blues albums.

There are already more than enough discussions of Robert Johnson in the four published biographies, a screenplay, and several videos about his life. It is interesting that the life of this obscure Mississippi blues artist has aroused so much interest and controversy among scholars and blues fans.

The Blues Today

There are still older blues artists, mostly electric, who remain active. The most famous is B. B. King, who has his roots in the Mississippi Delta but whose guitar style is based more on the work of T-Bone Walker and the early electric blues than on folk styles. John Cephas and Phil Wiggins are guardians of the Piedmont style with their excellent guitar and harmonica duo. Younger white artists like Jonny Lang and Kenny Wayne Shepherd play loud electric blues and have more than one foot in the hard rock camp. A string of women artists such as Marcia Ball, Angela Strehli, Lu Anne Barton, and Sue Foley have been connected at one time or another with Antone's Blues Club and the Antone record label in Austin. Many of the blues festivals draw thousands of people, there are blues societies in most of the major cities, and the blues have their own version of the Grammies, with the annual W. C. Handy Award in Memphis.

In fall 2003, Martin Scorcese presented seven films about the blues on the PBS television network. He also put together a number of CD releases and a book that coincided with the films. The films varied from impressionistic to business-like, novelistic, or factual. There were seven different directors, including Scorcese himself. It is difficult to imagine a current series along these lines devoted to American folk music. I suppose we could say that, commercially at least, the blues have come of age.

As is the case with some of the urban folk revivalists, a number of the performers who made their early reputations in the blues, like Rory Block, Ben Harper, and Bonnie Raitt, have also expanded their repertoire by becoming singer–songwriters.

Sadly the younger black artists still find their audience in the white middle-class. Whatever the blues represent to the average African American, they are seemingly more interested in rap, soul music, and gospel.

*   *   *

I first met Gary Davis in 1955, when I was on winter break from college. I went down to East 10th Street in New York and climbed some stairs in a typically shabby New York apartment building. I could hear the music floating down the stairwell as I rang the doorbell.

I was greeted by Tiny Ledbetter, Leadbelly's niece, who gave me a warm welcome. Over the next six weeks I'd go up there every Tuesday night and I ran into various young revival musicians that I knew, like Barry Kornfeld and Erik Darling. Gary's prize student at the time was John Gibbon, who ended up not going into music, but becoming a psychologist. One night Woody Guthrie was there with his third wife, Anneka.

At the time, I primarily played banjo. Trying to play with Gary was like going to music school. An early injury to his left hand had left him with a crooked arm, and it was difficult to follow the chords from just watching him. You just had to feel it. It was an amazing experience because I found myself playing things way out of my depth that I didn't remember later. It certainly was a permanent influence on my playing, even though I would not describe myself as a blues player, and I never actually took lessons from Gary.

A few years later, I had my first important nightclub gig in New York. It was at Gerde's Folk City, and I opened for Brownie McGhee and Sonny Terry. About a hundred people came to the party, including Brownie and Sonny and John Lee Hooker.

The house was a miserable old tenement and it had DC current. You had to use a converter to make any normal electrical appliance work. Brownie was a sophisticated guitarist and John Lee was a sort of unique, but primitive, kind of player. Hooker started to get angry and he went out to the car to get his amplifier. I tried to explain to him that if he plugged the amp into the wall, it would burn out. I believe he thought that I was lying, but he didn't plug it in. I thought this was pretty funny—a young graduate student living in a slum apartment is telling a black blues artist that he couldn't use electrical current because the apartment was too primitive.

A neighbor called the police complaining about the noise, and we gave the cop a beer and he briefly joined the party.

BLUEGRASS

Bill Monroe is generally referred to as the father of bluegrass music, but there is some disagreement as to the exact origin of the music and who should actually get credit for originating it. During the 1920s and 1930s string-band music was common in the southern Appalachians. The bands, as I have mentioned earlier, usually consisted of some combination of fiddle, five-string banjo, and guitar. Mandolin and dobro, a resonator guitar played with a metal bar, were sometimes in these string bands, and there were also acts that featured two guitars, or guitar and mandolin.

By the late 1930s, a style of singing became prevalent that featured the melody sung in the tenor register with another vocal part above it. The string bands began to play at more aggressive tempos. There were several bands that formed a sort of bridge between the old-time music bands and the style that was about to be born. The Mainer Brothers, Wade and J. E., and the Morris Brothers were two of these transitional groups. The Morris Brothers' band had a banjo player named Joel Martin, who was one of the pioneers in establishing a new picking style that involved use of the thumb and two fingers of the right hand. Both Don Reno and Earl Scruggs, the two men most responsible for early bluegrass banjo, did gigs with the Morris Brothers. The transitional bands included both fiddle and mandolin and their repertoire included not only traditional songs, but also original compositions.

Meanwhile Bill Monroe, who was a mandolin player, originally played with his brother Charlie, a guitarist. Realizing that he would always be "second fiddle" to his older brother, Bill came to the conclusion that he needed to form his own band. He recruited a fiddler named Art Wooten and an old-time banjo player named Dave Akeman, known as "Stringbean." Akeman was fine as long as he was singing and accompanying himself, but he didn't fit too well into the band context.

Monroe was able to get his band onto the *Grand Ole Opry* radio show in Nashville, but he wasn't entirely satisfied with the sound of his band. In 1943, he happened upon a young banjoist named Don Reno. Reno was working on a new banjo style that featured two fingers and the thumb. This style was much more suitable for playing solos than the old-time style that Stringbean played, and Monroe offered Reno the banjo chair in his band. Unfortunately for Don, he got drafted and that position ended up going to Earl Scruggs.

Scruggs's banjo technique became known as "Scruggs style," and it electrified other country musicians as well as audiences. Between Earl's powerful playing, the voice of Lester Flatt (recruited just before Scruggs joined the band), Monroe's impassioned tenor voice and his use of the mandolin as a lead instrument, and Wooten's dynamic fiddling, the style that became known as "bluegrass" made the old-time string bands obsolete.

In 1948, Flatt and Scruggs left the Monroe band and formed their own group, the Foggy Mountain Boys. Details of the various reasons that they left and the resulting bitterness between them and Monroe are described in great detail in Barry Willis's encyclopedic book, *America's Music: Bluegrass*. It is generally agreed that Monroe was a tough boss who was not particularly generous to the members of his band. It was obvious to Flatt and Scruggs that economic opportunities would be greater if they ran their own band. Besides not paying musicians especially well, Monroe expected them to play on his baseball team and to do chores on his farm on off-days.

Monroe was able to keep the Foggy Mountain Boys off the *Opry* for years by politicking the management of the show. He pointed out that the show only featured one band in a particular style, and he asserted that Flatt and Scruggs were imitating his style. They struck back by gaining sponsorship from Martha White Flour in 1953, and this sponsorship assisted them in getting personal appearances on radio and television programs. They made their way onto the *Opry* by taking over a Martha White–sponsored portion of the program that had belonged to a western string band.

There are a number of musicians who dispute Monroe's preeminence in bluegrass. They point out that the sound of bluegrass only emerged when Flatt and Scruggs joined Monroe. There are several other factors that support this argument. Monroe was an excellent songwriter, but none of his vocal or instrumental compositions crossed over into a broader market except for Elvis Presley's rockabilly revision of Monroe's "Blue Moon of Kentucky." Scruggs wrote an instrumental called "Foggy Mountain Breakdown," which became a standard in the world of bluegrass, was a hit on the country music charts, and reached a new audience with its appearance in the successful movie *Bonnie and Clyde*. They gained further exposure with their theme for *The Beverly Hillbillies* television show, which also became a country-hit record. Earl Scruggs then wrote a banjo instruction book. It was published in 1968, and within five years it had sold over a million copies. A new edition of the book was released in 2005.

Another difference between Monroe's band and the Foggy Mountain Boys is that Louise Scruggs was the manager for the Mountain Boys, while Monroe did not have consistent or professional management of equal caliber. Monroe's career was somewhat salvaged when Ralph Rinzler, a young musician and folklorist, took on the task of publicizing Monroe's pioneering role in bluegrass in an article in *Sing Out!* magazine in 1963. He then took over management chores for Monroe and successfully introduced him into the folk song revival, with numerous appearances at folk festivals.

This is not the place, nor am I the proper person, to deliver a definitive statement as to who was the most influential person in bluegrass. However, as important a role as Monroe played, there are still relatively few bluegrass bands where the mandolin is the lead instrument. Furthermore, Scruggs's banjo patterns have been adapted to the mandolin—by Jesse McReynolds of the band Jim and Jesse—and to the guitar by the superb musicians Doc Watson and, later, by a young West Coast guitarist named Clarence White. Aside from Monroe's use of the mandolin as a rhythm instrument, it is difficult to point to a single instrumental technique used by Monroe that has proved influential.

Record producer–musician Jim Rooney wrote a book called *Bossmen* in which he pointed out the significance of Bill Monroe's influence as a bluegrass bandleader and the similar importance of Muddy Waters in the blues. Practically every significant bluegrass musician, except the youngest ones, at one time or another played with Monroe. Monroe thus had an important role as a teacher from everyone from Scruggs himself to singer Jimmy Martin, fiddler Kenny Baker, and even a bunch of Yankee musicians including Bill Keith and Peter Rowan. Monroe was the first bandleader to hire northern and western players, thus integrating the urban revivalists into bluegrass.

Bluegrass to Newgrass

In the late 1950s, a creative young banjo player named Bobby Thompson was a member of the band Jim and Jesse. Some remarks made by fiddler Benny Sims during Bobby's previous gig with Carl Story led Thompson to experiment with playing fiddle tunes note for note on the banjo. As powerful as the Scruggs style was, because it consisted of a series of right-hand patterns called *rolls,* the melody was often subordinated into the rolls, rather than the rolls developing out of the melody itself. By interrupting the rolls with flurries of notes and fingering the short fifth-string of the banjo with the left hand, Thompson was able to simulate the role of the fiddle. Unfortunately, Thompson became discouraged when bluegrass audiences expressed no interest or appreciation for his efforts.

A few years later, Monroe hired New Englander Bill Keith, who had developed a similar approach to the banjo seemingly without knowing what Thompson was up to. Keith proved to be a sensation, and Thompson resumed his earlier work with newfound enthusiasm. Thompson went on to become a very successful studio musician, and Keith has had a long and fruitful playing career, moving into more of a jazz banjo style.

Another positive step in circulating bluegrass to a broad audience occurred when the Dirt Band, a West Coast folk–country–pop group, recorded an album called *Will the Circle Be Unbroken?* Dirt Band multi-instrumentalist John McEuen recruited Earl Scruggs, country legend Mother Maybelle Carter, fiddler Vassar Clements, and *Opry* star Roy Acuff for this roots-oriented record, which sold over a million units.

By the early 1970s, young musicians such as fiddler Byron Berline, mandolin player Sam Bush, guitarist Dan Crary, and banjoist Alan Munde were experimenting by expanding bluegrass into a music that became known as "newgrass." By 1971, Bush had started the band Newgrass Revival. Ten years later, banjoist Courtney Johnson was replaced by a young New York banjoist named Béla Fleck. Fleck was a spectacular player, and John Cowan, the band's new lead singer, blended rock and soul influences in his vocal stylings. The band ended up with a major label deal at Capitol, but never sold enough records to really excite the label.

The newgrass musicians were a rebellious bunch. Many had long hair and their habits bordered on the rock 'n' roll lifestyle. Their music included jazz and rock influences, and some of the older musicians and fans had the same attitude toward newgrass that dixieland musicians had when bebop became popular just after the end of World War II. New bands emerged, notably Colorado's Hot Rize, whose career lasted from 1978 until 1990.

In 1990, bluegrass had a resurgence on the country music charts through the work of multi-instrumentalist and singer Ricky Skaggs. For several years, all of the country labels were looking for traditional musicians who had crossover appeal to the country-pop audience. Bluegrass was then relegated back to the world of summer festivals and a niche audience, until a midwestern fiddler named Alison Krause took the country music market by storm. Her mid-1990s album on an independent label sold over a million copies, an astounding performance by a bluegrass musician. Krause has branched out into different musical genres, but remains essentially influenced by bluegrass. She is a reliable country chartmaker; she still records for Rounder, and they even do videos with her.

The most astonishing development in bluegrass was the success that accompanied the sound track recording from the movie *O Brother, Where Art Thou?* To date, the set, which consisted of a number of bluegrass cuts including the work of traditional singer Ralph Stanley, has sold over seven million copies. The album has received virtually no airplay on country music radio as program directors were nervous that listeners would find the music too harsh for their taste. Certainly the success of this album indicates that the market for bluegrass and roots music exceeds anyone's guesstimates.

Many of the musicians mentioned above have gone on to achieve significant careers in music. Béla Fleck has moved far beyond his bluegrass roots into a sort of experimental rock–bluegrass–jazz trio and tours and records extensively. Alan Munde teaches bluegrass at South Plains Community College in Levellend, Texas, along with his old bandmate, guitarist Joe Carr. Tim O'Brien of Hot Rize has had some of his songs recorded on multiplatinum albums by Kathy Mattea, Garth Brooks, and the Dixie Chicks. His bandmate Peter Wernick has played an important role in the growth of the International Blugrass Music Association (IBMA) and has written best-selling banjo instruction books. Another Hot Rize alumnus, Nick Forster, has a successful syndicated radio show, *E Town*, which features music from various roots music genres. Dan Crary tours with several different guitar ensembles, and Sam Bush tours, records, and does extensive studio work in Nashville.

And there are many other significant musicians who we don't have the space to cover, such as banjoists Tony Trishka and Allison Brown, fiddlers Byron Berline and Vassar Clements, bandleader–singer–guitarist–banjoist Lynn Morris, and such traditional musicians as Jim and Jesse and the Osborne Brothers. There are hundreds of bluegrass festivals all over the world, and bluegrass bands also appear at many folk festivals that do not specifically feature bluegrass. Several magazines are devoted to bluegrass and to specific instruments used in the music, and there are several record companies that specialize in it.

*   *   *

In 1989, I interviewed Bobby Thompson for an article published in *Frets* magazine. He told me that when he was on tour with Jim and Jesse, every morning they would get on the bus at dawn and Jesse would start to play a new tune that he had dreamed up. Bobby told me he would give a lot to hear some tapes from these on-the-bus jam sessions.

Bobby also revealed that every once in a while he would come from a recording session that was so wonderful he would get wired and couldn't sleep. I asked him what happened to those recordings. He wryly commented that most of them were never released.

A few years before our interview, Bobby had complained to his doctor that he was having trouble moving his right hand. After several medical referrals, all the doctors told him that it was all in his head. One day he went to a session and he was completely unable to move his right hand. A doctor diagnosed him with multiple sclerosis. Bobby had to give up his career as a session player and has never played again. From time to time, Rounder Records is rumored to be releasing an album of tunes that Bobby played on. Bobby was one of the few melodic banjo players whose rhythmic playing was as powerful as Earl Scruggs's playing in the early part of his career. Ampersand Records has just recently released a Thompson retrospective CD. Bobby succumbed to MS in May 2005, after a twenty-year struggle with that disease.

*   *   *

Tim O'Brien left Hot Rize in 1990. He had written several hit country songs for Kathy Mattea and the two recorded a duet. It was agreed that the single would be released on Mercury, the label Kathy recorded for, and the song would appear on an album Tim was making for RCA. The song, "The Battle Hymn of Love," got up to about number ten on the country charts and Tim felt that it would make a great launching pad for him.

Tim had been signed by RCA Nashville record chief Joe Galante. Joe was promoted to head of the entire RCA operation, and left Nashville. Unfortunately, the new people didn't like Tim's record, and chose not to release it. They apparently decided he wasn't going to be the next Ricky Skaggs. For some months, Tim would get a bill from RCA claiming that he still owed the label over $100,000—the cost of recording the album. The reader should understand that this is not a normal debt, it simply means that if Tim ever made any money from RCA, they would charge it against the debt.

Tim is now touring, recording, and doing studio work in Nashville. As Tom Waits put it, the large print giveth, and the small print taketh away.

*   *   *

It is interesting that the biggest sellers in contemporary bluegrass are Alison Krause and Nickel Creek. Krause herself sings a wide variety of music, and her voice is sweet rather than harsh. The bluegrass vocal element comes from the singing of her band members, especially Dan Tyminski. Nickel Creek's vocals also have a pleasant sound that is acceptable to audiences who are not fans of the harsher high lonesome bluegrass vocal style. Fans are drawn into Nickel Creek by the instrumental virtuosity, especially the mandolin playing of Chris Thiele. Both of these bands have remained in favor among bluegrass aficionados, but have developed a wider audience that is less oriented toward traditional-bluegrass vocal style.

Gospel Music

Gospel music is a particularly strong influence on bluegrass due to its emphasis on vocal harmony. Most bluegrass festivals have Sunday morning gospel singing, and many bluegrass artists record religious as well as secular songs and albums.

Religious songs date back to the eighteenth century psalm books and the various evangelical movements known as Great Awakenings. A tradition developed in which melodies were printed in songbooks where the notes were identified by shapes, rather than by standard musical notation. This enabled musicians to read music without any formal training. The tradition continues to a minor degree today, with gatherings of "singing schools" singing religious songs. Kip Lornell has pointed out the connections between the Pentecostal movement and southern white string bands. Certain composers of religious music, like Alfred E. Brumley, published songbooks and some of his songs, such as "I'll Fly Away" and "Turn the Radio On," became widely known by country and folk musicians.

A parallel tradition developed among African Americans. A number of the blues musicians such as Blind Lemon Jefferson and Josh White recorded religious songs as well as blues numbers. Some of the religious singers, like Blind Willie Johnson or Gary Davis, essentially sang tunes close to blues songs, but with religious lyrics. During the 1930s, a number of black vocal groups like the Golden Gate Quartet became quite popular. Jazz-blues pianist and composer T. A. Dorsey transformed black religious music from a concentration on traditional spirituals to a focus on newly composed songs. Singers like Roberta and Sallie Martin and Mahalia Jackson sang songs by Dorsey and other composers. A few of Dorsey's songs, such as "Peace in the Valley" and "Take My Hand Precious Lord," were also recorded by white country artists, notably Red Foley's best-selling version of "Peace in the Valley."

In recent years, black gospel music has become popular with white audiences, and groups like the Dixie Hummingbirds and the Blind Boys of Alabama have recorded with Paul Simon, Ben Harper, and other contemporary urban revivalists, both white and black.

One of the idioms that has recently emerged in gospel music is the genre called "sacred steel." It seems to have originated in Florida churches, and Arhoolie Records has released several albums of this type of music.

A gospel-related folk group is Bernice Reagan's vocal ensemble Sweet Honey in the Rock. Reagan is a folk song scholar, political activist, and a veteran of the civil rights movement. She is also a scholar of African American music and has written books and recorded albums that are gospel-influenced.

CHILDREN'S MUSIC

Children's songs, or at least songs for young children, usually have the same construction as older folk songs do. They generally contain only a single melody, or they have a verse and a chorus with melodies that are similar if not identical. This makes the tunes easy to remember. It is therefore not surprising that quite a few of the artists who perform for children use folk songs or songs that are written in a similar style.

Several of the major figures in the folk song revival have been quite involved with writing and/or performing music for kids. Woody Guthrie wrote a number of children's songs, and Folkways issued three volumes of them between 1951 and 1961. A few of them, like "Car, Car," are still performed. Pete Seeger's stepmother, Ruth Crawford Seeger, put together two volumes of folk songs for children that are particularly notable for her simple but inventive piano arrangements. Pete has recorded a number of children's albums, along with his many other recording projects. Ruth's children—Peggy, Penny, Mike, and, on one album, Barbara—recorded a number of these songs. In addition to these songs, Pete has created a number of song-stories that include music and narration. Malvina Reynolds also wrote, performed, and recorded songs for children as well as material intended for adults.

Besides the records described above, there were a handful of artists who were making records specifically for children. Chicago artist Ella Jenkins recorded twenty-two albums for Folkways, starting in 1956. Her *I'll Sing a Song* album, recorded in 1966, was the best-seller in the entire Folkways catalog. Jenkins concentrated on rhythm activities for children, using various percussion instruments. Tom Glazer, who had sung with the Almanacs, moved entirely into children's music, recording songs for Young People's Records even before the LP medium existed. He subsequently had one hit record with his parody of "On Top of Old Smokey," which he renamed "On Top of Spaghetti." He continued to record and play concerts for many years, and also put together collections of folk songs for children.

Los Angeles–based Marcia Berman and Patti Zeitlin also recorded and wrote songs, together and separately, for young children. They were teachers themselves, so they had a good understanding of what songs children would enjoy singing. They even became active in a sort of Los Angeles music commune called CAMEL (Children's Music Artists Making a Living).

When a Canadian performer named Raffi visited record stores in the mid-1970s, he found that most of the children's records in the bins were movie sound tracks or music used in Disney cartoons, or as he writes in his autobiography, *Raffi: The Life of a Children's Troubadour,* "dry and instructional or syrupy, sweet and condescending." Raffi started out as a performer who sang for adults, but he soon realized that he seemed to be much more successful performing for children. He tried to model his records along the lines of the albums recorded by the Babysitters, a group that featured Alan Arkin (formerly in the Tarriers), Lee Hays (a Weaver), and Doris Kaplan.

Raffi proved to be incredibly successful. He set up his own label, Troubadour, and sold his albums at children's book, toy, and music stores. He soon made a distribution deal with A&M Records in Canada, and a deal with their mother company in the United States followed. Raffi sold hundreds of thousands of albums, and his concerts sold out all over the United States and Canada. The music included some original songs along with folk songs, in simple but attractive arrangements. Raffi was so successful that he started to record other artists on his label, including Fred Penner. Penner was on CBC television and the show was also picked up by Nickelodeon in the United States. Penner's albums also did quite well. With the Canadian children's market on fire, three singers started a trio called Sharon, Lois, and Bram. They started their own independent label, Elephant.

Raffi made a video in 1984. It was played on the Disney Channel and ended up selling over a hundred thousand copies. Raffi's core audience was very young, mostly two-to-seven-year-old children. In 1986, just as Pete Seeger had done, he became more and more concerned with environmental issues, and he recorded an album for older children. A&M was not thrilled with the notion of marketing to a new group, and the album ended up not selling nearly as well as his earlier ones. This led Raffi to move to MCA Records for six years, and eventually to American independent label Rounder.

There are a number of artists with folk roots who have entered the children's market. Peter Alsop has a PhD in educational psychology and he has recorded a number of albums on his own Moose Head label dealing with children's issues, "In the Hospital" for example. Harry Chapin's brother Tom had a national children's TV show in the '70s called *Make a Wish*. Since that time he has done a number of albums, mostly for children. Lui Collins, Anne Dodson, Jon Gailmor, Bill Harley, Kathy Kallick, John McCutcheon, Tom Paxton, Peter, Paul & Mary, and Carla Sciaky are all revivalist artists who have recorded occasional children's albums alongside their more typical adult fare.

Multi-instrumentalists Cathy Fink and Marcy Marxer started out as adult artists, but have primarily moved into children's music and have been finalists for what would have been well-deserved Grammy awards. Many other children's artists, like Katherine Dines in Denver and Joe Scruggs in Austin, have their own labels and tour widely.

There is a small infrastructure for the children's music market. *Parent's Choice* gives annual awards for the best children's records, and many of the artists listed have won these awards. An organization called the Children's

Music Network publishes a magazine called *Pass It On!*, holds annual meetings, and in general provides a forum for exchanging ideas about children's music. Folksinger Sally Rogers, another artist who started out writing and performing for adults, is the president of the organization.

As the children's music market became a viable commodity, the major record labels showed more interest in it. The influence of television shows and movie sound tracks has to some extent tended to push the folk aspects of the music aside. Heavy-grossing films like *The Lion King* and *Shreck* vastly outsell even the top children's folk performers' work. Some rock 'n' roll artists have also begun to record records for children. Dan Zanes, who was in the rock band the Del Furgos, is now recording and performing folk-influenced music for kids. Music for Little People, an independent label, has issued a number of anthologies by folk-oriented children's performers. An Australian band called the Wiggles are the current superstar of children's music.

COWBOY POETRY AND MUSIC

The tradition of cowboy poetry dates back to the late nineteenth century and the work of such "cowboy poets" as Badger Clark and D. J. O'Malley. John Lomax's first serious song collection was his book of cowboy songs published in 1910, and "Cowboy" Jack Tharp self-published his collection of traditional songs along with some of his own songs two years earlier.

These early cowboy poems and songs reveal the romanticized image of the lonely, manly cowboy that became heavily promoted by the movie industry. Carl Sprague was the first "radio cowboy," singing his songs on the radio. He also made records starting in 1925. Such movie cowboys as Gene Autry and Roy Rogers spread good cheer and nobility on America's movie screens, stopping to sing songs from time to time. These songs also became successful through the medium of records. A vocal group called the Sons of the Pioneers sang in many of these movies. The Sons of the Pioneers were a vocal group that utilized jazz-influenced harmonies, but their lyrics stuck with western themes, as can be seen from the titles of some of their most famous songs: "The Tumbling Tumbleweeds" and "Cool Water." During the late 1920s, a new sound developed in Texas and Oklahoma. It was called "western swing." Western swing was an odd combination of country music that often featured multiple fiddles and pedal-steel guitar along with brass and reed instruments. It was like a shotgun marriage of country music and Kansas City jazz. The musicians donned western attire, including cowboy hats. The most famous of these bands was Bob Wills's orchestra, but the music became something of a Texas tradition through the work of such musicians as Hank Thompson.

Throughout the 1930s and the 1940s, America retained its fascination with the "wild west" not only through the medium of movies and singing cowboys, but also in the form of such radio shows as *The Lone Ranger, The Cisco Kid, Tom Mix,* and *Red Ryder*. These shows did not involve musical performers, although the instrumental music themes were intended to convey a western ambience. These programs also became television shows in the early post–World War II days of black-and-white TV.

The cowboy poetry aspect of things was thought to have disappeared until the 1970s, when folklorists working in the western states discovered that cowboys were still writing poetry. In the 1970s, a visual artist who had an interest in western lore named Sarah Sweetwater arranged for some of these cowboys to recite their poetry at a small folklife festival in Elko, Nevada. Starting in 1983, this festival became an annual event. It is now a high-profile tourist event that brings thousands of people into Elko, and it includes many musical performances, as well as poetry recitations. Hal Cannon, who was the Utah state folklorist, went on to found the Western Folklife Center and to edit collections of cowboy songs and poetry. The event has also developed many unofficial satellites, and there are similar festivals all over the western United States. Baxter Black, a veterinarian–cowboy poet–humorist has helped to fuel the cowboy poetry boom with his best-selling books, CDs of his humorous poems, and his newspaper columns and public radio appearances.

The cowboy poetry and song explosion led to an interest on the part of record companies. Warner Brothers established a Warner Western label in the 1990s to handle cowboy artists. Michael Martin Murphey proved to be the most successful commercial artist, but the label had limited success with such western staples as the Sons of the San Joaquin, a sort of Sons of the Pioneers tribute band, and a mellow-voiced cowboy singer named Don Edwards.

Murphey had achieved a reasonable level of success as a sort of pop–western–folk artist. He refocused his career on cowboy songs and on a annual Colorado festival called West Fest, which he still headlines. He also does an annual Cowboy Christmas tour of forty cities and has established his own record label. A booking agent in Colorado Springs named Scott O'Malley is a tremendous fan of cowboy music and when Warner dropped their label, he set up his own record company called Western Jubilee Records. Besides Edwards and the Sons, he has also issued albums by Red Steagull, Waddie Mitchell, and Cowboy Celtic.

Ian Tyson, the Canadian who partnered with Sylvia Tyson during the 1960s, has gone onto a successful solo career as a cowboy singer and songwriter. He often appears at the Elko gathering and his records are issued by Stony Plain in Canada and Vanguard in the United States. Tyson's two most popular songs are "Four Strong Winds," which refers to Alberta and conveys a western ambiance, and "Someday Soon," a song about a rodeo rider. His friend singer–songwriter Tom Russell has also recorded some western albums, along with his other work.

Ex-rodeo star the late Chris Le Doux was another cowboy song artist. He wrote numerous songs about rodeos, some of which have been recorded by Garth Brooks. Cowboy music is often featured at or around the major rodeos, like the Western Stock Show in Denver, Frontier Days in Cheyenne, and the Calgary Stampede. Skip Gorman, a former member of the Utah group the Deseret String Band, has also recorded albums of cowboy songs. The western swing idiom continues through the work of mandlin-fiddle virtuoso Johnny Gimble and such groups as the Amazing Rhythm Aces and Asleep at the Wheel.

Cowboy, or western, music is one of the many branches of the contemporary folk song tree. As a commercial entity it is definitely a niche market, but one with its own coterie of artists and fans who retain a devotion to a western landscape of the imagination.

INSTRUMENTAL AND NEW AGE MUSIC

Earlier in this book, I discussed the instrumentalists in the early part of the folk revival. John Fahey cut his first record in 1959. He was an early "do it yourself" exponent, releasing the album on his own Takoma label. His initial interest in country music was superseded by his discovery of the blues. This led to his role in the rediscovery of Bukka White and Skip James, followed by a master's degree in folklore and mythology at UCLA. Fahey wrote his thesis on delta blues artist Charley Patton.

Fahey led a rather disordered life, spending ten years in psychoanalysis, living in a Buddhist monastery in India, and becoming ill with chronic fatigue syndrome, followed by a bout of alcoholism. Because of these personality blips, Fahey hardly ever played music live and his career was more a function of word-of-mouth and legend rather than hard work. Along the way, he continued to record his guitar music for his own label, which he later sold to Chrysalis Records, and for other record companies as well. His Christmas album supposedly sold 200,000 copies, a phenomenal sale for as obscure an artist as Fahey. His playing was abstract and improvisational, and in the sense that he wasn't especially inclined toward melodic figures, he was a pioneer in the so-called new age music idiom. He was more rhythmic, however, than most of the new agers, and he also was sloppy, inspired, and he sometimes he played out of tune. He certainly wasn't careful and pretty in his approach.

Takoma also released albums by other guitarists, notably Leo Kottke, and Indian music–influenced Robbie Basho. Fahey died in 2001. Toward the end of his life, Fahey recorded dissonant almost industrial-style music, and he also cofounded Revenant Records, an extremely eclectic label that released everything from banjoist Dock Boggs to a fourth volume of Harry Smith's *Anthology* collection and avant-garde jazz pianist Cecil Taylor.

Leo Kottke made one obscure album in 1969 before hooking up with Fahey at Takoma. Kottke has spectacular technique, which he uses on six- and twelve-string guitar. He is also an entertainer and a storyteller who does some capable singing, which he has laughingly described as "goose farts." He uses vocals as a break from his instrumental music in reverse ratio to the usual performer, who might play an occasional instrumental solo in what is basically a vocal performance.

New Age Music

The term "new age" when applied to music is essentially a meaningless one, designed to create space in record stores. The first new age artist was Will Ackerman. He began to play guitar for his own amusement and made a record to fulfill requests from his friends. He pressed three hundred copies, and he named the label Windham Hill Records.

Ackerman was a guitarist whose style was sort of halfway between Fahey and Kottke, more attentive to tone and intonation than Fahey, but not as rhythmically powerful as Kottke at his best. Somehow the album got to a Seattle radio station, where a young disc jockey named Jeff Heiman began to play it on a regular basis. The radio station's switchboard lit up and people started asking where they could buy the album. Finally, Heiman had to call Ackerman and explain that if the record wasn't available in record stores in Seattle the station wouldn't be able to continue playing it.

One thing led to another and soon the label was recording Ackerman's cousin, Alex De Grassi, an excellent guitarist, and an unknown piano player named George Winston. George really saw himself as a guitarist, but Ackerman became entranced with his piano work. He album ended up becoming a best-seller, and the label succeeded beyond his wildest dreams.

Winston was about as close to being a "folk" piano player as anyone could be. His technical abilities on the piano weren't outstanding, but his repeated left-hand figures with the right hand improvising over them became much in demand. Windham Hill set up its own distribution network, selling through health food stores and bookstore as much as in record stores. The early covers were almost all black-and-white photographs. The label had stumbled upon an image that distinguished it from any other record company. Ackerman signed Liz Story, another pianist; Shadowfax, an experimental jazz group; and a guitarist named Michael Hedges. Hedges was exploring a technique called "tapping," where the player actually picked notes with both hands rather than using the left hand for the traditional method of fretting the strings. Hedges was using an acoustic-electric guitar, because the left hand notes don't sustain well on an acoustic guitar. Tapping wasn't unique to Hedges, Stanley Jordan was exploiting the technique in his jazz playing and Eddie Van Halen was exploring it in the world of rock guitar.

Windham Hill sold out to RCA/BMG, Ackerman left the label, and over the years new age music became something of a cliché. Narada Records in Milwaukee and Silver Wave in Boulder, Colorado, picked up some of the slack, but none of their artists reached the heights of popular acceptance that Winston had scaled.

COUNTRY PICKERS

Earlier, I discussed the strong influence that Merle Travis had on folk revival musicians. Two other country guitar players were also important figures in terms of their influence on the folk pickers. Chet Atkins was often attacked as a purveyor of the Nashville schlock sound—heavenly background choirs and pat instrumental work. Nevertheless, he made many solo guitar albums on which he demonstrated his mastery and extension of some of Merle Travis's innovations. Many of the folk players could be heard noodling their own versions of Atkins's tune "Windy and Warm." Chet played virtually every imaginable style of music, ranging from ragtime to old country tunes to blues, jazz, and Latin-influenced music. Jerry Reed was his protégé, but Jerry played a much funkier and more rhythmically powerful style of guitar, and his humorous story-songs, like "Guitar

Man," along with his Hollywood acting career, exemplified by *The Dukes of Hazzard,* made him a household name.

Mark O'Connor is a phenomenal musician. As a teenager he won many contests at the Weiser, Idaho, fiddlers' gathering. Among the instruments he mastered are banjo, fiddle, guitar, and mandolin and he is a monster player on all of them. He was a Nashville studio ace during the 1970s, but in the mid-1990s he began to play music with cellist Yo Yo Ma and bassist Edgar Meyer, recording *Appalachian Waltz,* a successful classical crossover album.

More than any other musician, O'Connor brought folk and country music into the classical realm, where he proved he could hold his own with the best.

INSTRUMENTALISTS AND INSTRUMENTS

John Hartford crossed over into many categories. His greatest commercial success was his song "Gentle on My Mind," recorded by Glen Campbell. But Hartford was an excellent banjo, guitar, and fiddle player who did one-man concerts across the country. He was very open to new musical styles and some of the musical fusions on his recordings anticipated developments that are just now coming to fruition. Two other important guitarists are David Bromberg and Pierre Bensusan. Bromberg accompanied Jerry Jeff Walker during the mid-1960s and went on to a solo career and yet another incarnation as the leader of his own band. Along the way he played on albums by Bob Dylan, Carl Simon, John Denver, and Chubby Checker, among others. Bromberg then organized a band that included a trombone player, a multireed instrumentalist, and a rhythm section. By 1980, Bromberg moved to Chicago and became a violin builder and has only occasionally appeared in public since that time.

Pierre Bensusan is a superb finger-style guitarist whose music reflects various world music styles. He was one of the first guitarists to extensively explore the DADGAD tuning that is often used in playing Celtic music.

During the 1970s and 1980s, some other instruments began to come into play in the folk revival. The mountain dulcimer had been used early on by Kentucky singer Jean Ritchie. It has three or four strings. Another instrument, the hammer dulcimer, is played with mallets, and has either triple sets of strings or double sets. The grand total comes to either 58 or 87 strings. One of the earliest important exponents of the instrument was Howie Mitchell, whose records for Folk Legacy included an instructional album. More recent dulcimer players include Colorado dulcimer maker and artist Bonnie Carol; Celtic music performer and hammer dulcimer player Maggie Sansone in Annapolis, Maryland; Oregon musician Mark Nelson; California-based Neil Hellman; and David Schnaufer, who is possibly the world's only studio dulcimer player in Nashville. He also teaches the instrument at Vanderbilt University's Blair School of Music, where he is an adjunct professor alongside fiddle instructor Mark O'Connor.

Concertina is another instrument that has a small but devoted coterie of followers. Bertram Levy, a Port Townsend, Washington, physician who is also a fine nylon-string banjoist and a tango orchestra leader(!), recorded an instructional album for concertina. The concertina is a sort of folk cousin of the accordion with a reedier, smaller-volume sound.

The Irish harp, which is used in Celtic music and is a smaller folk version of the concert harp, also has a place in today's urban folk movement. The Seattle duo Magical Strings is one of the more prominent groups utilizing the Irish harp. Phil Boulding builds his own harps and he and his wife, Pam—who plays hammer dulcimer, harp, piano, and other instruments—have made a number of recordings using these instruments.

The hammer dulcimer and Irish harp represent niche markets in the folk revival. Dulcimers in particular seem to inspire an almost cult-like devotion, and there are festivals devoted specifically to the dulcimer. Some modern instrument makers, notably Dusty Strings in Seattle, produce excellent versions of the hammer dulcimer and Irish harp.

chapter 11

Roots and Branches, Part Two: Ethnicity

Many of the people who emigrated to America came to escape political or religious persecution. Many others came in search of economic opportunity. Nineteenth century America was viewed as a place where "the streets were paved with gold." The immigrants prided themselves on quickly adjusting to American life and learning to speak fluent English. They often tended to suppress the memories of their original homelands, and this included their music. The children of the immigrants, those who either came here at an early age or were born in America, were even less likely to be interested in their parents' customs, language, or music.

This section of the book will concentrate on the music of these immigrants, a music not usually sung in English. There simply isn't room here to publish a detailed description of the music of every immigrant group, so this section will include a brief discussion of cajun and zydeco music, Celtic music, klezmer music, and the music of Mexican-Americans and Native American groups. Books are available that discuss each of these musical genres in depth, and some of them are listed in the appendix of this work.

CAJUN AND ZYDECO MUSIC

Cajun and zydeco music are two musical styles found in southeast Texas and in Louisiana. There are similarities and also differences between the two styles, and the racial composition of the two groups is dissimilar. In 1755, the British expelled the French from Acadia in Nova Scotia because they refused to pledge allegiance to the British crown. Some of the settlers returned to France, some went to Quebec, and hundreds more made their way to the French territory of Louisiana. These settlers spoke a version of seventeenth century rural French, and they formed the same sort of isolated pocket around Lafayette, Louisiana, that the British settlers in the southern Appalachians had. They developed a music that included the fiddle as the lead instrument and used simple percussion instruments, such as the triangle or spoons. The music changed when the settlers adapted to the accordion that German settlers brought to the area a hundred years later. Gradually, the accordion replaced the fiddle as the primary instrument. The accordion used was a single-row diatonic instrument. Like the harmonica, it played in a limited number of keys, especially C and G. The fiddle was often tuned down a whole tone in order to facilitate playing with the accordion, because the common normal fiddle keys are D and A.

By the beginning of the nineteenth century, there was an influx of black settlers into the area. Some were slaves imported from the French West Indies and some were free citizens who arrived in the area after the Haitian revolution of 1803.

Since segregation prevailed in Louisiana, contact between the two groups was somewhat limited. Over the years, zydeco absorbed strong blues influences, while cajun music learned more toward country music styles. Ethnomusicologist Kip Lornell, in his excellent survey *Introducing American Folk Music: Second Edition,* points out that cajun music tends to emphasize the first and third beats of a 4/4 measure, while zydeco usually accents the second and fourth beats. Zydeco bands do not generally include a fiddle.

The first recordings of both cajun and zydeco were made in 1928, with cajun music preceding zydeco by a few months. During the 1930s, cajun music was influenced by western swing and pedal-steel guitar was sometimes added to the musical mix. The influence sometimes went in the other direction; Hank Williams's song "Jambalaya" was "borrowed" from "Grand Texas," by cajun artist Papa Cairo. Iry LeJeune, another cajun artist, returned the favor by doing a French version of Hank's "I Can't Help It If I'm Still in Love with You."

Alan Lomax collected cajun music for the Library of Congress in the 1930s and twenty years later, Harry Oster, an English professor at Louisiana State University, did the same.

In the ensuing decades the use of the French language had started to decline, and so had interest in the music. In 1964, musicians–folklorists Mike Seeger and Ralph Rinzler served as advocates for presenting cajun music at the Newport Folk Festival. Oddly, the Louisiana press was terribly afraid that the music would be regarded as junk, and they were amazed at the positive reception that it received. A fiddle player named Dewey Balfa was a last-minute substitute in the band and three years later, he came back with his own band, mostly consisting of family members. This time, the music created a sensation that resulted in a revival of the music and worldwide tours, recordings, and even videos about the music. Another factor in helping to keep the music alive was the founding of CO-DOFIL, the Council for the Development of French in Louisiana, by James Domengeaux in 1968.

Meanwhile, sensational accordion player and singer Clifton Chenier emerged as the major figure in zydeco, making his first records for pop label Specialty in 1955, followed by a long series of albums on Chris Strachwitz's roots music label Arhoolie. Chenier abandoned the old-style accordion and played the modern piano-accordion, with a full keyboard. Chenier also used a saxophone and a drummer in his band. The music had elements of zydeco mixed with rhythm and blues. The old washboard that had been used for percussion evolved into a metal washboard worn as a sort of vest around the player's neck and played with thimbles that acted like fingerpicks on a guitar.

Another hybrid music called "swamp pop" developed in Louisiana. It was an amalgamation of blues, cajun, and zydeco, with a dash of country music, sung in English. Some of its practitioners anglicized their names, like Robert Charles Guidry, who adopted the name Bobby Charles, hitting paydirt with his song "See You Later Alligator."

Cajun and Zydeco Today

Dewey Balfa was a key figure in the revival of cajun music, and he also played alongside zydeco musicians in Louisiana schools. Michael Doucet is another major figure in the development of worldwide interest in Louisiana music. His band, Beausoleil, which was formed in 1973, has toured all over the world and has recorded a Grammy–winning album, and dozens of other records as well. Beausoleil, by cajun standards, is a big band, featuring Doucet on fiddle, his brother David on guitar, a drummer, an accordion player, a percussionist, and a multi-instrumentalist who even sometimes adds banjo to the mix. Doucet is an indefatigable musician who has played on many cajun and zydeco recordings, and has a side project with Marc and Ann Savoy. Marc Savoy is an accordion maker who owns a music store that is a center for the teaching and playing of cajun music. His wife, Ann, besides playing guitar in the band, has also written an important book about cajun music, *Cajun Music: A Reflection of a People, Volume 1.*

Zydeco has had its moment of mass exposure, like its role in the movie *The Big Easy,* and the quirky hit pop record "My Toot Toot" by Rockin' Dopsie. Boozoo Chavis, Geno Delafose, Rosie Ledet, Buckwheat Zydeco, and California émigré Queen Ida all tasted some success in their careers.

Younger bands, including Zachary Richard, Tereance Simien, and Clifton Chenier's son, C. J., continue to spread the zydeco message.

Dewey Balfa's daughters carry on the family musical tradition with the band Toujours Balfa. A female quintet called the Magnolia Sisters, which includes Ann Savoy and Christine Balfa, along with Steve Riley's Mamou Playboys, also do their part to keep the music alive.

Cajun and zydeco music have never entered the mainstream folk revival, but they definitely constitute an important niche market within it. Some musicians, like guitarist Sonny Landreth, who has played with Clifton Chenier, retain cajun or zydeco roots in their more widespread musical repertoire. There are also a number of revivalist cajun and zydeco bands in relatively unlikely places such as Denver's Zukes of Zydeco or the Bayou-Seco band in Silver City, New Mexico.

CELTIC MUSIC

The term "Celtic music" usually refers to the music of Ireland, Scotland, Wales, Cape Breton Island in Nova Scotia, Brittany in France, and Galicia in northern Spain. There are at last as many differences as similarities in the music of these far-flung areas, but for purposes of convenience in labeling that suits the needs of record companies, record stores, and radio stations, all of this music as classified as "Celtic." Historically, the word "Celt" comes from a tribe that emerged from central Asia around 1000 BCE.

Celtic music in general, and Irish music in particular, has a considerable built-in audience in the United States, with an estimated forty-four million Americans of Irish descent. There are two components to the Celtic music movement in the United States. The first is the arrival of the Clancy Brothers and Tommy Makem in the United States. Tommy, Paddy, and Liam Clancy were all actors who came to the United States in search of acting careers, but ended up as a very successful singing group. The original impetus for their success came from their friend Diane Hamilton, who set up Tradition Records in Greenwich Village. Hamilton was an heir to the Guggenheim fortune. She chose to devote her resources to music, while her sister Peggy played a major role on the New York City visual art scene.

The Clancy Brothers recorded a relatively rough and informal album for Tradition in 1958. Many other recordings followed, and so did an appearance on the *Ed Sullivan Show*. The group toured internationally, went on to record for Columbia Records, and performed regularly at Carnegie Hall.

The Clancy Brothers and Makem sparked an interest in Irish folk music as an alternative the sort of denatured pub-fare that Irish music had degenerated to at that point. Tommy Makem left the group in 1970 and continues to record and to tour today, appearing with his son.

*   *   *

During the late 1960s, I got a call asking if I could do a Carnegie Hall concert with the Clancy Brothers. Usually, Tommy Makem played banjo with them, but he was having some problems with bursitis. They said they would send me some records so I could learn the songs. There were about two months to go before the concert, so I put it out of my mind until I happened to notice that it was only about a week or so away and I had no idea what I was supposed to do. I concluded that Tommy had gotten better, or that they got someone else to do the gig. About two days before the concert I got a call confirming the gig, and they told me just to show up shortly before the concert and we would "go over a few songs." The night of the concert we rehearsed three or four of the songs, and then it was time to go on stage.

I was in a fairly serious state of panic. It turned out the concert was sold out and they had placed several rows of seats on the stage. I thought to myself that this was an incipient disaster; not only would thirty or forty people be staring at me trying to figure out why the band had decided to hire this flaky incompetent, but for all I knew, Robert Shelton of the *New York Times* would probably have a few well-chosen words to describe the "accompanist."

As it turned out, the concert was a lot of fun, but it proved even worse for me than I had expected. I knew about three-quarters of the songs that they sang, but the problem was that the versions I knew always seemed to have slightly or substantially different tunes than the ones that they were doing. The *Times* didn't review the concert, and I managed to get through it more or less uneventfully. So much for my career in Irish music.

In 1964, a Canadian folk-pop group called the Irish Rovers entered the Irish music scene. If the Clancy Brothers were enthusiastic and theatrical, the Rovers were more of a Kingston Trio sort of operation. They had a big American hit record with Shel Silverstein's song "The Unicorn" and toured the United States and Canada. They had a weekly Canadian TV show, and ultimately were more popular in Canada than in the United States.

Later in the book, I turn to the interchange between the English and American folk revivals, but the connections between the American and Irish roles in the Celtic music revival are more profound and continue today. Celtic groups like the Chieftains and the Boys of the Lough became internationally popular and continue to tour in the United States.

Some of the most famous Irish musicians emigrated to the United States, like fiddler Kevin Burke, a member of the Bothy band, who now lives in Portland, Oregon.

Another important émigré is Mick Moloney, who was active in the bands Planxty and the Bothy Band and toured with a successful folk-pop group called the Johnsons. This led to Moloney's studying folklore and receiving a PhD from the University of Pennsylvania. Moloney has functioned as a teacher and mentor and has helped a younger group of Irish-American musicians by organizing various bands and also playing in some of them. The interested reader is referred to Fiona Ritchie's recent book, *The NPR Curious Listener's Guide to Celtic Music.* Ritchie herself has had a Celtic music show, *The Thistle and the Shamrock,* on NPR for over twenty years

There are a few things about Celtic music that are worth mentioning here. The role of melody is crucial in the music. The singer or player ornaments the music in a style that fiddler Eileen Ivers describes as "subtle, yet intricate." There is considerable unison singing and playing in the music. Because the island is largely populated by Scottish émigrés, the music from Cape Breton Island is rooted in a Scottish tradition. A few of the Cape Breton musicians, such as Ashley MacIsaac and Natalie McMaster, have become internationally known.

Celtic music seems more malleable than some of the other folk styles covered in this book. For example, in the early 1970s, an Irish musician named Johnny Moynihan brought a bouzouki—a sort of long-necked lute—back from Greece. He gave it to Alec Finn of the group Da Danann. The bouzouki now plays a significant role in a number of Irish bands. Similarly, the bodhran, a frame drum that had only an occasional presence in Irish bands, is now a regular presence in Irish bands. An American shop, the Bucks County Folk Shop, makes a number of bodhrans and sells them all over the world. Some American musicians have adopted the bouzouki. Tim O'Brien, a singer–songwriter, fiddler, mandolinist, and guitarist, uses it in his shows to play both Celtic music and other tunes as well.

Another example of the apparent ease for Celtic music to cross over into new directions is the successful folk-rock bands that have emerged from the Celtic music revival. Clannad has had a strong international presence and its music has reached the pop charts. The group consists of two families and one of the original members, Enya Brennan, has become one of the most successful new age artists in the world, with million-selling albums. Solas is a successful American band that performs in Europe as well. They are a dynamic band with a strong percussive feel, but still essentially a folk-based group.

Irish rockers U2 are a good example of a band that is certainly not a folk group, yet songs like "Sunday Bloody Sunday" retain a strong Irish flavor and also represent an interest in topical music that has been so much a part of American folk music.

The 1990s saw the production of an enormously popular show called *Riverdance.* The show has toured internationally and uses elements of Irish folk music and dance molded into an extremely theatrical presentation. Although it is possible to view this as a bit of a bowdlerization of the tradition, in the same way that American folk-pop groups tended to be, it certainly stimulated an enormous interest in Celtic music and dance and created commercial opportunities for musicians in that genre.

The Irish guitarists generally play in the tuning DADGAD, and many fine guitarists have experimented with this tuning. Algerian-born Pierre Bensusan is one of its foremost exponents, and he now plays entirely in that tuning. Many other guitarists use the tuning to play in other genres of music.

There are many local and regional Celtic music bands, such as Beltaine in Portland, Oregon; Craigmore in Los Angeles; and Colcannon in Boulder, Colorado. Some of them consist entirely of members who are not ethnically Celtic but simply love the music. Others, like Colcannon, whose lead singer is Irish émigré Mick Bolger, are a mixture of Irish and non-Irish musicians. Celtic music at its best is both soulful and energetic, and it has generated its group of fans in the folk revival. Space limitations have prohibited discussion of some of the other Celtic musicians, like fiddler Aly Bain, the Tannahill Weavers, or Brittany harpist Alan Stivell.

KLEZMER

From 1880 until 1920, many Eastern European Jews emigrated to the United States, especially to New York. They brought with them the musical traditions of their native countries, fused with their own traditions. There was a thriving Jewish community on the Lower East Side of Manhattan and in Brooklyn. This provided musicians with a considerable amount of work. They played weddings, bar mitzvahs, and dances; they played on five different radio stations and made records. The most famous of these musicians was clarinetist Dave Tarras, who not only recorded Jewish music but made dozens of records where he played the music of other national groups, sometimes having his picture taken in the appropriate ethnic dress. The word "klezmer," according to musician–scholar Henry Sapoznik, writing in his authoritative book, *Klezmer! Jewish Music from*

Old World to Our World, is a Hebrew word that combines the words "song" and "instrument."

Like Irish music, Yiddish music used a great deal of musical ornamentation, imitating the vocal embellishments of Jewish cantors. The music was also influenced by a thriving Jewish theater, where plays were presented in the Yiddish language. At the turn of the twentieth century there were many pop songs that described and even made fun of various ethnic groups, and Jewish-American composers like Irving Berlin wrote material of this sort as well. One example is Berlin's song "Yiddle on Your Fiddle Play Some Rag Time."

Some of the musicians who played Jewish music were also actively involved in Dixieland jazz music. There were even some attempts to combine the music, as in Joseph Cherniavsky's Yiddish American Jazz Band. Some musicians were fluent in both musical genres, but others really only mastered one style, like Tarras, who was comfortable improvising Jewish music but not jazz.

By the end of World War II, the Yiddish theater declined, most of the radio stations went off the air, and many of the pioneer Jewish musicians were aging. Jewish music became only a small component of the repertoire for these musicians, even at such events as bar mitzvahs. During the 1950s and 1960s the music was almost forgotten. Through an odd sidelight of the folk song revival, several Jewish urban revivalists became active in reviving klezmer.

Sapoznik was an excellent five-string banjo player who spent some time collecting songs and learning instrumental styles in the southern Appalachian mountains. On one of his trips to visit banjoist Tommy Jarrell in 1977, Henry told Jarrell that he was Jewish and Jarrell, noting that many of the folk song enthusiasts and collectors were Jews, asked him if Jews didn't have their own music. This almost casual comment totally changed Sapoznik's life. He went back to New York and began to inquire seriously into the whereabouts of the older Jewish musicians. He also began to collect old klezmer records, set up an archive through a federal grant, and started a camp called KlezKamp in 1985. He also started a klezmer band called Kapelye.

At about the same time, a bluegrass mandolinist named Andy Statman chanced to find one of clarinetist Dave Tarras's records. He was able to locate Tarras, and overcoming Tarras's initial reaction that the music was old-fashioned, he convinced Tarras to be his mentor and teacher. Tarras even gave him an old clarinet.

But even before these revivalists started their careers, a band in Berkeley called Klezmorim recorded their first album, *East Side Wedding,* for the independent folk label Arhoolie. Over the course of the following twenty-five years, there has been a revived interest in the klezmer idiom. Most of the bands feature clarinet and/or violin as the lead instruments, but others are less concerned with literal authenticity. Some of these bands used the older musicians as their mentors while they were still alive. KlezKamp, which occurs during Christmas week, has grown to include hundreds of participants. Many of the younger musicians begin as students and, some years later, end up in a teaching role. Sapoznik also included older Jewish music scholars, like Ruth Rubin, a performer who sang unaccompanied and edited several collections of Jewish folk songs. According to Sapoznik, the atmosphere at KlezKamp was very welcoming, and soon Jewish lesbian and gay musicians joined the mix.

Today, klezmer bands exist all over the United States, Canada, and Europe. There are even several female klezmer bands, like Klezmeydlekh and Mikveh in New York and KlezMs in Philadelphia. Bands like the Klezmatics and the Klezmer Conservatory Band perform, tour all over the world, and make recordings.

Some bands, like Klezmorim, play a repertoire that is not restricted to klezmer, but includes gypsy music and other Eastern European music. The same inevitable arguments about authenticity versus change crop up in klezmer music that we have seen throughout the reinterpretation of music in the revival at large. I particularly like the comments of klezmer musician Alicia Svigals, writing in *American Klezmer: Its Root and Offshoots*, edited by ethnomusicologist Mark Slobin. Svigals is a founding member of the popular Klezmatics and of Mikveh. She comments that, "My hope is now that we're becoming fluent in our language, we can go beyond simply reciting a received text to speak spontaneously in our own voices."

Composer John Zorn has been active in composing klezmer music and the Knitting Factory, an enterprise that includes a club as well as a record company, is a hotbed of klezmer music. A recent Knitting Factory record called *Yid Vicious Forverts!* includes songs from various cultures and even electric guitar.

Although klezmer was not included in the folk revival of thew 1960s, it has become yet another appealing ethnic style with its own supporters and musicians. As I have already pointed out, some of the major figures in the revival had their own roots in the urban folk revival.

MEXICAN-AMERICAN MUSIC

If the most significant influence on American vernacular music in the twentieth century was African American music, it is almost inevitable that

Hispanic musical styles will have similar significance in the twenty-first century. On the basis of population alone, this is virtually a certainty.

The bulk of this brief section will deal with the music of Mexican-Americans. They constitute about half of the Spanish-speaking population of the United States and about two-thirds of the record sales of the music of Spanish-speaking groups. Obviously, there are quite a few other Spanish- (and Portugese-) speaking groups that are part of the ethnic mix in the United States, but their relationship to the folk music revival is less direct. There are some exceptions to this generalization. Pop-folk group Bud & Travis customarily sang some Mexican songs and they had a reasonable mastery of Mexican guitar techniques. During the '60s revival there were several songs, particularly "La Llorena" and the Cuban "Guantanamara," that made it into the repertoire of a number of singers. Nevertheless, it would be fair to say that the folk revival proceeded without much awareness of Mexican music. The United Farm Workers Union integrated music and theater into its organizing campaigns. This music was sung in Spanish and existed independently of the folk revival.

This particular musical odyssey begins with the Spanish settlers who came to New Mexico and Colorado in the sixteenth century from Mexico. The late J. Donald Robb documented the music of these settlers in his huge volume, *Hispanic Folk Music of Old New Mexico and the Southwest*. Jenny Wells Vincent was an active member of People's Songs and is the only fairly well-known singer in the revival who performed any of these songs.

Another Spanish-speaking group with their own musical traditions are Puerto Ricans, thousands of whom have settled in New York City from the 1920s to the present day. New York developed its own Latin nightclubs and dance halls, and records were sold in the barrio in barbershops and pharmacies. The meeting of Cuban and Puerto Rican musicians produced a new Latin dance music called *salsa*, which has essentially overwhelmed traditional Puerto Rican music. In any case, Puerto Rican music was essentially ignored during the folk music revival of the '60s.

The Puerto Rican influx to New York was mostly predicated on a desire for economic improvement. Extensive Cuban immigration to Florida was based on political disagreements with the Castro regime. The Florida Cuban music scene has been dominated by Gloria and Emilio Estéfan and the Miami Sound Machine. This is a slick, commercial operation that has little to do with anything even remotely related to the folk revival. A more recent development is Ry Cooder's recordings and film with the Buena Vista Social Club. That particular musical sidebar will be discussed when

I turn to the current world music explosion, and the recent work of Ry Cooder, among others.

There are numerous musical sub-genres present in Central and South American music. In Paraguay, there are many harp and guitar combos, in Argentina it is customary to play the guitar in several dozen different tunings, and in Bolivia, Peru, Ecuador, and Chile there are many small combos that feature guitar and guitar-like instruments, percussion, and some sort of wood flute or panpipe. Many of these groups travel back and forth between their homelands, the United States, and Europe. I have seen such groups playing on the streets of Boulder and Denver, and in various cities in Belgium. Besides performing on the streets, they sell CDs. Even before his *Graceland* album, Paul Simon used one of these groups as the backup band for one of his songs. All of this music was essentially ignored during the folk song revival, and it still is. Other South American musical styles that have been exported to the United States include the cumbia from Columbia and the merengue from the Dominican Republic. And of course, Brazilian music is a persistent and important presence on both the American jazz and pop scenes.

In Central America, calypso music and steel-band music are styles that have their adherents in the United States. Other musical styles, like Haitian music, zouk music, and reggae, have had more influence in rock music than on American folk musicians,

A number of Mexican music styles are represented on the American music scene. Mariachi bands, with trumpets, guitars, and a bass guitar called a *guitarron,* are popular in various parts of the southwest. There are also regional styles present in Mexican music, like the harp-based Vera Cruz style that is relatively rare in the United States. Traditional Mexican ballads are called *corridos,* and it is these songs that come closest to relating to the subject matter of this work.

Christ Strachwitz of Arhoolie Records has reissued several dozen albums of Mexican-American music, together with booklets that extensively document the music. Corridos follow a particular structure. Maria Herrick-Sobek, in her book *Northward Bound: The Mexican Immigrant Experience in Ballad and Song,* points out that they often start with a direct message from the singer to the listener and the place, date, and name of the protagonist is then given. The song then transmits some sort of message or story, a farewell from the protagonist, and another from the singer. It is common for the song to contain the name of the author.

Originally, the subject matter of these corridos discussed everything from illegal border crossings to problems of immigrant workers, various romantic situations, and injustices committed by gringos. Other corridos celebrate heroes like union leader César Chavez, who organized migratory farm workers. There are even corridos that discuss John F. Kennedy.

Musician–scholar–author Elijah Wald has documented the use of corridos that discuss various aspects of the narcotics trade in his unusual book *Narcorrido: A Journey into the Music of Drugs, Guns and Guerrillas.* Wald hitchhiked and rode a bus all over Mexico, interviewing various corrido composers and performers. He traces the first narcorrido to 1934, but the boom in the style began the late 1960s, when Los Tigres del Norte (The Tigers of the North) adopted drugs as their primary subject matter.

Wald documents not only the creative aspects of narcorridos, but also the business itself. He discusses Musart, a Los Angeles record label that has done very well. Pedro Rivera, the owner, writes many of the songs, and his son Lupillo and daughter Jenny have written and recorded a number of their own songs as well. None of the family members are directly involved in the drug trade; they are simply capturing young people's interest in the drama of drugs and violence, in the same way that not all gangsta rap artists are in fact gangsters.

Another Mexican musical style is *conjunto,* or *tejano* music. This is the music that evolved during the 1920s and 1930s in and around San Antonio. Many well-known tejano musicians live there, including accordion virtuosos the Jiminez Brothers, Flaco, and Santiago. Norteño started with the accordion and bajo sexto, a version of the twelve-string guitar. As was the case with Cajun music, the accordion was adapted from German immigrants in Texas. During the 1940s and 1950s, the bands expanded to include bass and drums in the rhythm section. Most tejano artists are men, perhaps because the musicians, rightly or wrongly, are identified with the abuse of alcohol and drugs and a promiscuous lifestyle. Ry Cooder has used Flaco Jiminez on some of his albums and so has Paul Simon, bringing tejano music to wider audiences. Elijah Wald has pointed out that the San Antonio music has relatively little popularity in Mexico itself. Albuquerque is another center for this music, with local record labels and Spanish-speaking artists who record there.

The most prominent Mexican-American artist who has achieved some popularity in the folk music movement is Tish Hinojosa. She has recorded for several major record companies and has toured widely. She sings in both Spanish and English, and her songs move from the personal to the political. Alexandro Escovedo is another chicano artist who has had some success in the folk marketplace.

Sol y Tango is a Boston-based trio that performs Spanish and Caribbean music and has recorded a number of CDs for Rounder, including a bilingual children's album. They tour widely and are one of the few Spanish-speaking groups that has found a place in the revival movement.

Irene Ferrera is a Venezuelan singer who lived in the United States in the 1980s and '90s, but she quit the music business and returned to Venezuela in 2004.

Bertram Levy, a musician of considerable curiosity, played traditional southern mountain music on a nylon-strung banjo, mastered the concertina, and currently has an Argentine tango band that operates out of Seattle.

The inevitable question is why music of the Spanish-speaking groups hasn't achieved a stronger position in the folk music movement. Part of the problem is the lack of linguistic skills on the part of most Americans, college-educated or not. Denver, for example, has a very large Spanish-speaking population, comprising about thirty percent of the total demographic. The Swallow Hill Music Association is the second-largest folk music organization in the United States, and it has virtually no connection to the Spanish-speaking community, although it has presented Tish Hinojosa in concert. For some ten years, then-Swallow Hill director and musician John Neilsen, who is fluent in Spanish, was active in presenting several concerts by a Vera Cruz Trio for the organization. Since he left that position, the organization is basically unconnected to the Spanish community, with the exception of flamenco guitarist Rene Heredia. A couple of years ago, the Denver weekly *Westword* did a lengthy article on the Spanish-speaking music scene. It highlighted clubs, venues, musicians, and promoters that I had never heard of. I had only lived in the area for about twenty-five years!

The late Lalo Guerrero served as a mentor to the Mexican-American rock group Los Lobos. Guerrero was a very successful songwriter who recorded hundreds of songs in both Spanish and English and also wrote children's songs, which he recorded with Chipmunk-style children's background singers. Some of his songs were used in the Luis Valdez play and film *Zoot Suit,* which concerned the so-called zoot suit riots, where Mexican-Americans were attacked by American soldiers in 1942.

Los Lobos was founded in 1973 and had a major pop hit with the song "La Bomba" in 1987. This song was previously recorded by young Mexican-American rocker Richie Valens. Rather than moving deeper into the pop maelstrom, Los Lobos decided to stay in their community and investigate the roots of Mexican music. Although one could hardly call the band a folk group, they have done a wonderful job integrating various aspects of

Mexican, rock, blues, and country music into their repertoire. After achieving a considerable degree of pop-rock music success, Los Lobos immersed themselves in traditional Mexican music and instrumental styles, and did some recording with Guerrero. The one band that has best integrated Mexican-American musical styles into American music is Los Lobos.

*   *   *

Toward the end of the 1990s, the musicians' union became interested in the fact that there was a considerable recording scene in San Antonio but that none of the recording was done under union contracts. Musicians were paid absurdly small amounts of money and, of course, got no pension payments or other benefits. They began to organize the musicians and lobby the record companies, many of which were subsidiaries of major companies like Sony, which had agreements with the union. The major labels maintained that their subsidiaries were independent operations.

The union got major Hispanic political figures and artists to publicize the campaign, but the record companies held firm in their unwillingness to negotiate with the union. In 2001, the Hispanic caucus in Congress announced that it would hold congressional hearings about the exploitation of chicano musicians. The companies, after five years of stonewalling the union, all then signed union agreement guaranteeing a specified wage scale and benefits. This may be the most significant victory that the union achieved in many years. Unfortunately, it occurred at about the same time of the 9/11 tragedy. Consequently, there was essentially no public recognition of the victory.

NATIVE AMERICAN MUSIC

American Indian music can be classified in a number of musical styles. There are traditional songs sung in various tribal languages, usually accompanied by drums. Peyote songs are connected to the use of that drug and also are sung only to the accompaniment of drums. Powwow music is music sung at powwows, which are intertribal ceremonies. Powwows are not traditional, but are a development of the twentieth century. Some powwow songs are accompanied only by drums; others are "49ers," songs with something of a humorous twist.

Country and western music is popular on some reservations, and there are groups like the Sundowners who perform frequently on the Navajo reservation. Indian blues and rock bands started to appear during the 1960s.

XIT was popular on the reservations. They also toured in Europe and, oddly, they recorded for Motown Records. Redbone had a giant hit in the early 1970s with a song called "Come and Get Your Love," and the current blues band Indigenous has had some success. A number of artists move back and forth between these categories. Keith Secola's powwow song "Indian Kars" was a sensation on the two-dozen Indian radio stations. Bill Miller is a country-rock artist who tours nationally and has recorded several albums for Warner Brothers Records. Miller also plays the Indian flute. Jack Gladstone is more of a country-folk artist. He sings, writes songs, plays guitar, and tours with a slide show. Joanne Shenandoah has more of a folk approach and has been called the Indian Joan Baez.

Indian culture in general, and the music in particular, has been adopted by new adherents. They seem especially fascinated by the Indian flute, an instrument that was relatively rare in traditional Indian music. Some of the flute players, especially Kevin Locke, maintain a traditional approach, while R. Carlos Nakai has integrated his music with both jazz and classical styles. He has recorded a number of classical compositions written by Arizona State University professor James de Mar, and Nakai also has a side project called Jackalope, which is a flute-synthesizer combo. A number of the people playing the Indian flute and recording with it are not American Indians, but they tend to take pseudo-Indian names and capitalize on an alleged new age identity rooted in the earth.

A number of American Indian artists perform protest music. John Trudell, a former leader in the American Indian Movement (AIM), is probably the best known of these artists, who also include Red Thunder and Julian B. These artists perform spoken word music to rhythm backgrounds, some of which are essentially rap music forms. Actor-singer Floyd Westerman's protest songs are written and performed in a country music style.

Unlike Mexican-American music, American Indian music has some direct connections to the urban folk revival. Peter La Farge and Buffy Sainte-Marie have both recorded. La Farge's "The Ballad of Ira Hayes" became such a big hit for Johnny Cash that Cash recorded an entire album called *Bitter Tears.* Ira Hayes was one of the half-dozen American soldiers who raised the flag at Iwo Jima. When he returned home he was briefly lionized, then he became a forgotten alcoholic who drowned in a ditch while drunk. The album included a half-dozen songs by La Farge. La Farge was a fixture on the Greenwich Village folk scene. He recorded five albums for Folkways and one for Columbia, but none of them became popular.

Sainte-Marie wrote a number of outspoken protest songs, not only about American Indian rights, but also protesting the war in Vietnam. Her songs have gone back and forth between the subject of American Indian rights and into such rarified areas as title songs for movies, the latter coauthored with her late husband, Jack Nitzsche. She has also written music for the *Sesame Street* television show, on which she appeared regularly in the late 1970s.

Social Conditions

America Indians have the lowest average income of all American minority groups. Unemployment on reservations varies from fifty to eighty percent; housing and medical conditions are deplorable; drugs, alcohol, and gangs are yet another present from the white man. A number of folk artists have been involved in the movement to free Leonard Peltier, who is a serving a life term in prison for allegedly killing two FBI agents on the Sioux reservation. For whatever reason, most of the famous names in the folk field have stayed away from this and most other issues involving American Indians.

The American Indian Music Business

Folkways Records has a number of albums of traditional American Indian songs, but there are two companies that dominate the contemporary market. One is Canyon Records in Phoenix, which was originally founded to record "chicken scratch" music, a strange hybrid style that includes elements of German and Mexican music as well as 1950s rock 'n' roll. It has gone on to release music in all of the various musical styles mentioned above. Canyon's biggest artist is R. Carlos Nakai. Its biggest competitor is SOAR Records in Albuquerque. SOAR was founded by Tom Bee, who had been in the American Indian rock band XIT. He started the company by selling off a Rolex watch and has gone on from there to record dozens of albums. Bee started out selling cassettes out of his station wagon in the reservations. Bee's son Robbie has recorded several rap albums featuring two American Indians and an African American. Another interesting SOAR artist is South Dakotan Vince Two Eagles, who is an excellent guitarist and Indian flute player and writes some interesting protest songs. Boulder, Colorado-based Silver Wave Records has also released some American Indian music, including albums by Joanne Shenendoah.

Because the cost of recording and duplicating has become relatively reasonable, there are many American Indian artists who have issued their own albums, selling them at performances. Blackfire is a hard rock band that performs very strong protest music set to a beat somewhere between hard rock and punk music. Primitive Tribes is an Indian punk group in Flagstaff. In recent years, sisters Priscilla and Rita Coolidge have formed a trio called Walela, and Robbie Robertson, formerly a member of The Band, has recorded several albums for Capitol on Indian-related issues.

As far as the urban revival goes, sadly, there is little attention paid to American Indian artists or their music in folk festivals, coffeehouses, or on most of the folk record labels.

*   *   *

Sometime in the 1980s, I was driving from Denver to Los Angeles. I stayed at a friend's house in Durango, a small town in western Colorado. I woke up at six AM and resumed the long drive. I turned on the radio and heard the "all nations station." The format reminded me of the 1960s free-form FM radio stations in San Francisco. They mixed Indian music from various tribes with Willie Nelson and rock 'n' roll. At the time I was not even aware that there were native radio stations, but I later discovered there are twenty-six such radio stations, many on reservations.

OTHER GROUPS

Hawaiian music is a combination of dance, vocal chants, and the so-called slack-key guitar. Slack key is guitar in open tunings. It is played with a slide, but the slide is used to get a sweet almost syrupy sound rather than the intense style of Missisippi Delta guitar. According to ethnomusicologist Kip Lornell, in his excellent survey *Introducing Folk Music*, the guitar was brought to Hawai'i in the 1830s by Mexican and other Hispanic immigrants. By the late 1880s, Hawaiian musicians had gravitated to playing the guitar tuned to an open chord, just as blues musicians were doing in the United States. A Hawaiian guitarist named Joseph Kekuku supposedly started Hawaiian slide playing by holding the guitar on his knees and sliding a comb across the stings of the guitar.

During the 1960s, reacting to the popularization and stereotyping of Hawaiian music and dance in Hollywood and the relegation of music and dance to a tourist phenomenon, musicians began to revive traditional Hawaiian styles. "Gabby" Pahinui had kept the slack-key guitar tradition alive during this period, and he was active in the revival. Today, his sons perform together and they have recorded with American guitarists Ry Cooder and David Lindley. Bob Brozman is an American steel-guitar virtuoso. He has recorded a number of albums on his own and also in collaboration with Hawaiian musicians. Because Brozman is a familiar figure at folk festivals, many folk fans have heard Hawaiian guitar music. New age pianist George Winston is a big Hawaiian guitar fan, and he has released a number of albums on his Dancing Cat record label.

SCANDINAVIAN MUSIC

Scandinavian music traditions have been maintained in the areas of the United States where Norwegians, Danes, Fins, and Swedes live. Such native instruments as the hardanger fiddle, a fiddle with extra sympathetic strings that was popular in Norway, and the Finish *kantele*, a small zither-like instrument, were played in Scandinavian communities. There was also a dance music tradition.

In recent years, there has been a massive folk revival in Scandinavia and groups like the Finnish band Vartina have toured widely. The music integrates elements of traditional Scandinavian music with other musical styles. Although many of these bands have appeared at American folk festivals or concerts, so far the groups playing this music are generally "imported."

POLKA BANDS

Polka bands usually feature accordion, horns, and a drummer. Polka music is dance music that is found in much of the midwestern United States. There are differences in the instrumentation of these bands according to whether the music is German, Scandinavian, Polish, or if it comes from other areas of Eastern Europe. For example, the Slovenians prefer the accordion to the concertina, the Dutch and Czechs add tuba or sousaphone, while the Norwegians feature the fiddle. This is a working-class music that is still featured in taverns and social clubs throughout the midwest, and the artists often sell their own recordings during performances.

The American urban revivalist Rik Palieri has learned to play the Polish bagpipes by studying with teachers in Poland. Rik tours widely in the United States and Europe.

RECENT WORLD MUSIC ADAPTATIONS

There has been an increasing amount of Asian immigration to the United States since the end of the war in Vietnam. Music from Vietnam, Laos, Cambodia, Thailand, China, and Japan can be found wherever these groups have settled. Most of the music remains invisible in the folk revival, although a few festivals, such as the Seattle Folk Life Festival and the festival sponsored by the Smithsonian Institute in Washington, have featured a variety of groups from various ethnic communities. The presence of specific remarkable musicians has led to a widespread interest in their music. For example, when African drummer Abbo Addy moved to Portland, Oregon, a community of drummers and even music stores developed.

Some ethnomusicology departments of colleges, like the programs at UCLA and the University of Washington, import visiting professors and create ensembles that are dedicated to preserving such far-flung traditions as Javanese gamelan orchestras. Duquesne University in Pittsburgh has a tamburitza ensemble that was established in 1937. They tour nationally, performing music from various parts of Eastern Europe. This particular ensemble is not made up of music students, but of interested students in other disciplines.

THE BRITISH FOLK REVIVAL

The folk music revival in England is another subject that is beyond the scope of this work; however, it is important to underscore some of the connections between the American and British revivals. There was a certain amount of intermarriage—British singers or bands touring in the United States, and vice versa. There were also Americans who moved to England, like Jackson C. Frank and African American singer Doris Henderson. American musician–scholar Jennifer Cutting studied English folk song in England. Ramblin' Jack Elliott lived in England throughout the mid-1950s, and he performed with American expatriate banjo player Derroll Adams, who remained in Europe when Elliott returned to the States in 1961.

Part of the impetus for the British revival of the 1960s was Alan Lomax's British sojourn during the period from 1949 to 1958. Lomax immediately fell in with playwright Ewan MacColl and folk song scholar A. L. Lloyd. According to Breeta Sweers's book *Electric Folk*, MacColl, under Lomax's influence, sought out traditional English and Scottish songs.

Since Lloyd and MacColl were both communists, they shared some of Lomax's politically radical leanings as well. English scholar Michael Brocken has recently written a book on the British revival that points out the factional disputes in the British folksong revival. They ranged from the ballad enthusiasts centered in the English Folk Song and Dance Society, to the politically motivated Lloyd and MacColl, and to the more pop-oriented folk-rock musicians like the artists in Fairport Convention and Steeleye Span. The ballad protagonists were almost violently antipolitical, while Lloyd and MacColl were extremely wary of any pop music connection (despite the fact that several of MacColl's songs, especially "The First Time Ever I Saw Your Face," became successful pop-rock recordings by others).

England also experienced a brief but important craze for skiffle music with Lonnie Donegan's 1954 hit version of Leadbelly's version of "Rock Island Line." The skiffle bands used guitars, banjos, and homemade instruments like the "tea chest" one-string basses. The craze led to a 1957 BBC radio show that had an audience of two and a half million. More importantly, it inspired numerous English youth, including the Beatles, to take up music as a possible profession. Like the punk music that emerged some twenty years later, it clearly didn't require advanced musical training or skills to play or sing this music.

MacColl turned against the performance of American music by British artists. Partly influenced by his wife, Peggy Seeger, who found British blues performances a bit grotesque, MacColl founded one of the first folk clubs and he initiated a policy that performers could only sing songs that reflected the place where they had grown up. In May of 1961, there were forty folk clubs and by May of 1962, there were eighty-one such clubs. MacColl took on the role of commisar of folk culture and his edict proved influential, even though it provoked some resentment. It strongly influenced young singers to abandon the American model and to seek out their own music. There were a number of young artists on the scene, including Steve Benbow, Robin Hall and Jimmy McGregor, Martin Carthy, Davy Graham, Bert Jansch, and John Renbourn. MacColl also wrote and produced a series of radio ballads for the BBC. The ballads focused on various occupations and included much traditional music, performed by MacColl, Peggy Seeger, and others.

In the late 1950s, American folklorist Kenneth Goldstein issued a multivolume series of recordings of Lloyd and MacColl singing Childe ballads on Riverside Records. Goldstein also issued other recordings by Lloyd and MacColl, including an influential album of sea shanties. These albums were not big sellers, but they were instrumental in making the young

American revivalists aware of the influence of English folk song on American folk music. In 1961, Pete Seeger was finally able to get a passport after his travails with the American government, and he performed an influential concert at the Albert Hall in London.

In 1965, guitarist Davy Graham recorded an album called *Folk, Blues and Beyond.* The album was released by British Decca Records and Graham's fusion of folk, blues, jazz, and Indian music influences on guitar was extremely influential in England. Graham wrote an instrumental called "Anji," which Paul Simon recorded on *Sounds of Silence,* and which Bert Jansch also plays. The guitar gauntlet was taken up by Bert Jansch and John Renbourn, who developed what became referred to as "baroque guitar." This finger-style approach to the guitar incorporated the influences of blues and lute music.

*   *   *

In 1965, I was on vacation in Europe. I had read about Les Cousines somewhere, and my wife and I went to this rather dingy club in a basement on Greek Street. Davy Graham was the featured performer. He did an exceptionally long set, and although I was intrigued by his guitar playing, I was considerably less excited by his singing. His stage persona was something between incoherence and a drug-induced haze. The British audience was incredibly respectful during the set, hardly making a peep. At the next table from us were four young French tourists. They delivered a running commentary in French on the music for over a half hour. Whenever Graham would start a new song, they would say something to the effect of "What, another one, when is this bastard going to quit? Tell him to get out of here." For some reason the contrast between the almost sycophantish respect of the British audience with the rude nastiness of the French tourists had a strong effect on me. I couldn't decide whether to tell them to shut up or tell them that, to a point, I agreed with them.

ELECTRIC FOLK

Britain's Springfields and Australia's Seekers scored worldwide hits with their pop-folk sounds. The versatile Dusty Springfield went on to forge a successful career in R&B-flavored pop music. The Seekers featured the dynamic vocals of Judith Durham and had a good run in the pop-folk world.

Jansch and Renbourn recorded a number of albums together and separately. They teamed up with singer Jacqui McShee, bassist Danny
Thompson, and drummer Terry Cox to form the band Pentangle. Pentangle, along with Fairport Convention and then Steeleye Span, pioneered a
musical style that scholar Britta Sweers called *electric folk*. She uses that
term rather than "folk rock" because these groups were performing folk or
folk-based music using electric instruments, rather than original rock
songs, as Dylan was doing, in a style related to folk music.

All of these groups had a good ride during the late 1960s. They had
records on the British charts and toured widely in America as well as in
Europe. Pentangle maintained the same personnel throughout their heyday from 1968 until 1972. Jansch dropped out because of his drinking
problems but would occasionally return to tour with the group. Renbourn
left to pursue solo projects as well as an occasional duo with American
blues guitarist Stefan Grossman. McShee occasionally tours with the
group as the only original member, using the name Jacqui McShee's Pentangle. As I am writing this book in 2005, she is doing an American tour
with Renbourn.

*   *   *

I had a good friend in Denver named Wesley Westbrooks. Westbrooks
was a composer of gospel songs, several of which were recorded by the
Staples Singers. One of these songs was called "Hear My Call Here." It
was about an experience Wesley's daughter Tara had. She saw white kids
in Denver throwing snowballs at black kids as they were boarding a school
bus to be bused to a school in a white neighborhood. Wesley cleaned air-
planes for United Air Lines in Denver, and with his flying privileges he
would fly to Chicago and teach songs to Pop Staples. One early morning
while working at the airport, he came up with the song describing what
his daughter had seen. One of the songs they recorded was "Hear My Call
Here." Apparently, the Pentangle got hold of the record, learned the song,
and recorded it.

Wes was very moved by the recording. He felt that it was a perfect rep-
resentation of what he had been hearing in his head.

*   *   *

Any number of important British musicians and singers have passed
through Fairport and Steeleye, including dynamic guitarist–songwriter
Richard Thompson, singer–songwriter Sandy Denny, Martin Carthy,
fiddler–mandolinist Dave Swarbrick, singer Ian Matthews, singer Maddy

Prior, and vocalist–bass player Ashley Hutchings. *Dirty Linen*, one of two nationally distributed American folk music magazines, was originally founded in 1981 as a Fairport fanzine.

The electric folk movement certainly paralleled the American folk-rock explosion, but it was much more specifically rooted in folk song traditions. Some of the American folk-rock bands would occasionally perform folk material, such as Jefferson Airplane's version of "The Blood Stained Bandits" (titled "Good Shepherd"), but essentially they were songwriters. From the business aspect of things, all three of the British groups began their recording careers on independent record labels and then moved on to major labels. Pentangle broke up after one album for Warner Brothers, Fairport went from independent labels Island Records, and Steeleye moved from independent labels to Chrysalis. Pentangle and Steeleye were managed by American expatriate Jo Lustig, who apparently had some of the aggressiveness and nastiness of his American compatriot Albert Grossman. By the early 1970s the electric folk movement had peaked, and the major labels lost interest in the bands. All of them still exist, albeit as part-time operations. Fairport performs at an annual festival that draws close to twenty-thousand people.

Influence

Although American folk song is essentially a fusion of British and African American musical styles, I think it is fair to say that the American folk revival had more influence on the English revival than the other way around. Certainly, MacColl and Lloyd had an influence on the revival, and the various British guitarists and folk-rock groups did as well. Bob Dylan, however, seemed to influence everyone on both sides of the water.

MEANWHILE, BACK IN CANADA

Canada is larger than the United States in area, but has about one-tenth of its population. The distances between most of the major Canadian cities are huge, which makes it difficult for musicians to make a living through touring. Consequently, many Canadians gravitate to the United States for the obvious economic advantages. Some, like Joni Mitchell and Neil Young, stay in the States. Others, like Bruce Cockburn, Gordon Lightfoot, and Raffi, tour extensively in the States but live in Canada. Ian and Sylvia had dual residency for a while before returning to Canada. Many more Canadian folk musicians are comparatively unknown in the United States.

Canadian folk styles include many of the same influences as those found in the United States. There are singer–songwriters such as Rita McNeil, Murray McLauchlan, Bob Bossin, and Marie Lynn Hammond, a number of children's artists, and women's music artists like Heather Bishop, Ferron, and Lucie Blue Tremblay. Folk-rock artists the Cowboy Junkies have definitely developed an audience for their music in both the United States and Canada. There are Celtic artists such as Natalie McMaster and Cape Breton fiddlers, and any number of fine instrumentalists such as multi-instrumentalist Harry Manx or the excellent guitarist Amos Garrett. Quebecois musicians are one unique part of the Canadian folk scene; they sing in French and seem to have the same energy as Celtic bands.

There is something quirky and left-of-center about the Canadian songwriters and some of the younger bands. The Be Good Tanyas and the Dukhs are two groups that are difficult to characterize, but sound only like themselves. Kate and Anna McGarrigle are sisters who have been singing and writing their bilingual songs for some years now in Montreal, and Anna's song "Heart Like a Wheel" was a big hit for Linda Ronstadt.

The Canadian folk scene has been nurtured by a series of summer music festivals that present music from all over the world but particularly feature Canadian artists. The Vancouver and Winnipeg festivals are enormous events and are partly funded by the government. The government also has a unique program called FACTOR. It began when laws were passed that compel radio stations to play a certain percentage of Canadian music on the radio. The record companies replied that there weren't enough Canadian records being produced to enable them to accomplish this. The government then set up the FACTOR fund. It provides grant support to help artists make records. If the records make money, then the money must be returned to the fund. The Be Good Tanyas, for example, have benefited from this fund. It is difficult to imagine the government of the United States offering similar financial support for folk (or rock) music.

Most of the major American record labels have Canadian companies as well. My American friend Tom May, for example, made his first records for Capital of Canada while he was living in Toronto. There are also several important independent record labels, notably Stony Plain. Northern Blues is a relatively new company that specializes in contemporary blues recordings.

The strongest Canadian influence on the American folk scene has been through children's music, as I have already discussed in the section on children's music.

chapter 12

The Folk-Music Business

As contradictory a notion as it might seem, there is indeed a folk music business. Obviously, people like Pete Seeger and Leadbelly were doing paid gigs as early as the late 1930s or early 1940s, but I suppose we can trace the real beginnings of a folk-music business infrastructure to the hit recordings of the Weavers, beginning in 1949. At that point, it became clear that just as pop or jazz musicians could perform and record, so could folk musicians, or at least pop-folk artists. The Weavers recorded for Decca, a major label, and the original group had two managers, Harold Leventhal and Pete Kameron. Music publishing companies were set up to publish their original compositions and arrangements of folk songs.

Clearly there was money to be made, and when Harry Belafonte, followed by the Kingston Trio and its various progeny, emerged, the folk business was off to the races. Although the popularity of folk-based music is not as great today, the infrastructure of the business has expanded in a variety of ways.

ORGANIZATIONS

Organizations devoted to the spread of folk music include both local and national groups. Folklore societies, or organizations with names such as the "friends of folk music," exist in many major cities. These groups have meetings, publish newsletters, and sponsor song circles where people sing with one another; they promote jam sessions and open microphones at local clubs, and organize concerts of local and visiting musicians. Not all of the local organizations fulfill all of these functions, and some go further. The Seattle Folklore Society, for example, has released a CD of the work of some of its members and has sponsored tours that group several acts together in a single performance.

In Chicago and Denver, there are two large nonprofit organizations that give music lessons and sponsor concerts and master classes. Both of them own their own buildings. The Old Town School of Music in Chicago also owns a music store, while the Swallow Hill Music Association operates a recording studio. Both groups operate with financing from their members and through grants and contributions. A number of revival musicians are supported by these organizations, mostly through giving lessons. Both organizations have a full-time paid staff as well. A much smaller organization exists on Vashon Island near Seattle. Although other cities have discussed forming similar organizations, I am not aware of any others that have done so. Victory Music is a co-op in the Seattle–Tacoma area that sponsors concerts and open-mic nights at local clubs, but it does not own a performance and teaching facility.

The Folk Alliance

The North American Folk Alliance was founded in 1989. Since then, the organization has run annual conferences that include workshops on the business aspects of folk music, panels on subjects of interest, and an exhibition area that has booths run by record companies, managers and agents, CD pressers, artists, and anyone who wishes to reach the several thousand people who attend the conference. Attendees include all of these groups plus many amateur musicians, scholars, and fans. There are also regional conferences held in various parts of the United States. The conferences move back and forth between different cities, although the organization plans to find a permanent site in Memphis. Every few years the conference moves to Canada, because the organization represents members from Canada as well as the United States. The paid staff of the organization works out of suburban Washington, D.C.

The national conference features musical showcases, and all members are eligible, although inevitably most applications are not accepted. For those who don't make it, there are many informal showcases available, sponsored by various groups such as record companies or performing rights groups.

There are 2,400 members of the organization. In addition to the conference, the organization gives lifetime achievement awards, sponsors showcases where artists perform, provides lists of business resources for members, and lobbies on behalf of the membership in order to achieve greater government support for the folk arts.

Because the logistics of running a four-day conference in a different city each year have been complex, attendance at the conferences has become relatively expensive. For those who do not live in the city where the conference is located, by the time conference fees, exhibition fees, hotel rooms, and airfare are added in the cost of attending the conference can be as high as $1,000. Although a few scholarships are available, this is rather a high cost for young or struggling performers. This year, the organization announced that after 2006, the conference will always be held in Memphis, except for periodic visits to Canadian cities. Perhaps this will reduce some of these expenses. There are also far more conference attendees and exhibitors who are artists than record companies or agents and managers. The nonofficial showcases are of questionable value because so many of them occur simultaneously that the audiences are relatively small.

Yet the conferences are enjoyable to many of the attendees because people from different parts of North America who rarely see one another get together and there are many informal jam everywhere.

IBMA

The bluegrass community has its own organization, the International Bluegrass Music Association. It currently boasts over 2,500 members, and has moved its headquarters to Nashville, the center of country music. Like the Folk Alliance, it has an annual conference with exhibits and educational events, and gives awards.

Local 1000, American Federation of Musicians

For many years, the American Federation of Musicians required musicians to join a local of the union in the location where they lived and worked. Consequently, many folksingers didn't bother to join the musicians' union. This was particularly ironic, since many of them were singing songs about unions and strikes. Folksingers were traveling musicians who worked in many different localities and they lobbied to establish their own local.

The union has a number of benefits, including pension provisions; contract guarantees, which give members protection if an employer fails to honor a contract; and health, dental, and instrument insurance. Recording companies are subject to national agreements with the union. These agreements provide pension contributions, wage minimums, and bonus funds based on the sales of all records. Because the folk labels are relatively small companies, most of them are not union signatories, and therefore do not offer these benefits.

RECORD COMPANIES, MUSIC PUBLISHERS,
AND PERFORMANCE RIGHTS

There are a handful of relatively small record companies that issue the bulk of folk-based recordings. The largest of these companies, Rounder, has issued a number of successful recordings, notably its million-selling Alison Krauss CDs. They are also embarking on a major reissue of Alan Lomax's field recordings, which will eventually amount to over one hundred and fifty albums. Other companies active in the folk world are Minneapolis' Red House Records, Smithsonian-Folkways—the successor to Moe Asch's Folkways label—Appleseed Records, Shanachie Records, June Appal Records, and Folk Era/Wind River Records. Many recordings from the 1960s revival have been reissued on the Fantasy label, which owns Riverside and Prestige Records (now owned by Concord Records), or on Laser Light, which has picked up Tradition Records and other labels.

Specific genres of folk-based music have their own labels, such as Sugar Hill for bluegrass, Alligator for blues, and County for old-time music. Singer–songwriters are the artists most apt to end up with major label contracts, because their records usually have the biggest commercial potential.

Very few folk musicians receive royalties of any significance. This is a subject all its own. If you wish to learn more about how this works (or doesn't work), I recommend the autobiography of Ruth Brown. Ms. Brown was the first big R&B artist to record for Atlantic in the 1950s. She never received a penny in royalties until a chance meeting with a corporate lawyer named Howell Begle. Begle enlisted Jesse Jackson and the black congressional coalition to pressure record companies to pay past royalties, plus new ones based upon CD reissues, and to contribute to the founding of the Rhythm & Blues Foundation. That organization celebrates R&B music and assists ill or poverty-stricken R&B musicians.

Several of the Grammy categories involve folk and folk-related musical styles, like world music and bluegrass. In order to participate in the Grammy Awards, a voter must have worked on a half-dozen recordings. Since there are multiple nominations in every category, despite the organization's proclamations, it is usually the popular records that win the award, whether or not they are the most artistically interesting, though possibly obscure, recordings.

Music publishing involves a number of royalties that are paid to the songwriter and music arranger. In the folk music heyday of the 1960s, and even to some extent today, the rearranging of traditional songs results in the payment of royalties for these adaptations. Among the rights available to songwriters are performing rights, paid through ASCAP, BMI, and SESAC. Folk music records generally do not show up with much frequency in the surveys of these organizations, which focus on commercial radio stations. In recognition of this problem, ASCAP has a Special Awards program that pays money to songwriters who fill out applications showing that their music is actively performed in public. SESAC also pays an advance for songs that are on recordings that have national distribution. Oddly, when folk songs appear on radio in foreign countries, the writer usually *does* get paid. Many countries own and control radio stations and they pay on all airplay, rather than through the sophisticated logging systems that ASCAP, BMI, and SESAC use. These logging systems are akin to polling in that they are representational rather than specifically accurate.

*　　*　　*

An example of this process is something that happened to my fellow Journeyman, Scott McKenzie. He recorded one of the biggest pop hits of all time, John Phillips's "If You Go to San Francisco (Be Sure to Wear Some Flowers in Your Hair)" in 1967. The record sold over thirteen million copies worldwide, and when the CD format appeared it was placed on dozens of compilation reissue albums. For many years, Scott wasn't paid for any of these reissues, until Lou Adler, who had produced the record along with many, many other hits, decided that he wanted to get paid. Scott got a sizeable settlement.

Bob Bowers is an arranger–record producer who produced a number of albums with the Serendipity Singers, a band that had a few hit records and performed widely. A number of these albums have been reissued on CD in the Unite States and Europe, and Bob has gone to great lengths to pursue royalties that are obviously owed to them. So far this knight's quest has not proved successful.

The point is that record companies indulge in what I like to call "the culture of nonpayment." Many of them seem to regard royalties as a privilege, rather than a contractual necessity. At a music business conference that I attended, a business manager for a major rock group remarked that he had experienced similar problems in collecting royalties.

MAGAZINES

There are two national magazines devoted to folk music, *Dirty Linen* and *Sing Out! Sing Out!* is the heir to the People's Songs mantle, although over the years it has become much less politically oriented. Both magazines have feature articles, record reviews, and advertisements for records. There are also some regional publications, like the *Victory Review* in the Tacoma–Seattle area, that promote folk-based music in a particular section of the country. Other magazines, like the *Banjo Newsletter, Acoustic Guitar,* or the *Old Time Herald,* deal with specific musical instruments used in folk-based music. The British magazine *Folk Roots* covers folk music with a world music emphasis. Many of the local folk societies, including the San Francisco Folk Music Club and the Portland Folk Music Society, publish periodic newsletters.

MUSICAL INSTRUMENTS

Along with the folk revival came a tremendous interest in folk instruments. The guitar is the most popular folk instrument, and sales are in the hundreds of thousands. Martin and Gibson were the traditionally strong names in the field, but Taylor has made a strong impact and employs a half-dozen players, including Artie Traum and Chris Proctor, as clinicians. Fender, Guild, Larrivee, and Takoma also are important players in the marketplace. Such smaller companies as Collings, Breedlove, Gallagher, Goodall, Huss & Dalton, and Santa Cruz sell guitars that are closer to the handmade instruments that some players prefer. Similarly, companies like Deering, Gibson, and Ome are the major players in the banjo market. Smaller companies like Stelling, Ramsey, and Wildwood produce a more limited number of instruments. Gibson is one of the important mandolin manufacturers, and Weber, Rigel, and Mid-Missouri are other important makers.

A large part of the moderate-to-medium-priced instruments are imported from China under various brand names. Saga and Johnson are two of the companies that sell these instruments in the United States. Yamaha and Takamine are two Asian-owned companies that sell thousands of guitars in the United States.

Some of the more famous musicians, particularly guitarists, endorse certain instruments or even help to design models named after them. Similarly there are a half-dozen string makers that provide strings for musicians. The string makers, instrument builders, and such accessory makers as Rick Shubb, Capos, and Breezy Ridge exhibit at the various musical conferences and also advertise in the folk magazines. As such, they are important to the music scene. String companies also use famous players as endorsers.

PRINT MUSIC

In the original folk boom, Oak Publications was the primary company publishing instruction books for folk instruments or styles of playing. Their output has been surpassed by Mel Bay Publications, Hal Leonard, and Alfred Music. Alfred has also recently acquired the print division of the giant Warner Brothers Music. Many of the instruction books contain either CDs or DVDs, and they have helped two whole generations of players to learn the styles of important traditional musicians, as well as some of the innovative new artists in the field. One of the pioneers in folk and blues guitar instruction was People's Songs veteran guitarist and New Yorker Jerry Silverman, who wrote a number of instructional books for Oaks and others.

One of the great success stories of the folk business has been the odyssey of Homespun Tapes. The company was started by Happy Traum when some of his students expressed frustration at his abandoning their lessons when he went on tour. He started to duplicate reel-to-reel tapes in his living room.

Over a thirty-year period, operating out of his home base in Woodstock, New York, Happy has expanded through cassettes, CDs, DVDs, and instruction books. Among the many artists offering instructional work through his company are Béla Fleck, Mike Seeger, Artie Traum, and Happy himself.

Several other companies compete with Homespun Tapes. Guitarist Arlen Roth's Hot Licks and Ridge Runner in Texas are two companies that sell a number of instructional DVDs and CDs.

MUSIC STORES

Earlier in the book I discussed how such music stores as the Denver Folklore Center provide a network of instruction, gigs, and a supportive community for folk musicians. There are far too many of these stores to mention each one by name, but the Folk Music Center in Claremont, California, the Blue Guitar Workshop in San Diego, the Folklore Center in Colorado Springs, the Candyman in Santa Fe, Matt Umanov in New

York, Dusty Strings and McCabe's in Santa Monica, Westwood Music in Los Angeles, Intermountain Banjo and Guitar in Salt Lake City, the Folkstore in Seattle, and Rufus' Guitar Shop in Vancouver, among many others, are places where such a community has developed.

Elderly Instruments in Lansing, Michigan, is possibly the largest and most successful of all these stores. It is situated in a huge building and has a large mail-order catalog of books, records, and musical instruments. Some other stores, like Gruhn Guitars in Nashville; the Mandolin Brothers in Staten Island, New York; Vintage Instruments in Philadelphia; and Norm's Rare Guitars in Reseda, California, are shops that specialize in the vintage instruments that so many folk musicians covet.

Despite the popularity of acoustic instruments, many of these stores are experiencing problems due to the proliferation of big-box chain stores like Guitar Center, mail-order discount catalogs, and the dozens of individual entrepreneurs who sell instruments on eBay. None of these operations do anything to promote a sense of community, and if they drive acoustic music stores out of business, it will severely impact the folk music movement.

RADIO

Folk radio shows are generally found on noncommercial NPR, community radio stations, or satellite radio. Some of these folk disc jockeys, such as Mary Cliff in Washington, D.C., Howard and Roz Larman in Los Angeles, Gene Shay in Philadelphia, Matt Watroba in Detroit, and Norm Pellegrini in Chicago, have been on the air for years. Many local stations, like KBOO in Portland, Oregon, have folk shows at specific times of day.

Two other outlets also exist for folk-based music. One is the so-called American format, formerly known as AAA Radio. These are stations that feature a free-flowing roots-based musical format that allows the inclusion of folk-based music. The other radio possibility is through syndicated radio. Nick Forster's *E Town* program, based in Boulder, Colorado, features a great deal of acoustic music. Songwriter–performer Tom May has a show called *River City Folk* that started out in Omaha. Tom moved to the Portland, Oregon, area several years ago, and the show is now carried through the WFMT satellite. He records the show in various locales.

Garrison Keilor's *Prairie Home Companion* has been an extremely successful radio show for years. It is not a music show as such, but it features many musicians and there is a quality house band that includes such excellent musicians as guitarist Pat Donahue and fiddler Andy Stein.

GIGS AND THE BUSINESS OF GIGS

A few years ago, Mike Seeger made a casual remark to me when I asked him how he was doing. He commented that the folk music pie was about the same size, but the number of people sitting at the table had grown much larger. Since folk is a niche market in terms of the overall market for nonclassical music, the sort of coffeehouses and clubs where performers work don't tend to draw large audiences or pay serious money. There are a dozen booking agents who specialize in folk-music gigs, like Folklore Productions in Santa Monica or Real People's Music in Chicago. They are able to book performers at art centers, colleges, and folk festivals. It is possible for performers to attempt this on their own, but it is a difficult process requiring patience and persistent follow-up. Folk festivals are particularly good gigs, not necessarily because they pay that well, but because the audiences are very large. Most of them are outdoors, and not all artists are at their best in outdoor venues, where volume may be more important than subtle artistry. Many Borders bookstores and Starbucks coffee shops feature live music, and folklore societies often sponsor concerts as well.

With the advent of home recording and computers, it is possible to make CDs at a relatively modest cost. Without CDs, it is almost impossible to get gigs of any consequence. Some innovative musicians survive by creating alternative markets for their music. These include church work, writing instructional materials for the music print publishers listed above, and attempting to get music into film and television. There are more and more prerecorded songs and instrumentals used in movies and cable-TV programs. Unfortunately, this work is best accessed by agents who deal with these outlets.

Grants are another possibility for musicians. The NEA has various grant programs in the Folk Arts. They typically go to traditional musicians, not to revivalists. Their largest grants are the $20,000 Folk Heritage grants. Some of the artists who received these awards in recent years include fiddler Kevin Burke, blues man David "Honeyboy" Edwards, and cowboy singer Don Walser. Many of the grants, which date from Bess Lomax Hawes's tenure as head of the Folk Arts program, go to preserve traditional folk art forms. They not only provide money for artists, but also finance teacher-student relationships that enable traditions to continue to thrive. One of the rare revivalists to receive an award was dobro player Jerry Douglas in 2004. Since Douglas is a successful studio musician in Nashville, I would have to regard this as a very peculiar choice.

The very idea of the folk business becoming a business is probably enough to give any folk musician with a conscience serious second thoughts. But the fact is that making a living as a musician is indeed a serious business. In the folk community, some of the folk festivals, like the Seattle Folk Life Festival, are wonderful events, but they do not pay musicians. This works out for some of the part-time ethnic musicians who live in the area, but it is a serious problem for those who actually want to make a living playing music. It is also difficult to understand how an event with a large budget cannot allocate money for professional musicians. Because folk music for many participants and fans involves a feeling of a community, many people have difficulty factoring money into the equation.

*   *   *

Recently I found a restaurant near where I live in Portland, Oregon. It does not pay musicians, but requires them to sign a contract. The artist is required to do his/her own publicity and is strongly leaned upon to encourage friends to come to this not inexpensive restaurant. In return, musicians get a fifty percent discount on food, two free soft drinks, and are allowed to set up a tip jar and to sell CDs. I was tempted to ask the owner if they would like to cook at my club. All the food would be free, so I couldn't pay them, but I'd encourage them to invite all their friends and I'd give them a fifty percent discount on CDs!

chapter 13

Up to Now

American popular music went through various stylistic changes during the 1970s and 1980s. Rock 'n' roll moved from folk-rock to art rock, and punk music developed as a sort of allergic reaction to the art rock bands, who were mostly British. The basic punk ethic was to keep music as simple and loud as possible. If the art rockers were proud of their training and technical skills, then the basic punk ethic maintained that "anyone could do this." Meanwhile, the singer–songwriter movement experienced a temporary slump, punk was refined into New Wave, glam rock had its day, and heavy metal music, and then rap, came into vogue. Interest in folk music became more and more specialized by genre, and it was definitely a niche market.

But the musical climate was changing. The punk ethic wasn't all that different from what brought people into folk music in the first place. Most of the pop-folk groups were defunct or reduced to playing secondary gigs. Many of the bands, like '50s and '60s rock bands, began to tour with replacement members, and in some cases there were more replacements than founding members.

During the early 1980s, there was a brief vogue for reviving traditional country music. Ricky Skaggs was the leader of the pack and he moved from country-folk labels like Rounder and Sugar Hill to Columbia Records subsidiary Epic. Ricky had played in Emmy Lou Harris's band. He had authentic bluegrass musical chops, and it was odd to hear hit country records with his high, lonesome singing style and hot bluegrass licks along with it.

The younger artists who started to infiltrate both rock and country music were much more open-minded about musical style than the early revivalists had been. Some of them were rockers as teenagers, but they also had some familiarity with country and folk music. By the mid-1980s bands like the Jayhawks and Uncle Tupelo were developing a genre that became known as "alternative country." In 1995, *No Depression* magazine was born. The magazine was named after a Carter Family song that was re-

recorded by Uncle Tupelo. The movement was informed by Harry Smith's old *Anthology* reissues on Folkways and it covered a broad musical spectrum. It even made fun of itself, something the sincere early revivalists were loath to do. A collection of articles from the magazine is titled *No Depression: An Introduction to Alternative Country Music. Whatever That Is.*

Another revolution was going on in the bluegrass movement itself. Béla Fleck carried the innovations of Bill Keith and Bobby Thompson to a whole new level. After studying with Tony Trischka, himself an innovative and creative banjoist, Fleck set the bluegrass world on its ear. His first records were for Rounder and then in 1981, he joined the leading newgrass band, the innovative New Grass Revival, which featured Sam Bush on mandolin and John Cowan on vocals. During the 1980s, the bluegrass group was divided between the older, more traditionally oriented musicians and the younger, longhaired performers. It paralleled what had happened in jazz when bebop came along; the older swing and Dixieland musicians didn't care for the music and felt threatened by its complexity.

Soon, the younger musicians turned to the newer styles and the newgrass players moved farther and farther to the musical left wing. In 1988, Béla Fleck started his own group, the Flecktones, which featured the Wooten Brothers playing electric bass and an electronically triggered drum set. He also began to integrate jazz influences into the music, adding oboe and English-horn player Paul McCandless to the band. Meanwhile, Mark O'Connor cut down on his studio work and started performing fiddle concertos with symphony orchestras. He formed a trio with cellist Yo Yo Ma and bass player Edgar Meyer, and they played folk-based classical music together, culminating in the best-selling classical crossover album, *Appalachian Waltz.* Fleck has also recorded classical music with Meyer.

It seemed as though the musical floodgates had opened; musical styles that were always considered to be very specific became part of larger musical picture. On the West Coast, a bunch of musicians were attempting to stir the musical pot by stirring in helpings of rock, country music, folk music, and jazz.

David Grisman is a virtuoso mandolin player. In his East Coast days in the mid-1960s, Grisman performed with the Even Dozen Jug Band, and later he and guitarist-singer Rowan were in the psychedelic folk-rock band Earth Opera. During the 1970s, he was in the bluegrass band Old and in the Way with Grateful Dead member Jerry Garcia. From there, Grisman essentially invented a folk-jazz style that became known as "Dawg music." Grisman's original quintet featured superb guitarist Tony Rice and fiddle virtuoso Mark O'Connor. Fiddler Darol Anger and mandolinist Mike

Marshall are also alumni of the group, which was a sort of chamber folk-rock-jazz quintet loosely reflecting the influence of Django Reinhardt and Stéphan Grappelli and the Hot Club of France. Grisman also started his own Acoustic Disc label, largely to release mandolin music of his own and the work of other, often neglected, artists.

Among a bunch of other forward-thinking West Coast musicians, banjoist–guitarists Herb Pederson and Bernie Leadon and mandolinist Chris Hillman were in and out of various folk–country–rock groups, including the massively successful Eagles, the Flying Burrito Brothers, the Byrds, and the Desert Rose Band. If it was hard to define folk music before the '60s revival, it became next to impossible by the end of the 1970s.

THE RETURN OF THE SINGER–SONGWRITERS

During the mid to late 1980s, another group of singer–songwriters emerged. For some reason, the most popular of these artists were women. 10,000 Maniacs featured Natalie Merchant. The band began recording for Elektra in 1985 and they sang about a variety of political and social issues, such as child abuse, the criminal justice system, and the environment. Merchant left the band to pursue a solo career in 1992.

Suzanne Vega and Tracy Chapman were among the most important of the singer–songwriter soloists, and their songs touch on social issues as well as personal odysseys. Chapman's records feature relatively simple productions, with her twelve-string guitar as the centerpiece. Her songs "Fast Car" and "Talking 'bout a Revolution" were extremely successful. Of all the singer–songwriters, her songs are possibly the closest to the style of the urban revival, both in terms of lyrical content and her consistent use of the twelve-string guitar as the musical centerpiece of the songs. Vega's song "Luka" brought the issue of child abuse to the radio waves of America. Californian Kate Wolf is less well-known, partly because of her premature death in 1986. She and her songs still retain a sizeable niche audience.

Amy Ray and Emily Saliers formed a duo, the Indigo Girls, and saw their first major label release in 1989. Their songs reflect environmental and political concerns, and they came out as lesbians. The women's music movement had changed, and it had become acceptable for women with same-sex preferences to include men in their audiences. Ray also founded a record label, Daemon, with the goal of issuing music that she felt was artistically valid, but not necessarily commercial. Both of the Indigo Girls are good guitarists, and their instrumental work is the primary musical feature of their accompaniments. In other words, unlike some other singer–songwriters, they have not allowed the obligatory electric bass and drums sound to dominate their music.

All of the above artists had major label recording contracts and achieved a considerable amount of commercial success. For some reason, there are a couple of dozen (mostly) male singer–songwriters who never broke through to the major record labels, but whose work is reasonably available on various smaller, independent labels. There is a whole contingent of writers from the New England area—Bob Francke, Patty Larkin, David Mallett, Bill Morrissey, and Ellis Paul. Another singer-songwriting community grew up in New York's Greenwich Village, sparked by the organizational efforts of Jack Hardy, himself a performing songwriter. He established a songwriting magazine called *Fast Folk*. The magazine came with a recording. A double-CD reissue album of the magazine on Smithsonian Folkways includes songs composed and sung by thirty-three artists, including Shawn Colvin, Steve Forbert, John Gorka, Jack Hardy, Lucy Kaplansky, Christine Lavin, Rod McDonald, Richard Shindell, and Suzanne Vega. *Fast Folk* started in 1982, and there were live shows as well as the recording sessions sponsored by this loose co-op. In 1997, the magazine suspended publication, but many of its writers had by that time established their careers.

Other singer–songwriters such as Spencer Bohren, Chuck Brodsky, Greg Brown, Eliza Gilkyson, Woody Guthrie's son Arlo, Iris DeMent, Jimmy La Fave, Tom Russell, David Wilcox, Jack Williams, and (unrelated) Victoria Williams came from, or live in, various parts of the country. Arlo Guthrie achieved considerable notoriety with his song "Alice's Restaurant," a spoof of his draft board experience, and his hit recording of Steve Goodman's song "City of New Orleans." Arlo is a witty songwriter whose career has never quite taken off. Greg Brown is renowned for his chronicles of midwestern life—a sort of folk Sherwood Anderson—and Jack Williams is a soulful singer and a superb guitarist whose luck has never matched his talent.

Eva Cassady was a wonderful singer who has developed a strong niche audience since her unfortunate early death. Her repertoire varied from folk to gospel music, jazz, and jazz-inflected pop. A half-dozen albums of her have been released sincer her death. Her posthumous popularity parallels that of British folksinger Nick Drake, except that Drake was a songwriter as well.

From Canada, there are versatile British Columbia–based Bob Bossin, his former singing partner Marie Louise Hammond, the McGarrigle sisters (from Montreal), pop-folk singer Gordon Lightfoot, and Ian Tyson, who has become a fixture at cowboy poetry gatherings. The McGarrigle sisters are widely respected songwriters who never have wanted to pursue an extensive touring career.

Another group of singer–songwriters including Mike Dowling in Wyoming, Mary Flower in Portland, and Artie Traum in Woodstock are superb instrumentalists whose recordings include numerous instrumentals as well as original songs.

There are also subject-specific singer–songwriters like Gordon Bok and the late Canadian artist Stan Rogers, whose songs celebrated the sea and sailors. Other artists worked in the original tradition of the Almanac Singers, recording songs about social and political issues. Charlie Brown, Anne Feeney, John McCutcheon, and Jim Page can be found singing on picket lines and at antiwar rallies, in the tradition of Pete Seeger and Woody Guthrie. McCutcheon and Feeney have also been activists in the Musician's Union, an organization that many radical folksingers have largely ignored.

The word "crossover" is a popular word in the music industry. It is used to describe artists whose work can fit into more than one radio format, or record bin. Artists such as Jackson Browne, James Taylor, and Lucinda Williams appear to fit into this noncategory. And then there are the "country" singer–songwriters, some of whom we met in the earlier discussion of singer–songwriters. Guy Clark, Nanci Griffith, the late Mickey Newbury, Townes Van Zandt, and Steve Young are among these country-folk artists.

Another kind of crossover has been attempted by Bruce Springsteen and John Mellancamp. Springsteen's albums *Nebraska* and *Ghost of Tom Joad* are essentially attempts to transform Bruce into a Woody Guthrie sort of artist. Mellancamp in a sense went even further, using a country-folk band to back him up on such albums as *The Lonesome Jubilee*. It is a matter of opinion as to how successful these transformations have been. For my own taste, Springsteen, who is by all indications one of the most pleasant and unassuming of superstars, was more convincing on his ominous *Nebraska* album than in his more recent *Ghost of Tom Joad*. He was probably less familiar with folk music during the *Nebraska* period, and aside from his Dylan-inflected harmonica, less subject to other influences. The energy of his rock band seems to blend better with his own vocal abilities than these more exposed efforts. Canadian Bruce Cockburn seems to move comfortably between folk-rock and topical songs, anchored by his own excellent guitar work.

In the course of writing this chapter, I have listened to dozens of singer–songwriters. In my readings, I ran across a comment by Dave Van Ronk, who claimed that the music scene would be much better off if there were ten artists who interpreted the songs of each songwriter. Van Ronk himself is a case in point. Although he was perfectly capable of writing interesting songs, for the most part, he sang traditional songs and the songs of other composers. The prevailing cliché is that the songwriter is the best interpreter of his or her own song, because he or she is so invested in expressing the emotions of the song. To hear the big, gruff-voiced Van Ronk sing a Joni Mitchell song, however, is to grasp a whole dimension of the song that Mitchell herself might not imagine or attempt. Presumably, she would appreciate and enjoy his efforts. At one time Judy Collins, Tom Rush, and Van Ronk introduced the work of many young songwriters. Who is playing this role today?

The assumption that the writer is the best one to interpret her own work seems to be simplistic, and not necessarily accurate. Add to this the seemingly obvious fact that some people simply sing better than others do. I am thinking, for example, of the wonderful and effortless version of Joni Mitchell's "Help Me" performed by k. d. lang on a televised tribute to Mitchell.

Distinctions and Judgments

In writing about singer–songwriters, I have wrestled endlessly with the question of what artists stand out because of their unique talent and vision. Any observer or critic risks imposing his or her own tastes and prejudices on this sort of judgment. One test, I think, is whether other artists have been compelled to record the songs of a particular singer–songwriter. I suppose one could make the argument that song X by artist X is such a wonderful interpretation that no other artist would dare to compete with the original version.

But isn't the validity of a song tested by whether it *can* survive other interpretations with its core intact? (Now we can argue about what the "core" means.) I suppose that another test is the question of what songs come to mind when you think about a particular artist.

One of the reasons that I think some of the songwriters, especially the male ones, have not found a wider audience is that their songs tend to fall into familiar subjects and patterns. There are the personal romantic song about marriages, divorces, family tragedies, and affairs; observations about being a musician and going on the road, examinations of loneliness and despair, and generally liberal political songs about environmental issues or against war. A writer like Christine Lavin shines out like a beacon because of her sense of humor, whether she is writing about herself, human relationships, or people who she has run into or invented.

Someone like Daniel Johnston of Austin, who by music-school standards can't sing or play very well, somehow manages to draw you into his tortured world. So does the eccentric approach of Michael Hurley, who *can* sing and play, but whose work is thoroughly unpredictable and at the same time engaging. Possibly because so many of the singer–songwriters are guitar players, and the styles they play in are somewhat predictable and defined, it really is hard to focus one's attention on their particular artistry. And those who move in a more pop direction often have their lyrics and subtlety obliterated by the thud of loud, metronomic, and unimaginative rhythm sections.

I think part of what Van Ronk was getting at was that some people who sing shouldn't write songs, and some people who write songs shouldn't try to perform them. Why? Because many artists who do one of these things well really don't do as well with the other.

THE JAM BANDS

Jam sessions are a long tradition in jazz. The basic jam session puts players together who don't generally play in the same band or combo. The atmosphere varies between bitter "cutting contests," where one player tries to best the other players on his particular instrument, and situations where a bunch of musicians get together and play improvised solos on tunes that they are all more or less familiar with.

Jam bands are bands that generally do play together. They take a particular tune, often one that they have written, and they play it for considerable lengths of time. The Grateful Dead is the model for all of the jam bands. The Dead were famous for their lengthy concerts. They attracted a group of fans, called "Deadheads," who would follow the band around the country whenever possible. The social world of the Dead included large-scale ingesting of drugs and/or alcohol. The fashion world featured the obligatory tie-dyed T-shirts and the Dead's more or less leader, Jerry Garcia, even designed a line of ties. Several of the members of the dead, especially Garcia himself, had a fairly broad background in folk and country music, and Garcia also recorded some neo-bluegrass albums with his friend David Grisman (which, by the way are more focused and contain better musicianship than his work with the Dead).

A string of jam bands has grown up around Boulder, Colorado. The String Cheese Incident, Leftover Salmon, and the Yonder Mountain String Band have all toured widely and recorded. The degree of their folk influence is varied; essentially they are all a kind of outgrowth of the newgrass scene with an admixture of Grateful Dead sauce.

Possibly the most famous jam band aside from the Dead was Phish. Phish's music, along with other blues-oriented jam bands such as Government Mule and the very popular fringe-jam group the Dave Matthews Band, does not exhibit a whole lot of folk influence, although Matthews has utilized Béla Fleck on some recording sessions.

For this particular listener, jam bands present a fundamental musical problem. Most folk and country tunes simply don't lend themselves to extended jamming because of the musically simple structure of the tunes. Consequently, the jam bands need to rely on a combination of speed, playing everything as rapidly as possible, and a certain amount of bombast in terms of their approach to the vocals.

WORLD MUSIC

World music is literally music that comes from different parts of the planet. The term is used today to represent fusions of music from different cultures, usually anchored by some sort of rock rhythm. In the United States, there has been a considerable amount of recording in foreign languages practically from the beginning of the recording medium. This is because of the large number of immigrant groups found in this country.

In terms of the folk revival, the Weavers were the first folk group to dip into the world music repertoire. They sang and played music from Hungary, Israel, the West Indies, and Africa. Their 1949 recording of South African Solomon Linda's song "Mbube" was a big hit. It was retitled as "Wimoweh" and in 1961, a rock group called the Tokens reworked it as "The Lion Sleeps Tonight" and had their own hit with it.

The calypso boom of the 1950s was initiated by the Tarriers, but it took wing with the recordings of Harry Belafonte. In the urban revival, as we have already seen, Theodore Bikel, Cynthia Gooding, and Martha Schlamme all sang in multiple languages, and a number of California pop-folk groups did a Mexican song or two. In his solo performances, Pete Seeger performed music from everywhere—Korea, India, French Canada, Latin

America. All in all, the folk revival played comparatively little attention to music from most world cultures.

British rock 'n' roll artists seemed to pay closer attention. Short-lived Rolling Stone Brian Jones recorded Moroccan musicians in 1969, even before that the Beatles were hooked on Indian music. George Harrison, who had briefly studied with Ravi Shankar, played sitar on some Beatles records. Stevie Winwood recorded with Nigerian high-life musicians in the early 1970s in what may have been the earliest example of integrating world music musicians into pop music. In 1982, Peter Gabriel, then the lead singer of the British rock band Genesis, formed the World Music and Dance Organization (WOMAD). This led to Gabriel's establishing a record label called Real World, a multimedia company, and recording studio. David Byrne of the Talking Heads followed suit with his Luaka Bop label in 1989.

In 1986, Paul Simon brought world music to the attention of American music fans with his *Graceland* album. Simon used South African musicians and singers on the record, and he also toured with some of them. The album won several Grammy Awards, sold well, and revived Simon's flagging career. It also introduced the notion that world music could find a mass audience. According to Chris Nickson, writing in *The NPR Curious Listener's Guide to World Music,* Simon's album resulted in a London skull session of several entrepreneurs involved in the merchandising of music from around the world, and the term "world music" was adopted as the key to selling the music to consumers.

The American World Fusion Urban Revivalists

Taj Mahal and Ry Cooder were two American folk-blues musicians who had an early involvement in integrating various music styles into their recordings and performances. Cooder internationalized American music by combining music styles that would probably never have been attempted together otherwise. He has very broad musical taste, so he would toss in a Tex-Mex accordion with a slide guitar, for example. Cooder later made a number of recordings with musicians from far-flung cultures. He played with Indian musician C.M. Bhatt, with African guitarist Ali Farka Toure, and with Cuban musicians on an album called *The Buena Vista Social Club.* The latter project also involved a documentary film made by director Wim Wenders. The *Buena Vista* album was a worldwide hit, selling over seven million copies to date. Cooder's latest CD is the brilliant *Chavez Ravine.* The album is a sort of historical novel telling the story of the destruction of a Chicano neighborhood. Cooder cowrote most of the songs, and he enlisted the participation of a number of outstanding musicians like the late Lalo Guerrero, Little Willie, guitarist David Hidalgo from Los Lobos, and vocalists Juliette and Carla Commagere. The CD includes a lengthy and well designed booklet that greatly enhances the recording itself.

Meanwhile, Taj Mahal played with Hawaiian musicians and in 2003 recorded an album on which he integrated an American drummer and electric bassman Billy Rich with a number of musicians from Zanzibar. Hawaiian guitarist Bob Brozman similarly played with a variety of musicians from around the world, including an Okinawan guitarist, and Los Lobos guitarist David Hidalgo also played on the record.

Last, but definitely not least, guitarist Henry Kaiser and multi-instrumentalist David Lindley recorded and played with musicians in Madagascar and later in Norway. Lindley had been experimenting with world music styles ever since his 1960s tenure with the rock band Kaleidoscope, possibly the first rock band to integrate music and instruments from various parts of the world.

How do we judge the musical experiments described above? With difficulty, I would say. Sometimes the musicians betray the fact that they have spent relatively little time together. On some of Taj Mahal's experiments, frankly, the banjo sounds out of place. Cooder tends to be uniformly tasteful, but sometimes the *Timbuktu* record slows down into musical situations reminiscent of the jam bands. The Cuban record works well, since the main performers are so musical and so enjoyable and because Ry manages to add to the proceedings without getting in the way. Sometimes, Cooder and Brozman's use of slide and Hawaiian guitars makes me wish for other musical choices, but I always admire their spirit of adventure.

Kaiser and Lindley's Norwegian album *The Sweet Sunny North* is one of the most exciting CDs that I have heard in years. Lindley seems to be able to play anything with strings, whether it's an oud a saz or a bouzouki. Plowing some of the same ground that Cooder has farmed, he seems to make the most unlikely or absurd musical combinations work well together.

I think it is much too early to draw conclusions about the value of these off-the-wall experiments. A British band called Three Mustaphas and an American "polka" band called Brave Combo are mining some of the same terrain. Both of these bands have a strong humorous element to their work. Down the road, I anticipate that musical groups will emerge whose members come from different cultures and teach one another their traditions. Until then, I think of the musicians mentioned in this section as intrepid explorers, some of whose voyages are more valuable than others.

chapter 14

Today and Tomorrow: What's Going On

There have been a number of interesting developments in what has to be seen as the aftermath of the folk revival, from the 1990s halfway through the first decade of the twenty-first century.

All of the remaining pop-folk group members are a bit long in the tooth. Many have retired from touring, including Bob Shane, the last holdout of the original Kingston Trio. The group slogs on without any of the original members, although banjoist George Grove has been a replacement so long he is practically an original. Similarly, the Brothers Four and the Limeliters continue to tour, with an ever-decreasing number of original band members. Peter, Paul & Mary continue to perform with the three originals intact, including regular fundraisers for WNET in New York City, even though Mary is currently being treated for leukemia. Harry Belafonte has become the elder statesman of the civil rights movement in music. Erik Darling continues to make occasionally brilliant records, and also works as a counselor.

The original revivalists have also slowed down their activities, and their ranks have begun to be thinned through the ravages of disease and death. The late Dave Van Ronk, the supreme iconoclast of the revival, would probably be vastly amused to see the city of New York naming a street after him. Joan Baez and Judy Collins continue to perform and record, if on a somewhat reduced basis. Now in his mid-eighties, Pete Seeger has finally slowed down, but he still makes occasional records and concert appearances. Bob Dylan has his Neverending Tour.

The significance of all of this is that the recent, aging group of folksingers is essentially the last one that had any direct contact with the original blues and country music performers who formed the inspiration for the revival. Of the major folk artists, such as John Hurt, Son House, Gary Davis, Dock Boggs, Bill Monroe, and so many others, only Doc Watson is still active as of this writing. Some of the early heroes of bluegrass, like Earl Scruggs, are still alive, but partly or entirely retired.

A whole new generation of folksingers, blues artists, bluegrass musicians, and singer–songwriters have emerged to take their place in the current incarnation of the revival. It would be fair to say that the music hasn't died, but it would be equally correct to see it as having been transformed through the attitudes and styles of new artists, the changing face of the folk music business, and the cross-pollination of other musical styles.

Possibly the most striking of these various transformations has been the career of Ani DiFranco. Considerable attention has been paid to her independence—ownership of her own successful record company, Righteous Babe, and her refusal to deal with the various large record labels that would love to reverse their initial skepticism about her "commercial potential." All of this is interesting enough in its own right, but it fails to deal with her artistry, rather than her commercial success. What DiFranco has done for folk, in my eyes, is make it a viable form of music for young people, as opposed to a forum for people sharing old memories.

Ani writes about herself, about her friends, about life as she sees it. At first she was embraced by the contemporary version of the women's music community. When she came out as a bisexual, rather than a lesbian, these fans became thoroughly confused.

To return to the subject of the music, Ani uses various vocal devices—whispering, talking, reading poetry, and performing so intensely that she almost borders the heavy metal genre. The production on her records is suitably adventurous, even though it doesn't always quite work. The listener gets the feeling, the "l'il old folksinger," as she calls herself, is not fooling around. Her guitar playing is also creative and adventurous, varying from original figures that she has worked out to almost frantically beating the guitar in performance with a self-made plastic tool she calls a "claw."

There is also the aspect of community. Ani operates her record company in her hometown of Buffalo. She splits the ownership with her long-time manager and friend, and she employs local people to print the jackets, make the T-shirts, and so forth. I mention this because I think it represents a sincere attempt to walk the walk, something not all of the urban revivalists have had the courage to do.

Ani has also produced an album with Dan Bern, a sort of simpatico fellow punk-folker. For my taste, Dan is a talented writer who is overcome with the idea of shock value—using four-letter words and direct sexual references that guarantee a lack of radio play but, at the same time, don't necessarily reflect artistry. On the other hand, he sometimes displays a more sensitive side, as in his musings about his sister or the tennis player Monica Seles.

*   *   *

About five years ago, I went to see Ani perform at the *E Town* radio show in Boulder. Utah Phillips was performing with her. Utah is a singer–songwriter–storyteller–radical folksinger who is old enough to be Ani's father, and almost her grandfather.

The audience was a curious combination of young people with multi-colored hair and nose rings and middle- and older-aged fans who had come to see Utah. On the face of it, it was a very odd billing. However, Ani was a long-time admirer of Utah's songs, stories, and radical anarchist political stances and had put together an album of his stories interspersed with her own musical contributions. The audience was respectful for Utah's part of the performance, but when Ani started to play, the young people all got up and danced as she viciously attacked her acoustic guitar. At the time, I was the chair of the music department at the University of Colorado. I had the intense desire to force all of my faculty to go see Ani play. I knew quite well that many of them would have been confused by the jagged rhythms, by her clawing the guitar half to death, let alone by the subject matter of her songs.

OLD-TIMEY MUSIC AND BLUEGRASS

We are now in the third generation of old-time revival bands. The New Lost City Ramblers were the first generation, followed by groups like the Red Clay Ramblers and the Hollow Rock String Band, the Good Old Persons, the Boiled Buzzards, and the Highwoods String Band. In the last few years, a group of younger players, some with a rock 'n' roll or punk background, drifted into the old-time world. The Foghorn String Band in Portland, Oregon, is one example of such a group. Their repertoire is drawn from the same well as the Ramblers, and they perform with similar enthusiasm and energy. Many of these bands develop out of regular jam sessions where musicians meet one another, which probably parallels the way the original groups that recorded during the 1920s formed and evolved. There are similar bands throughout the western United States. For example, one group meets weekly at a coffeehouse in Denver. As is the case with Foghorn, their members are generally in their twenties and thirties. Since this is not music that receives much radio airplay, and it is

even a bit difficult to find in record stores, there is a certain specialness
about finding new tunes and working them out that was what the urban
revivalists were feeling forty years ago. It is probably too early to predict
whether this particular aspect of the revival will sustain itself over a period
of time.

Another group of old-time musicians, like Frank Lee and Brad Leftwich, grew up in the tradition, learning how to play from relatives rather
than from books or videos. A number of the old-time musicians such as
scholar–musician Alan Jabbour, Lee, or Leftwich expanded on their
knowledge of old-time styles by studying with such traditional musicians
as Tommy Jarrell and Fred Cockerham. In her book *A Hot-Bed of Musicians*, Paula Hathaway Anderson-Green describes various old-time gatherings like the Galax, Virginia, Fiddlers Convention, where these
traditions continue to be passed on. Lee performs and records with his
band the Freight Hoppers. Uncle Earle is a contemporary old-time music
band of female musicians.

There is a wonderful story about the recording of traditional music in
the book. A considerable part of her it is devoted to a discussion of a fine
fiddler named Albert Hash. As Green tells the story, a producer from
Rounder Records came down to the North Carolina–Virginia border to
record Hash and other musicians. According to Hash, the producer was
seeking a rough sound and "they didn't want it to sound too good. They
thought these mountain fiddlers was supposed to be rough and sound bad.
. . . There's some of those fellows that can really play it, you know, and
they do play it and they don't play rough." The point of this story is that
we need to revise the relationship between collectors and informants in
order to ensure that there is a climate of mutual respect and understanding.
The days of folklorists censoring their subjects or their songs need to disappear with the prejudices of the early twentieth century.

A group of urban revivalists has developed an extension of traditional
clawhammer banjo styles that to an extent parallels the melodic banjo
picking styles Bill Keith and Bobby Thompson pioneered. They play fiddle tunes note for note or even with embellishments of the melody, as opposed to the more rhythmic traditional clawhammer style. Many of these
innovations came through the work of banjoist Stu Jamieson, who taught
many revival banjoists. Another major influence on the style was the work
of banjoists Kyle Creed, Fred Cockerham, and Tommy Jarrell of Galax,
Virginia, and Mount Airy, North Carolina. Among the current practitioners of melodic clawhammer are Ray Alden, Paul Brown, Bob Carlin,
Walt Koken, Frank Lee, Brad Leftwich, and Ken Perlman. Other players

utilize aspects of melodic clawhammer, but are more difficult to categorize. Mac Benford, Howie Bursen, and Michael Miles are a few of these banjoists. A few other banjoists, such as Mark Johnson and Mark Schatz, integrate the clawhammer style into bluegrass bands.

Bluegrass remains an important niche market with a few rare exceptions of artists who have broken through to a wider country-pop-folk market. Alison Krause is a fiddler and singer who began winning fiddle contests at the age of twelve. By the mid-1990s, she had enjoyed a double platinum (two million units) album and had won Grammies and Country Music Association Awards. All of this was done for independent label Rounder Records, which has even done videos for her, something that would have defied credibility a few short years earlier. Today, Alison has become almost an easy-listening vocal artist, albeit one backed by a bluegrass band. To retain the band's original audience, her style mixes bluegrass instrumentals with hot picking, and the "high lonesome sound" of the band's male singer–guitarist–mandolinist Dan Tyminski. She still records for Rounder and her albums still sell half a million copies or more. Meanwhile, the trio Nickel Creek has enjoyed albums with sales of over half a million copies with their blend of excellent vocals and instrumental virtuosity. Although their songs don't range as far afield as Krause's do, they too are smooth-voiced vocalists who do not emphasize the traditional "high lonesome sound."

But two other things happened in the world of bluegrass music that could not have been predicted. The Coen brothers, two filmmakers, made the aforementioned *O Brother, Where Art Thou*. The sound track was released on CD in 2000. The record got virtually no airplay, because much of the music was unadorned bluegrass, old-timey music, and even a black work song. The album has currently sold over seven million copies! When radio station music directors were queried as to why they wouldn't play a record that had sold so many copies, their response was that although many people were enthusiastic about the record, others found it far too rough for their musical taste. Since what radio stations fear more than anything is that a listener will switch the dial to another station, they concluded that it just wasn't worth the risk.

A musical act that did get radio airplay (at least until Natalie Maines expressed her political views) was the Dixie Chicks. The Dixie Chicks albums sold as many as ten million copies. For their 2002 *Home* they recorded in Austin, rather than Nashville, took control of their own recording process, and featured themselves playing banjo, guitar, and fiddle on the record. This album sold over six million copies when the political "scandal" around Maines's remarks started to impact their airplay on country music radio.

The lesson of the *O Brother* record and the Dixie Chicks' albums is that there appears to be a much greater market for this music than anyone had previously considered. Other left turns in the bluegrass road include the use of old-timey banjo on records by such bluegrass stalwarts as Lynn Morris and Tim O'Brien. We will shortly turn to the "art folk" work of such artists as Béla Fleck and Mark O'Connor.

POP-FOLK AND PUBLIC TELEVISION

PBS has produced two fundraiser shows that feature sixties folk-pop artists, and Peter, Paul & Mary, as noted, are a constant presence. If Di-Franco and Krauss are bringing folk-based music to younger people, PBS executives seem determined to preserve the memories of their mature viewers and listeners.

NO DEPRESSION—ALTERNATIVE COUNTRY

A new generation of country–folk–rock artists began to emerge during the 1990s. Such bands as the Jayhawks, Uncle Tupelo, and Freakwater emerged in the Midwest. All of these bands were informed by the old *Anthology* records, but they were equally familiar with rock 'n' roll and country music. Uncle Tupelo eventually evolved into Wilco, the most commercially successful of these bands. A magazine called *No Depression* dedicated to alternative country music began publication in 1995.

In the *No Depression* reader, such disparate artists as songwriters Mickey Newbury, Guy Clark, Steve Earle, Gillian Welch, and Freakwater are all profiled. The subtitle of the book, *Whatever That Is,* pretty well defines the problem of alternative country: one person's alternative is another person's mainstream.

There is an interesting video about the making and selling of Wilco's *Yankee Hotel Foxtrot* album, as well as a book about Wilco, Greg Kot's *Learning How to Die.* The book and the video reveal the frustrations and personality conflicts between various group members as Wilco loses its Reprise Records contract and then signs with another company, Nonesuch, which, like Reprise, is owned by the Warner group of record companies. Ironically, Reprise gives the band its $85,000 album back, free, with no strings attached, and they proceed to sell the identical record to Nonesuch. The album goes on to sell 400,000 copies, far more than any other Wilco album up to that time.

In the video, we see how the band moves back and forth between acoustic and electric music, and how they use the recording studio to shape the music itself. We also see in both the book and the video the sort of personality conflicts that destroy bands, as Jeff Tweedy successively rids himself of his primary collaborator, Jay Farrar from Uncle Tupelo, and then Jay Bennett, who performs a similar role with Wilco. Drummers and other side musicians disappear along the way, as Tweedy, not the most articulate person in the world, struggles to retain control over the songwriting and musical direction of his band.

A radio format called Americana is essentially the only place outside of NPR radio where this music receives any airplay. As with bluegrass, it is evident that an audience exists for the music; it simply isn't currently large enough to persuade radio to hump on the bandwagon.

BLUES

The blues have had a few crossover hit artists as well. B. B. King had his big hit, "The Thrill Is Gone," more than thirty-five years ago, and he still has a viable performing career. Robert Cray enjoyed a hit crossover record, and white blues artists like Jonny Lang, Kenny Wayne Shepherd, and Stevie Ray Vaughan have experienced a life closer to rock stardom than to the life of the traveling blues artist. The blues has become a universal language—a recent book described the life of the blues in Russia. There are videos and biographies of blues artists living and dead, and the late Robert Johnson is a certified if belated superstar, endorsed by everyone from folkies to rock stars like Eric Clapton.

THE BOURGEOISIZATION AND COMMODIFICATION OF FOLK MUSIC

It is forty years since Dylan went electric at Newport. We have seen any number of musical styles, like folk rock, emerge and decline. The folksingers of the 1930s and 1940s were mostly closely tied into social protest, even to subverting the existing social order. Today's folksingers have websites; they self-produce CDs or records for major labels; they support a small army of booking agents, personal managers, music publishers, and, even if pitifully, the small independent record companies that are the primary sponsors of their works. Those that have emerged on the radar of the major labels—such as Raffi, Joni Mitchell, the Dixie Chicks, Wilco, Peter, Paul & Mary, and a dozen other acts—support a similar corps of publicists, accountants, and road crews. Studio musicians receive nice paychecks for adding parts to these records, and the successful acts get to be wined and dined by record company representatives and lionized by a handful of promoters who control the major venues in the United States.

The North American Folk Music Alliance holds its annual convention and trade show and gives classes in the business of folk music for putative booking agents, artists, managers, and the like. The IBMA does the same for bluegrass. The Grammies honor the winners of their annual talent contest, as do the Handy Awards for blues. The annual meetings are expensive to attend and at this point there are serious considerations as to whether they have much relationship to the real content of the music. On the other hand, they are opportunities for artists to make social and musical contact with one another.

There is talk of a folk music museum, possibly to be housed in New York City, and the guitar- and banjo-making companies thrive and expand, even if many of their wares come from China. Every year, they exhibit their wares two times, at the NAMM trade shows. Virtually ever major city has an acoustic music center. For those who prefer the box store approach, you can buy instruments online, through catalogs, from the music store octopus Guitar Center, or on eBay.

Recently, I saw a two-page advertisement in the *New York Times Magazine.* One page featured the Lincoln Navigator car, the other Bob Taylor and Taylor Guitars. I struggled bravely to figure the connection between acoustic music and Lincoln automobiles. The only relationship I could come up with is that both parties are trying to sell me something.

How did all of this commodification happen? It started whenever folk musicians became professionals and appeared on the stage. After all, the music started in communities of people who knew one another. Fathers and uncles and aunts taught the next generation how to play, and the cousin who played better taught a few more things. Music was played at picnics, in church, and on social occasions. Once recording began, basically during the 1920s, the situation inevitably changed. The music was now fixed in time at a particular period and it was this performance that was authoritative or "authentic." Then the audience wanted to hear what was on the record. The same situation prevailed in jazz. How in the world can we possibly know whether the greatest blues artists, the best guitar pickers, or the finest singers actually got to record? We have written our music history based on the evidence provided by recordings. Basically, musicians have been transformed into entertainers. Are the roles exclusive? Not necessarily, but more and more there seems to be an increasing contradiction between the two roles. One of the things that has happened in the world of folk music is that acoustic guitars simply aren't necessarily acoustic any more. First came the notion of plugging into a venue's sound system, a necessary evil when a concert is outdoors or at a large venue. The musicians started plugging into little sound-modifying boxes, because they didn't like the sound that was coming from plugging into a house sound system. Recently, I attended a performance by two guitarists at a fairly large venue. They had so many sound modifiers that their sound was at rock-star level. They played very rapidly, demonstrating technical excellence, although I would have to say the effect was not particularly musical. Because they were louder and faster than any of the preceding acts, most of the audience loved them. I couldn't help but think that this performance had little to do with folk music, or with music in general.

On the positive side, a relatively recent development in the "folk business" is the spread of house concerts. These are small-scale concerts held in private houses. The host or hostess is generally a fan of folk music, whose only desire is to create performing opportunities for musicians in a situation where people listen, and there is no smoking or drinking. The artist generally receives all or almost all of the proceeds. It's a great performing situation, without distractions, and the artist can generally sell quite a few CDs because of the intimacy of the relationship that develops between the performer and the audience. In a sense, it restores the music to a more personal and intimate role in the lives of the performer. Whether the audience is literally singing along or not, there is face-to-face contact and a feeling of dialogue between the artist and the audience.

These performances are usually advertised through e-mail lists, and the bulk of people in a community don't even know they are taking place. It is all done through e-mail and word-of-mouth. Since most living rooms have a small number of available seats, public advertising is out of the question. Performers seem to have developed a grapevine so that they know how to access the people who do house concerts. This may be as close as folk music is going to get to feeling like a community in the twenty-first century.

A sort of parallel development is the song circle movement active in a number of cities. These also often take place in people's homes. People sit together, exchange songs, and sing along with one another. For the most part, this activity seems to appeal to an older group of people, the sort of people who grew up going to Pete Seeger concerts, where singing along was a large part of the event.

During the course of an extensive and far-reaching conversation with Kate Power and Steve Einhorn—Portland songwriters, singers, musicians, and music store owners—I asked them what musicians they had encountered who they felt were not as well known as their talents justified. They replied that the best musicians they knew were probably people who had chosen not to be professional musicians because of other personal and/or professional commitments.

In another context, Portland musician Jane Keefer, who has drifted in and out of a professional music career between working first as a scientist and later as a librarian, cited sense of community as the principal virtue of folk music. Does such a community exist today? Who are today's Almanac Singers (given the ample existence of competition, jealousy, and downright unpleasantness in the ranks of the Almanacs themselves)? Mimi Fariña founded Bread and Roses, an organization that sponsors concerts in prison and other public facilities. Outside In, located in Santa Fe, is pursuing a similar vision. Participation can mean more than singalongs, it can indicate an involvement with the world of those who *need* music but aren't apt to receive it.

Finally, how does the nature of making a living as a professional musician intervene between the music that a musician loves and admires and what they do to make a living? There are presenters in the folk world who organize big-budget music festivals that combine local ethnic music groups with people who come hundreds of miles to perform. I am thinking specifically of the massive Seattle Folk Life Festival, held in the park near the Seattle Experience Music Project rock museum. There must be a budget in the thousands of dollars for this event, but not for musicians. Now, I have nothing against presenting local ethnic groups, people who are often fine musicians but who have other sources of income. So why do people apply to play? Possibly it is because folk musicians indeed still do search for that sense of community and mutual identity, and there is a certain amount of guilt about receiving money for performing music. Bar and restaurant owners take advantage of this attitude by hiring musicians to play for the questionable gross receipts that come from a door charge, or for that medieval absurdity, the tip jar, placing us back in the days of the troubadours. Now our financial recompense comes not from a single monarch, but from an entire audience.

PAYING THE COSTS

There are costs that come with the entry of folk music's relationship with rock 'n' roll. During the late 1960s, record company money was flowing freely. Many artists never understood that it was really their own money that was financing the limos, the tour support, the ads, the lunches, and whatever else was being offered to them. Folk-rock and the singer–songwriters brought the world of the folk revivalists into alignment with rock stardom. Some of us were lucky enough to write hit songs or make hit records. In the course of a particularly searching conversation, my friend Artie Traum described to me how during the mid-1980s he realized that his life was dissolving into a cocaine fog. He was able to stop and rethink his priorities and return his life to a reasonable direction. Many others were not able to exert that sort of discipline. There were drug casualties, alcoholics, broken marriages, families scattered to the four winds. Of course, I am thoroughly aware that half of the marriages in the United States end in divorce. The point that I am trying to make is that the life-style that rock 'n' roll entails is virtually *guaranteed* to cause personal dissolution, frustration, and in some cases premature death.

Recently, I read some comments from Joni Mitchell that reflected her opinions of the current market for music in the United States. She is now sixty-two years old, and is apparently bitter that she gets no airplay and the size of her audiences has greatly reduced. The fact is that she has done about a dozen-and-a-half albums and she has earned a tremendous amount of money through her songwriting royalties. How long does fame last? How many albums should even a devoted fan buy? How many recordings of a single artist should a radio station be expected to play? Obviously, in whatever ways her career has developed, Joni Mitchell wants to be treated like a superstar, not like a folksinger.

One of the problems that the hybridization of music has brought is that the artists expect the sort of adulation and financial remuneration that music superstars receive. This is not only unrelated to the essence of folk music, but for me it contradicts any sort of feeling that I associate with the music.

A wonderful corrective to the self-involved folksinger was the 2003 movie *A Mighty Wind*. It gently satirized the various folk groups, in some cases appearing to mimic the performing qualities of specific successful musicians from the folk revival. There are some wonderful moments that mimick the verbal diarrhea that certain performers manifest when they introduce songs. Amusingly enough, a good deal of the music in the film is performed at a higher musical standard than some of the groups satirized would have been able to pull off. The film led to actual live performances by the cast, and even more amusingly it helped to revive the careers of some of the aging pop-folkers who have been able to construct successful tours in the wake of the mighty wind.

INSTRUMENTAL VIRTUOSITY

There are a large number of excellent instrumentalists in the folk–country–blues world today. As noted, Béla Fleck has set new standards of technical ability with his banjo work, as has Mark O'Connor with his fiddle work. Bill Evans writes beautiful original bluegrass-based tunes. Evans, Tony Trishka, and Michael Miles all do concert programs on the history of the banjo, and Steven Wade has written and performed two theater pieces featuring the banjo and traditional music. Walt Koken has made several enjoyable CDs of traditional and original banjo music. Jerry Douglas is a musician who can make his dobro talk (even if I personally feel that he frequently makes it talk too much). Sally Van Meter, Cindy Cashdollar, and Mike Auldridge are other excellent dobro players. Tony Rice, Scott Nygaard, Kelly Jo Phelps, and Ry Cooder on the guitar, fiddler Darrol Anger and David Grisman, Mike Marshall, and Barry Mitterhoff on the mandolin are among today's talented instrumentalists, as is David Lindley on the many instruments that he plays. British-born Martin Simpson is adept at combining aspects of the English guitar styles of such players as John Renbourn and Martin Carthy with more American-flavored banjo and guitar playing. Garrison Keilor's *Prarie Home Companion* radio show regularly utilizes the services of such fine instrumentalists as guitarist Pat Donahue and mandolin player and fiddler Peter Ostrushko.

There is the matter of taste and economy, often called the "space between the notes." I sometimes think we should institute a system of fines for people who play too many notes, similar to what a basketball coach might come up with for someone who shoots the ball too much without regard to his teammates. Maybe we should offer folk awards for those who play the most economical solos, like Eric Weissberg. I also wish that more artists would limit the number of albums that they make. There is, I am afraid, simply a limit to how much good music can come out of a single source. Having said all of this, it is great to see so many talented people moving the music in so many directions.

WHERE DO WE GO FROM HERE

As I am writing this final section, I have just heard to two albums. One is by Conor Oberst, a contemporary singer songwriter whose albums are released under the name Bright Eyes. The other album is by Bruce Molsky, an excellent multi-instrumentalist and singer, who performs traditional folk music. Like Ani DiFranco, Oberst is involved in the ownership of his record company, Saddle Creek, in his hometown of Omaha, which he has recently left. Molsky began recording in 1996, and like Mike Seeger, was mentored by several excellent traditional musicians. Oberst is an interesting artist, because he makes some albums that are essentially acoustic, and others that are electric.

Artists such as Moby or Beck are not folk, but their music is informed by their knowledge of folk music and they sometimes use folk-music styles or samples of existing records to enhance their own musical innovations.

In various regions of the United State there are musicians such as John Saunders in Cleveland, Massachusetts; Steve Hansen in Lincoln, Nebraska; Bob Coltman in Massachusetts; Jody Stecher, Kate Brislin, Eric and Suzy Thompson in the San Francisco Bay area; or Joel Mabus in Michigan who are versatile multi-instrumentalists and/or singers who do not tour widely, but are an important source of inspiration to other aspiring musicians. Other folk-based musicians, like Peter Wernick in Colorado, have concentrated their efforts on teaching the next generation of musicians. Different instructional needs are now satisfied through the various summer workshops of the National Guitar Institute, and the programs at Davis and Elkins College in Augusta, Georgia; Woodrow Wilson College in Asheville, North Carolina; and the old-time music and guitar workshops at Port Townsend, Washington. Most of the folk festivals include workshop formats where excellent musicians and songwriters share their writing and performing skills. There is also a tremendous profusion of instructional material available in book, CD, and video formats through such companies as Homespun Tapes and music print publishers like Alfred, Mel Bay, Hal Leonard, and Music Sales. You can even get a two-year Associate Arts degree studying bluegrass and country music with fine guitarist Joe Carr and banjo player Alan Munde at South Bend College in Levellend, Texas.

It is the work of such musicians that makes me believe that the direction of American folk music need not be static or ossified, nor must it be unduly compromised or commercialized to have audience appeal. There are a number of musicians who have not been sufficiently recognized for their contributions to the folk-music revival. Mike Seeger has integrated so many traditional music styles into his playing, that in effect he has created his own version of tradition. It is rewarding to see Bob Dylan recognize Mike's abilities in *Chronicles*. Peggy Seeger, Mike's sister, has also been a figure of major importance in American folk music, even though she spent a good deal of her adult life in England. As for Pete Seeger, if there is a single person who typifies the best values of the revival, it is Pete Seeger. A good part of the reason for this would be that he himself would be least likely to suggest that this is true. Danny Wheatman, a Seattle musician and singer–songwriter, has written the music for a number of plays that have premiered at the Denver Center for the Performing Arts and have gone on to appear on Broadway and/or tour. The music ranges from blues to folk and traditional country music, and Wheatman himself is usually in the plays. He also uses other talented instrumentalists like San Francisco fiddler Tony Marcus in the shows. There are also many artists who don't choose to tour much but who are important sparkplugs in keeping the music alive. Ry Cooder has written a string of film scores that employ folk music styles as the basis for his compositional work. I am thnking particularly of his atmospheric score for the movie *Paris, Texas.*

There are so many talented singer–songwriters that it is almost foolish to single any of them out. Recently, I have been moved and fascinated by the work of David Edwards in Denver. Edwards performs in two groups, 16 Horsepower and Woven Hands. Some of these artists, like Mary Flower or Erik Darling, are hard to pigeonhole because they write and sing, interpret other people's music, and also do fine instrumental solos. Geoff Muldaur, with his varied musical interests and arranging skill, also deserves a place in the archives of the urban revival far beyond his work with Jim Kweskin's Jug Band.

One of the interesting developments among the younger singer–songwriters, such as Iron and Wine and Sufjan Stevens, is that they are modifying or abandoning the pop music form of verse–chorus, or verse–chorus–bridge, and substituting their own variations on the form. A number of young groups like the Mammals, the Dukh, and the Wailing Jennnies offer hope that the music can survive and move in new and valid directions.

FINAL WORDS

Traditional music was born of the desire of amateur—in the truest sense of the word—musicians to express their hopes, dreams, and despair. The purpose of this book is to examine the way that the American folk music revival developed and where it has gone. Along the way, I hope to have called attention to the people who for reasons of bias, ignorance, politics, or disagreements in taste have not found their way into other histories of the revival, and others, who by the same token, may have received more attention than they deserve.

From my point of view, we need to give more credit to the artists who have worked to keep the music alive, and to be tolerant of their musical experiments. If we don't try to move folk music in new and creative directions, the music will degenerate into a lifeless body of work that will hang in a badly attended museum. The reader needs to be guided by his or her own intuition and taste. A good deal of the best music today has to be sought out, since it is not on the radio and it is not heavily promoted. As for musicians, it is up to them to determine what there is in traditional music that is relevant to today's experience or tomorrow's dreams. In the words of The Band, "Take what you need, and you leave the rest."

Acknowledgments

Many people enriched this book by providing me with insights, facts, and their own life histories. Some of these conversations, like those with Erik Darling, Dan Fox, and Alan Shaw, occurred over a long period of time and weren't directly related to this project. In Denver, my good friend Harry Tuft shared quite a few stories of his own involvement in the revival and the role of the Denver Folklore Center and the Music Association of Swallow Hill. A trip to Woodstock, New York, resulted in a series of warm and useful interviews with Artie and Happy Traum and Eric Weissberg, and nonfolkie music videographer Burrill Crohn. A panel discussion at the Western region of the Folk Music Alliance provided some good insights to the history of the revival in Los Angeles, from booking agent–blues scholar Mary Katherine Aldin, musicians John McEuen and Alex Hassilev, and long-time radio hosts Roz and Howard Larman. In Portland, Oregon, Mary Elizabeth Rose shared her life in the feminist movement and her knowledge of women's music, Jane Keefer discussed her involvement in the folk music scenes in Salem, Victoria, and Santa Barbara, among others places. Singer–songwriter–radio host Tom May gave me a quick history of the folk scene in Toronto and Omaha, musicians and music store owners Kate Power and Steve Einhorn discussed the revival on the East Coast and in Portland, and musician–composer Michael Kersey shared his take on the singer–songwriter movement. Michael has promoted so many concerts with singer–songwriters that he's almost become one himself by osmosis. Folksinger Mark Ross reminisced about New York, and about his experiences in New York and Montana and Bob Bowers, an old arranger–producer–musician chum sent me some informative emails about the quaint royalty customs of various record companies. Bonnie Messenger provided information about the current state of children's music and Ken Perlman helped me to understand the evolution of clawhammer banjo in some informative emails. Pete Seeger took time out from his busy schedule to suggest various changes in this manuscript. Michael Keefe at Annie Bloom's Books in Portland kept me updated on various obscure neo-folk recordings. I tried to pay attention to all of these people, but the final result obviously reflects my own choices.

My editor, Evander Lomke, was enthusiastic about this book from the very beginning, and he has provided steady guidance in formatting the book and combining a historical approach with my own story in the revival. Susan Planalp lived through all of my various personal freak-outs as I tried to make sense of a project that could have gone on interminably. It probably seems to her that it did just that.

A book like this is bound to reflect the writer's own prejudices and value judgments. Over the years music has captivated me. There is something intangible about folk music when it is close to its original source or inspiration that is magical. As the music has become inextricably tied to a business infrastructure that supports record companies, music publishers, managers, agents, and promoters much of that magic has disappeared. It is my sincere hope that the reader will look for these intangible qualities by listening more closely to the music itself, rather than the clutter that so often surrounds it.

You can reach me at *r2s@comcast.net*, and you can listen to my own music at *cdbaby.com*.

Bibliography and Discography

There are entire books devoted to lists of CDs about folk music, so I see no need to list the hundreds of folk music–related recordings here. However, if you want to know where the urban revival began, you should listen to the Smithsonian-Folkways *Anthology of American Folk Music*, compiled by Harry Smith. In general, you may want to check out the catalogs of Arhoolie, County, Rounder, Smithsonian-Folkways, and Yazoo for roots music, Folk Era for pop-folk music, and such labels as Alligator, Red House, Rounder, Shanachie, and Sugar Hill for contemporary folk music. Rounder has begun to reissue, or issue for the first time, 150 CDs of music collected by Alan Lomax. This represents not only American folk music, but music collected from all over the world. Below are a few discographical books.

Lornell, Kip. *The NPR Curious Listener's Guide to Folk Music.* (2004) New York, Perigee Books.

Nickson, Chris. *The NPR Curious Listener's Guide to World Music.*(2004) New York, Perigee Books.

Ritchie, Fiona. *The NPR Curious Listener's Guide to Celtic Music.* (2005) New York, Perigee Books.

Stambler, Irwin & Lyndon. *Folk Blues: The Encyclopedia.* (2001) New York, St. Martin's Press.

Walters, Neil, Ed. *Music Hound Folk: The Essential Album Guide.* (1998) Detroit. Visible Ink.

If you want to order recordings by mail, below are three sources with addresses.

Andy's Front Hall PO Box 307 Voorheesville, NY 12186 www.andysfronthall.com

Down Home Music 10341 San Pablo Ave. El Cerrito, CA 94530 www.downhomemusic.com

Elderly Instruments 1100 N. Wisconsin, Lansing, MI 48906 www.elderly.com

BOOKS

I am only going to list a few songbooks in this bibliography, because once again there are simply too many books to list in a relatively brief section like this.

Alden, Grant and Peter Blackstook, eds. *No Depression: An Introduction to Alternative Country Music; Whatever That Is.* (1998) Nashville, Dowling Press.

Alarik, Scott. *Deep Community: Adventures in the Modern Folk Underground.* (2003) Cambridge, MA, Black Wolf Press.

Amatneek, Bill. *Acoustic Stories.* (2003) Sebastopol, CA, Vineyards Press.

Baez, Joan. *And a Voice to Sing With.* (1987) New York, Summit Books.

Bookbinder, David. *What Folk Music Is All About.* (1979) New York, Julian Messner.

Brend, Mark. *American Troubadours: Groundbreaking Singer–Songwriters of the 60's.* (2001) San Francisco, Backbeat Books.

Brocken, Michael. (2003) *The British Folk Revival: 1944–2001.* London, Ashgate.

Bufwack, Mary A. and Robert J. Oermann. *Finding Her Voice: The Saga of Women in Country Music.* (1993) New York, Crown Books.

Campbell, Gavin James. (2004) *Music and the Making of a New South.* Charleston, University of North Carolina Press.

Cantwell, Robert. (1996) *When We Were Good: The Folk Revival.* Cambridge, MA, Harvard University Press.

Carawan, Guy and Candie, eds. (1992) *Sing for Freedom: The Story of the Civil Righs Movement Through Its Songs.* Bethlehem, PA, Sing Out Corporation.

Carson, Mina, Tisa Lowes and Susan M. Shaw. *Girls Rock! Fifty Years of Women Making Music.* (2004) Lexington, KY, University of Kentucky Press.

Cohen, Ronald D. *Rainbow Quest: The Folk Music Revival & American Society, 1940–1970.* (2002) Amherst, University of Massachusetts Press.

Cohen, Ronald. D and Dave Samuelson. *Folk Music, Topical Songs and the Amerian Left, 1926–1953.* (1996) (a book that accompanies a 10-CD record set of the same name issued by Bear Family Records).

Cohen, Ronald D., ed. *"Wasn't That a Time!" Firsthand Accounts of the Folk Music Revival.* (1995) Metuchen, NJ, Scarecrow Press.

Cohn, Lawrence. *Nothing but the Blues: The Music and the Musicians.* (1993) New York, Abbeville Press.

Coles, Robert. *Bruce Springsteen's America: The People Lisening, a Poet Singing.* (2003) New York, Random House.

Collins, Judy. *Trust Your Heart: An Autobiography.* (1987) Boston, Houghton Mifflin Co.

Cray, Ed. *Ramblin' Man: The Life and Times of Woody Guthrie.* (2004) New York, W.W. Norton Co.

Crosby, David and David Bender. *Stand and Be Counted: Making Music, Making History.* (2000) San Francisco, Harpers.

Cunningham, Agnes "Sis" and Gordon Freisen. *Red Dust and Broadsides: A Joint Autobiography.* (1999) Amherst, University of Massachusetts Press.

Denisoff, R. Serge. *Great Day Coming: Folk Music and the American Left.* (1973) Baltmore, MD, Penguin Books.

Denisoff, R. Serge and Richard A. Peterson, eds. *The Sounds of Social Change: Studies in Popular Culture.* (1972) Chicago, Rand McNally and Co.

DeTurk, David A. and A. Poulin Jr. *The American Folk Scene: Dimensions of the Folk Song Revival.* (1967) New York, Dell Publishing Co.

Doggett, Peter. *Are You Ready for the Country: Elvis, Dylan, Parsons and the Roots of Country Rock.* (2000) New York, Penguin Books.

Dunaway, David. *How Can I Keep from Singing: Pete Seeger.* (1990) New York, Da Capo Press, reprint of the revised 1985 London edition.

Dylan, Bob. *Chronicles: Volume 1.* (2004) New York, Simon & Schuster.

Filene, Benjamin. *Romancing the Folk: Public Memory and American Roots Music.* (2000) Chapel Hill, University of North Carolina Press.

Finson, Jon W. *The Voices That Are Gone: Themes in 19ᵗʰ Century American Popular Song.* (1994) New York, Oxford University Press.

Fong-Torres, Ben. *Hickory Wind: The Life and Times of Gram Parsons.* (1991) New York, Pocket Books.

Fowke, Edith and Joe Glazer. *Songs of Work and Protest: 100 Favorite Songs of American Workers.* (1973) New York, Dover Publications.

Gellert, Lawrence. *Me and My Captain: Chain Gang Negro Songs of Protest.* (1936) New York, American Music League.

Gellert, Lawrence. *Negro Songs of Protest, Collected by Lawrence Gellert.* (1939) New York, Hours Press.

Gibson, Bob, and Carole Bender. *I Come for to Sing: The Stops Along the Way of a Folk Music Legend.* (1999) Naperville, IL, Kingston Korner, Inc.

Gilmour, Michael J. *Tangled Up in the Bible: Bob Dylan and Scripture.* (2004) New York, Continuum.

Gitlin, Todd. *The Sixties: Years of Hope, Days of Rage.* (1987) New York, Bantam Books.

Glassie, Henry, Edward D. Ives and John F. Szwed *Folksongs and Their Makers.* (undated) Bowling Green, OH, Bowling Green University Popular Press.

Goldsmith, Peter D. *Making People's Music: Moe Asch and Folkways Records.* (1998) Washington, D.C., Smithsonian Institution Press.

Goldsmith, Thomas, ed. *The Bluegrass Reader.* (2004) Urbana, IL, University of Illinois Press.

Gordon, Robert and Bruce Nemerov, eds. *Lost Delta Found: Rediscovering the Fisk University–Library of Congress Coahama County Study, 1941–1942.* (2005) Nashville, Vanderbilt University Press.

Gray, Michael. *Song and Dance Man III: The Art of Bob Dylan.* (2000) London, Continuum.

Green, Archie. *Only a Miner: Studies in Recorded Coal-Mining Songs.* (1972) Urbana, IL, University of Illinois Press.

Green, Archie, ed. *Songs About Work: Essays in Occupational Culture for Richard A. Reuss.* (1993) Bloomington, IN, Folklore Institute, Indiana University.

Green, Paula Hathaway-Anderson. *A Hot-Bed of Musicians: Traditional Music in the Upper New River Valley Whitetop Region.* (2002) Knoxville, TN, University of Tennessee Press.

Greenway, John. *American Folksongs of Protest.* (1953) Philadelphia, University of Pennsylvania Press.

Guthrie, Woody. *Bound for Glory: 101 Woody Guthrie Songs Including All the Songs from Bound for Glory.* (1977) New York, TRO.

Hadju, David. *Positively 4ᵗʰ Street: The Life and Times of Joan Baez, Bob Dylan, Mimi Baez, Fariña and Richard Fariña.* (2001) New York, North Point Press.

Halker, Clark D. *For Democracy, Workers and God: Labor Song-Poems and Labor Protest, 1865–95.* (1991) Urbana, IL, University of Illinois Press.

Hampton, Wade. *Guerrila Minstrels: John Lennon, Joe Hill, Woody Guthrie, Bob Dylan.* (1986) Knoxville, TN, University of Tennessee Press.

Harper, Colin. *Dazzling Stranger: Bert Jansch and the British Folk and Blues Revival.* (2000) London, Bloomsbury.

Harrah-Conforth, Bruce Conway. *Laughing Just to Keep from Crying: Folksong, the Field Recordings of Lawrence Gellert.* (1980) unpublished master's thesis, Bloomington, IN, University of Indiana.

Harris, Craig. *The New Folk Music.* (1991) Crown Point, IN, White Cliffs Media Company.

Havens, Richie, with Steve Davidowitz. *They Can't Hide Us Anymore.* (1999) New York, Avon Books.

Heilbut, Anthony. *The Gospel Sound: Good News and Bad Times.* (1985) Updated and revised edition, New York, Limelight Books.

Heylin, Clinton. *Behind the Shades Revisited: Bob Dylan.* (2001) New York, William Morrow.

Hinton, Brian. *South by Southwest: A Road Map to Alternative Country.* (2003) London, Sanctuary Publishing, Limited.

Isserman, Maurice. *If I Had a Hammer: The Death of the Old Left and the Birth of the New Left.* (1987) New York, Basic Books.

Ives, Edward D. *Joe Scott; The Woodsman-Songster.* (1978) Urbana, IL, University of Illinois Press.

Jackson, Laura. *Paul Simon: The Definitive Biography of the Legendary Singer–Songwriter.* (2002) New York, Citadel Press.

Klein, Joe. *Woody Guthrie: A Life.* (1980) New York, Ballantine Books.

Kornbluh, Joyce, ed. *Rebel Voices: An IWW Anthology.* (1962) Ann Arbor, MI, University of Michigan Press.

Kort, Michele. *The Music and Passion of Laura Nyro: Soul Picnic.* (2002) New York, St. Martin's Press.

Koster, Rick. *Louisiana Music.* (2002) New York, Da Capo Press.

Kot, Greg. *Wilco: Learning How to Die.* (2004) New York, Broadway Books.

Kutukas, Judy. *The Long War: The Intellectual People's Front and Anti-Stalinism, 1930–1940.* (1995) Durham, NC, Duke University Press.

Lieberman, Robbie. *"My Song Is My Weapon": Peoples' Songs, America Communism, and the Politics of Culture, 1930–50.* (1989) Urbana, IL, University of Illinois Press.

Lomax, Alan, Woody Guthrie and Pete Seeger. *Hard Hitting Songs for Hard-Hit People.* (1967) New York, Oak Publications.

Lomax, Alan, edited by Ronald D. Cohen. *Selected Writings, 1934–1997.* (2003) New York, Routledge.

Lomax, Alan. *The Land Where the Blues Began.* (1993) New York, Pantheon Books.

Lomax, John A. and Alan. *Negro Folk Songs as Sung by Lead Belly.* (1936) New York, Macmillan Company.

Lornell, Kip. *Introducing American Folk Music: Grassroots and Ethnic Traditions in the United States.* (2002 2nd edition) New York, McGraw Hill.

Mahal, Taj, with Stephen Foehr. *Taj Mahal: Autobiography of a Bluesman.* (2001) London, Sanctuary Publishing Limited.

Marcus, Greil. *The Weird Od America: The World of Bob Dylan's Basement Tapes.* (1997) New York, Henry Holt and Co.

McLauchlan, Murray. *Getting Out of Here Alive: The Ballad of Murray McLauchlan.* (1998)Toronto, Viking.

Metting, Fred. *The Unbroken Circle: Tradition and Innovation in the Music of Ry Cooder and Taj Mahal.* (1999) Lanham, NJ, Scarecrow Press.

Morgan, Ted. *Reds: McCarthyism in Twentieth Century America.* (2003) New York, Random House.

Near, Holly. *Fire in the Rain . . . Singer in the Storm: An Autobiography.* (1990) New York, William Morrow.

O'Brien, Karen. *Hymn to Her: Women Musicians Talk.* (1995) London, Virago Press.

Palieri, Rik. *The Road Is My Mistress: Tales of a Roustabout Songster.* (2003) Hinesburg, VT, Koza Productions.

Porterfield, Nolan. *Last Cavalier: The Life and Times of John A. Lomax.* (1996) Urbana, IL, University of Illinois Press.

Pratt, Ray. *Rhythm and Resistance: The Political Uses of American Popular Music.* (1994) Washington, D.C., Smithsonian Institution Press.

Quigley, Colin. *Music from the Heart: Compositions of a Folk Fiddler.* (1995) Athens, GA, University of Georgia Press.

Quirino, Raffaele. *Ani DiFranco: Righteous Babe.* (2000) Kingston, ON, Quarry Press.

Raffi. *The Life of a Children's Troubadour.* (1999) Vancouver, Homeland Press.

Reid, Jan. *The Improbable Rise of Rednock Rock.* (2004, new edition) Austin, University of Texas Press.

Reuss, Richard A. and JoAnne C. *American Folk Music and Left-Wing Politics, 1927–1957*. Lanham, NJ, Scraecrow Press.

Robinson, Earl with Eric A. Gordon. *Ballad of an American: The Autobiography of Earl Robinson*. (1998) Lanham, NJ, Scarecrow Press.

Rodger, Jeffrey Pepper. *Rock Troubadours*. (2000) San Anselmo, CA, String Letter Press.

Romalis, Shelly. *Pistol Packin' Mama: Aunt Molly Jackson and the Politics of Folksong*. (1999) Urbana, IL, University of Illinois Press.

Roscigno, Vincent J. and William F. Danaher. *The Voice of Southern Labor: Radio, Music and Textile Strikes, 1919–1934*. (2004) Minneapolis, University of Minnesota Press.

Rosen, David M. *Protest Song in America: More than a History: An Involvement with Freedom*. (1972) Westlake Village, CA, Aware Press.

Rosenberg, Neil, ed. *Transforming Tradition: Folk Music Revivals Examined*. (1993) Urbana, IL, University of Illinois Press.

Sandberg, Larry and Dick Weissman. *The Folk Music Sourcebook*. (1989, new updated edition) New York, Da Capo Press.

Sapoznik, Henry. *Klezmer: Jewish Music from Old World to Our World*. (1999) New York, Schirmer Trade Books.

Sawyers, June Skinner. *Celtic Music: A Complete Guide*. (2000) New York, Da Capo Press.

Schwartz, Ellen. *Born a Woman: Seven Canadian Women Singer Songwriters*. (1988) Winlaw, BC, Polestar Press.

Seeger, Pete and Bob Reiser. *Carry It On! A History in Song and Picture of the Working Men and Women of America*. (1985) New York, Simon and Schuster.

Seeger, Pete. *Where Have All the Flowers Gone: A Singer's Stories, Songs, Seeds, Robberies*. (1993) Bethlehem, PA, Sing Out Corporation.

Shelton, Bob. *No Direction Home: The Life and Music of Bob Dylan*. (1986) New York, William Morrow.

Simmons, Sylvie. *Neil Young*. (2001) Edinburgh, Scotland, Cannongate Books.

Slobin, Mark, ed. *American Klezmer: Its Roots and Offshoots*. (2002) Berkeley, University of California Press.

Slobin, Mark. *Fiddler on the Move: Exploring the Klezmer World*. (2000) New York, Oxford University Press.

Smith, Richard D. *Can't You Hear Me Callin': The Life of Bill Monroe, Father of Bluegrass*. (2000) Boston, Little Brown & Co.

St. John, Lauren. *Hardcore Troubadour: The Life and Near Death of Steve Earle*. (2003) New York, Harper Collins.

Sullivan, Denise. *Rip It Up: Rock and Roll Rulebreakers*. (2001) San Francisco, Backbeat Books.

Sweers, Britta. *Electric Folk: The Changing Face of English Traditional Music*. (2003) New York, Oxford University Press.

Tisserand, Michael. *The Kingdom of Zydeco*. (1998) New York, Arcade Publishing.

Unterberger, Richie. *Eight Miles High: Folk-Rock's Flight from Haight Ashbury to Woodstock.* (2003) San Francisco, Backbeat Books.

Unterberger, Richie. *Turn! Turn! Turn! The 60's Folk-Rock Revolution.* (2002) San Francisco, Backbeat Books.

Von Schmidt, Eric and Jim Rooney. *Baby Let Me Follow You Down: The Illustrated Story of the Cambridge Folk Years.* (1979) Garden City, NY, Anchor Press.

Wald, Elijah. *Narcorrido: A Journey into the Music of Drugs, Guns and Guerrilas.* (1998) New York, Harper Collins.

Wald, Elijah. *Josh White: Society Blues.* (2000) Amherst, University of Massachusetts Press.

Washburne, Christopher, J. and Maiken Derno. *Bad Music: The Music We Love to Hate.* (2004) New York, Routledge.

Waterman, Dick. *Between Midnight and Day: The Last Unpublished Blues Archive.* (2004) New York, Thunder's Mouth Press.

Weissman, Dick. *The Music Business: Career Opportunities and Self Defense.* (2003, 3rd revised edition). New York, Three Rivers Press.

White, Timothy. *Long Ago and Far Away: James Taylor, His Life and Work.* (2001) London, Omnibus Press.

Wilgus, D. K. *Anglo-American Folksong Scholarship.* (1959) New Brunswick, NJ, Rutgers University Press.

Willens, Doris. *Lonesome Traveler: The Life of Lee Hays.* (1988) New York, W.W. Norton & Company.

Willis, Barry. *America's Music, Bluegrass: A History of Bluegrass Music in the Words of Its Pioneers.* (1997) Franktown, CO, Pine Valley Music.

Wolfe, Charles and Kip Lornell. *The Life and Legend of Leadbelly.* (1992) New York, Harper Collins.

Wolliver, Robbie. *Hoot: A 25-Year History of the Greenwich Village Music Scene.* (1986) New York, St. Martin's Press.

Zwonitzer, Mark with Charles Hirshberg. *Will You Miss Me When I'm Gone? The Carter Family and Their Legacy in American Music.* (2002) New York, Simon and Schuster.

Zimmerman, Keith and Kent. *Sing My Way Home: Voices of the New American Roots Rock.* (2004) San Francisco, Backbeat Books.

Index